ECOTOURISM AND CONSERVATION IN THE AMERICAS

Ecotourism Book Series

General Editor: David B. Weaver, Professor of Tourism Management, George Mason University, Virginia, USA.

Ecotourism, or nature-based tourism that is managed to be learning-oriented as well as environmentally and socioculturally sustainable, has emerged in the past 20 years as one of the most important sectors within the global tourism industry. The purpose of this series is to provide diverse stakeholders (e.g. academics, graduate and senior undergraduate students, practitioners, protected area managers, government and non-governmental organizations) with state-of-the-art and scientifically sound strategic knowledge about all facets of ecotourism, including external environments that influence its development. Contributions adopt a holistic, critical and interdisciplinary approach that combines relevant theory and practice while placing case studies from specific destinations into an international context. The series supports the development and diffusion of financially viable ecotourism that fulfils the objective of environmental, socio-cultural and economic sustainability at both the local and global scale.

Titles available:

1. *Nature-based Tourism, Environment and Land Management*
   Edited by R. Buckley, C. Pickering and D. Weaver
2. *Environmental Impacts of Ecotourism*
   Edited by R. Buckley
3. *Indigenous Ecotourism: Sustainable Development and Management*
   H. Zeppel
4. *Ecotourism in Scandinavia: Lessons in Theory and Practice*
   Edited by S. Gossling and J. Hultman
5. *Quality Assurance and Certification in Ecotourism*
   Edited by R. Black and A. Crabtree
6. *Marine Ecotourism: Between the Devil and the Deep Blue Sea*
   C. Cater and E. Cater
7. *Ecotourism and Conservation in the Americas*
   Edited by A. Stronza and W.H. Durham

ECOTOURISM AND CONSERVATION IN THE AMERICAS

Edited by

Amanda Stronza

Department of Recreation, Park and Tourism Sciences
Texas A&M University
College Station, TX 77843–2261
USA

and

William H. Durham

Department of Anthropology
Main Quad, Building 50, 450 Serra Mall
Stanford University
Stanford, CA 94305–2034
USA

www.cabi.org

CABI is a trading name of CAB International

CABI Head Office	CABI North American Office
Nosworthy Way	875 Massachusetts Avenue
Wallingford	7th Floor
Oxfordshire OX10 8DE	Cambridge, MA 02139
UK	USA
Tel: +44 (0)1491 832111	Tel: +1 617 395 4056
Fax: +44 (0)1491 833508	Fax: +1 617 354 6875
E-mail: mailto:cabi@cabi.org	E-mail: cabi-nao@cabi.org
Website: www.cabi.org	

A catalogue record for this book is available from the British Library, London.

Library of Congress Cataloging-in-Publication Data

Ecotourism at work in the Americas / edited by Amanda Stronza,
William H. Durham.
    p. cm. -- (Ecotourism book series)
Includes bibliographical references and index.
ISBN 978-1-84593-400-2 (alk. paper)
1. Ecotourism--America. I. Stronza, Amanda. II. Durham, William H. III. Title.

G155.A45E26 2008
338.4'7917--dc22

2008004202

ISBN: 978 1 84593 400 2

Typeset by Columns Design Ltd, Reading, UK
Printed and bound in the UK by Cromwell Press, Trowbridge

The paper used for the text pages in this book is FSC certified.
The FSC (Forest Stewardship Council) is an international network to
promote responsible management of the world's forests.

Contents

Contributors

Alison Bidwell Pearce earned a BA in Earth and Environmental Sciences from Wesleyan University, Middletown, Connecticut and a PhD in Anthropology from Stanford University, California. She currently works in environmental education for the Audubon Naturalist Society in Chevy Chase, Maryland. She has an abiding interest in collaborative and community-based conservation efforts. *PO Box 66, Garrett Park, MD 20896, USA; abpearce@gmail.com*

Teresita Borges Hernándes is a PhD biologist and works on biodiversity, health and transportation policy in the Ministry of Science, Technology and Environment in Cuba. She has also been a member of the Scientific and Technical Review Panel of the Ramsar Convention on Wetlands since 2003. *Biologist and Senior Officer, Direction of the Environment, Ministry of Science, Technology and Environment– CITMA, Capitolio Nacional, Prado y San José, La Habana, Cuba; teresita.borges@infomed.sld.cu*

Randall Borman is Executive Director of the Fundación para la Sobrevivencia del Pueblo Cofan (FSC) and the Cofan Survival Fund. FSC was developed as a response to the needs of the Cofan Nation of Ecuador, a small indigenous culture that has survived since at least the time of the Spanish arrival in the New World. Randy is also the current 'Dirigente de Tierras' (which roughly translates as 'Director of Territories') for FEINCE, the Indigenous Federation of the Cofan Nation. *Founder, Fundación para la Sobrevivencia del Pueblo Cofan, Mariano Cardenal N74–153 y Joaquín Mancheno, Urb. Carcelén Alto, Quito, Ecuador; randy@cofan.org*

William L. Bryan is Co-Founder and Chairman of Off the Beaten Path, a custom travel planning company operating in the western half of the western hemisphere (www.offthebeatenpath.com). Bill is also the Executive Director of the Rural Landscape Institute (www.rurallandscapeinstitute.org) with the mission of furthering the economic viability of family-scale production agriculture in the Northern Plains and Rocky Mountains of the USA. *Co-Founder and Chairman, Off the Beaten Path LLC, 7 East Beall Street, Bozeman, MT 59715, USA; billb@offthebeatenpath.com*

Hector Ceballos-Lascurain is a Mexican environmental architect and international ecotourism consultant, credited for having coined the term 'ecotourism' and its preliminary definition in 1983. He has done pioneering work in ecotourism planning and development, design and construction of ecolodges, and sustainable architecture in 75 countries around the world. *International Consultant in Ecotourism and Environmental Architecture, Director General PICE (Program of International Consultancy on Ecotourism), Camino Real al Ajusco 551, Col. Xolalpa Tepepan, Mexico DF, 14649 Mexico; ceballos@laneta.apc.org*

Lourdes Coya de la Fuente is a biologist who serves as Deputy Director of the Direction of the Environment, Ministry of Science, Technology and Environment, Cuba. She is a specialist in biodiversity, tourism and the National Environmental Strategy. *Deputy Director, Direction of the Environment, Ministry of Science, Technology and Environment– CITMA, Capitolio Nacional, Prado y San José, La Habana, Cuba; chamero@citma.cu*

Julie Ivker Dubin is Co-Founder and Program Director of Global Explorers, a non-profit educational travel immersion programme for youth. The Global Explorers programme combines a strong preparatory curriculum and a required follow-up community service project with a one- to three-week international workshop. Similar to the Children's Environmental Trust Foundation, International, Global Explorers emphasizes responsible global citizenship through the study of science, culture, leadership and service. *Program Director and Co-Founder, Global Explorers, 420 S. Howes Street – Suite B300, Fort Collins, CO 80521, USA; julie@globalexplorers.org*

William H. Durham has a joint appointment in Anthropology and Human Biology at Stanford University, California and serves as Co-Director (with Martha Honey, also a contributor) of the bi-coastal Center on Ecotourism and Sustainable Development (CESD). Bill's interests focus on human ecology, evolution and conservation, with particular interest in the potential of ecotourism to combat poverty and promote environmental conservation. Recipient of a MacArthur Prize Fellowship, Bill has also served as editor of the *Annual Review of Anthropology* since 1992. *Bing Professor in Human Biology, Yang and Yamazaki University Fellow, Department of Anthropology, Main Quad, Building 50, 450 Serra Mall, Stanford University, Stanford, CA 94305–2034, USA; eb.whd@stanford.edu*

Megan Epler Wood is the principal of EplerWood International, which performs strategic analysis of sustainable tourism worldwide. Her consultancy has guided sustainable tourism projects in India, Sri

Lanka, Cambodia, Sierra Leone, Brazil, Mexico, Honduras, El Salvador and Peru. Megan founded The International Ecotourism Society (TIES) in 1990 and was its Executive Director and subsequently President from 1991 to 2002. *Principal, EplerWood International, 369 South Union Street, Burlington, VT 05401, USA; megan@eplerwood.com*

Javier F. Gordillo Jordan has a BSc in Industrial Engineering and an MA in Tourism and Sustainability from the University of the West of England, Bristol, UK. He served as the Peru Coordinator for the 'Amazon Exchange: Learning Host to Host' project, funded by the Critical Ecosystems Partnership Fund in 2002–2003. He was Posada Amazonas' Community Projects Coordinator from 2004 to 2007. *Community Projects Coordinator, Posada Amazonas, Rainforest Expeditions, Jr. Loreto 126, Puerto Maldonado, Madre de Dios, Peru; jfgordilloj@gmail.com*

Martha Honey is Co-Director of the Center on Ecotourism and Sustainable Development (CESD), based in Washington, DC, and Stanford University. She has written and spoken widely on ecotourism as a tool for development and conservation, including *Ecotourism and Certification: Setting Standards in Practice* (2002) and *Ecotourism and Sustainable Development: Who Owns Paradise?* (1999). For over 20 years she worked as a journalist overseas, based in Tanzania and Costa Rica. She holds a BA in History from Oberlin College, Ohio; an MA in African–American Studies from Syracuse University, New York; and a PhD in African History from the University of Dar es Salaam, Tanzania. *Centre on Ecotourism and Sustainable Development, 1333H St. NW, Suite 300, East Tower, Washington, DC 20005, USA; mhoney@ecotourismcesd.org*

Carter Hunt is pursuing a PhD at Texas A&M University, College Station, focusing his research on the impacts of ecotourism in Nicaragua on conservation ethics and institutions in the community. His work is part of a National Science Foundation-sponsored study that is being simultaneously conducted in three additional countries: Botswana, Brazil and Peru. He has also conducted fieldwork in Guatemala and Ecuador, and worked with ecotourism projects in Nicaragua and Peru. *PhD Candidate, Department of Recreation, Park and Tourism Sciences, Texas A&M University, College Station, TX 77843–2261, USA; chunt@tamu.edu*

Jon Kohl collaborates with the World Heritage Centre to introduce a new planning paradigm in protected areas around the world; and with Fermata, Inc. to promote the use of heritage interpretation as an important tool in site management. He also works with EplerWood International to promote ecotourism as a tool for conservation, community development and poverty alleviation. He writes about all these topics for a variety of audiences, mostly in Latin America. *Private Consultant, World Heritage Centre/UNESCO, Fermata, Inc., EplerWood International, Apdo. 12–2250, Tres Ríos, Costa Rica; jk-ecotourism@jonkohl.com*

Constanza Ocampo-Raeder was Watson Fellow at Grinnell College, Iowa, conducting undergraduate research in Tahiti, Belize, Brazil and Kenya. She earned her PhD in Anthropology at Stanford University, California and was a Graduate and Research Fellow of the National Science Foundation. Her research focuses on the ecological basis behind cultural belief systems. As an Assistant Professor at the University of Maine, she teaches and studies ecological anthropology, environmental justice, indigenous rights and conservation in the Amazon, USA and Central America. *Assistant Professor, Department of Anthropology, South Stevens 5773, University of Maine, Orono, ME 04469–5773, USA; constanza@umit.maine.edu*

Arnaldo Rodríguez is a sustainable tourism specialist, with over 20 years of experience in management, marketing, interpretation and consulting. He developed, marketed and operated the Kapawi Ecolodge and Reserve in the Ecuadorian Amazon between 1995 and 2004 and the Huao Lodge between 2005 and 2006. He has performed several consultancies in Latin America and Africa for several organizations, including the US Agency for International Development, the Belgium Agency for Cooperation, Conservation International, The Nature Conservancy, the Global Sustainable Tourism Alliance, WWF and the Inter-American Development Bank. *General Manager, Green Consulting Ecuador, Avenida Interoceánica Km. 81/2, Centro Comercial El Solar, Oficina 4, Cumbayá, Quito, Ecuador; arodriguez@green-consulting.com*

Susan C. Stonich is Professor in three departments (Anthropology, Environmental Studies and Geography) and the Interdepartmental Graduate Program in Marine Science at the University of California, Santa Barbara. She received a BSc in Mathematics from Marquette University, Milwaukee, Wisconsin; and an MA and a PhD in Anthropology from the University of Kentucky, Lexington. Her research focuses on the effects of economic development on human societies and the natural environment in Central America. She has concentrated on the consequences of non-traditional export growth along the Pacific Coast and the effects on human health and nutrition associated with intensified tourism development. *Professor, Anthropology, Environmental Studies, Geography, and Interdepartmental Graduate Program in Marine Science, University of California, Santa Barbara, CA 93106–4160, USA; stonich@anth.ucsb.edu*

Amanda Stronza is Assistant Professor in the Department of Recreation, Park, and Tourism Sciences at Texas A&M University, College Station. She has a BA in International Affairs from the George Washington University, Washington, DC and an MA in Latin American Studies and a PhD in Anthropology from the University of Florida, Gainesville. She was a Lang Postdoctoral Fellow in Anthropological Sciences at Stanford University, California. Her research focuses on community-based conservation and ecotourism in the tropics. Currently, she co-directs the NSF-IGERT programme in 'Applied Biodiversity Science' at Texas A&M. *Assistant Professor, Department of Recreation, Park and Tourism*

Sciences, Texas A&M University, College Station, TX 77843–2261, USA; astronza@tamu.edu

Fernanda de Vasconcellos Pêgas is a doctoral student at Texas A&M University, College Station. She is completing her dissertation on the outcomes of a 25-year 'Brazilian Sea Turtle Conservation Programme' (called TAMAR), which includes an ethnographic account of the project's presence in the fishing village of Praia do Forte, Brazil. Her professional goal is to continue working on community-based and ecotourism strategies in her native Brazil and other countries. *PhD Candidate, Department of Recreation, Park and Tourism Sciences, Texas A&M University, College Station, TX 77843–2261, USA; pegasf@neo.tamu.edu*

Karen Lee Wald has spent two decades doing research and writing in Cuba on a variety of topics, including environment and ecotourism. She holds a BS in Industrial and Labor Relations from Cornell University, Ithaca, New York; an MA in Education from Westminster College University Without Walls; and a bilingual teaching degree from California State University at Hayward. Her book *Children of Che: A Child's-Eye View of the Revolution* was published by Ramparts Press in 1978 and a Spanish version was published in 1986. *Writer and Journalist, 2803 La Terrace Circle, San Jose, CA 95123, USA; kwald@california.com*

Preface

Among today's contending conservation and development strategies, ecotourism is one of the most popular. It seeks to curb the often deleterious effects of large-scale, conventional tourism on local communities and ecosystems. But more than that, it holds the promise of overcoming a number of today's biggest environmental and social challenges. Ideally, ecotourism can help conserve biological and cultural diversity, alleviate rural poverty, strengthen ties between parks and neighbouring peoples, increase public awareness of environmental concerns, and manifest a new 'triple bottom line' for business that includes profit, social benefits and environmental conservation.

For these reasons, interest in ecotourism has never been greater. According to the World Tourism Organization, ecotourism is now the fastest growing segment of an already mammoth tourism industry. By some estimates, ecotourism generates as much as US$300 billion in revenues annually. International development and lending agencies channel millions of dollars into projects that include ecotourism. Major conservation organizations sponsor ecotourism projects in biodiversity 'hotspots' around the world. Most countries with parks and protected areas now have some kind of marketing strategy to attract ecotourists. Increasing numbers of universities in the USA and abroad now offer courses and degree programmes in ecotourism. The United Nations declared 2002 the 'International Year of Ecotourism' and marked it as a time to take collective stock of the lessons learned. At the Ecotourism World Summit in Quebec, Canada, thousands of delegates from over a hundred nations gathered to assess the pros and cons of ecotourism for peoples and ecosystems around the world.

But does ecotourism actually measure up to the environmental, social and economic ideals it has promised? Has ecotourism sensitized tourists to tread more lightly on the destinations they visit? Has it created economic incentives to conserve wildlife species and natural habitats? Has it augmented benefits to locals from established protected areas? What are the tangible impacts for people in surrounding human communities? Are there lessons for how to ensure net positive impacts in the future?

In preparing this volume, we gathered experts in the fields of conservation, ecotourism and community development to try to answer some of these questions. We first joined during the International Year of Ecotourism in a workshop entitled 'Ecotourism and Conservation in the Americas: Putting Good Intentions to Work', in the Department of Anthropological Sciences at Stanford University. Delegates came from the private tourism sector, community and non-profit organizations, research institutes and academia from seven countries. The 3-day workshop became the catalyst for this book. In the interim, we screened original contributions for current relevance to the field and worked with the authors to revise and update each of the chapters several times. We also selected a cross-cutting sample of topics and cases from the broad spectrum of geographic regions and ecosystems in the Americas.

We hope this book fulfils its mission, and offers professionals in conservation and ecotourism organizations, non-governmental organizations and government offices, particularly in the USA and Latin America, a worthy assessment of ecotourism's tangible impacts in the Americas. We also hope the volume will provide useful case studies, testimonies of 'ecotourism at work' in the field, and regional overviews for students and their professors in university classrooms. The time has come to take stock of what works and what does not in ecotourism, and ask why. This book is a step in that direction.

We gratefully acknowledge the support of the many people and organizations who contributed to this book. At Stanford, these include the Department of Anthropological Sciences, the Continuing Studies Program, the Center for Latin American Studies, the Center for Social Innovation at the Graduate School of Business and the Stanford Alumni Association. In the later stages of the book, we appreciated the support of the Center on Ecotourism and Sustainable Development based at Stanford and in Washington, DC. Thanks also to several students for their help at various stages of the process, particularly Audrey Davenport, Fernando Galeana, Joanna Levitt, Biasha Mitchell, Christina Shaheen, Thomas Kohnstamm, Nico Slate, Carter Hunt and Fernanda Pegas. We also thank our colleagues: Charles Junkerman, David Brady, Terry Karl, Duncan Beardsley, Pamela Matson, Flora Lu, Alison Pearce, Vernita Ediger, Constanzo Ocampo-Raeder, Emma Stewart, Susan Charnley, Dominique Irvine, Suki Hoagland, Larry Goulder, Cynthia Lang, Nancy Lonhart, Tracy Pizzo, Jen Paris and Tracy Robinette. Several participants from the original workshop provided important insights and made our original workshop especially worthwhile. These include: Ron Mader, Robert Healy, Daniela Vizcaino, Stephen Edwards, Alberto Mesquita, Eduardo Nycander, Candido Pastor, Zenon Limaco, Miguel Pesha, Kurt Kutay, John Shores and Sharon Matola.

Every book has its challenges and vicissitudes – we particularly enjoyed the opportunity afforded here to work through them together.

Finally, we thank the editors at CAB International, especially Sarah Hulbert, Claire Parfitt and Lesley King, for their support and willingness to invest in this book as a valuable addition to their Ecotourism Series.

Amanda Stronza
Texas A&M University

William H. Durham
Stanford University

Part I

Introduction

---

1 The Bold Agenda of Ecotourism

A. Stronza

Department of Recreation, Park and Tourism Sciences, Texas A&M University, College Station, Texas, USA

Introduction

A century into the age of modern travel and tourism, few corners of the planet remain truly off the beaten path. Tourism is a mammoth industry that generates an estimated US$300 billion in annual revenues and nearly 10% of all employment in the world (Honey and Rome, 2000). Under globalization, the numbers are expected only to rise, and by the year 2010, more than one billion tourists will be roaming the world (TIES, 2000; WTO, 2004). For environmentalists, development specialists and indigenous rights advocates, the predictions are both promising and worrisome.

A hundred years or more of tourism have revealed that the industry can, and often does, leave considerable 'baggage' for the people and natural environments of local destinations. Some of the problems introduced historically by tourists include crowding and disruption of local communities, commercial exploitation of cultural traditions, social conflict, entrenchment of ethnic stereotypes, disturbance to wildlife, degradation or outright conversion of habitats, increased economic dependency, the emergence of black markets, and increased illicit trade in everything from exotic pets to drugs and sex (Greenwood, 1989; Eadington and Smith, 1992; Giannecchini, 1993; Lanfant et al., 1995; Butler and Hinch, 1996; Stonich, 1998; Burns, 1999; Desmond, 1999; Chambers, 2000). In short, so many experiences with tourism, both on and off the beaten path, have proved disruptive, damaging and, in a word, unsustainable.

Ecotourism: A Better Path?

Today's approaches to tourism are aimed at eliminating the baggage and introducing an array of benefits to natural environments and local peoples. These alternative tours, variously labelled 'sustainable', 'eco' and 'responsible', strive to make tourism profits work for local environments and communities rather than against them. Among these new approaches, ecotourism stands out for its promise both to advance conservation goals and improve the livelihoods of local peoples. Ecotourism is thus broadly defined as nature-based tourism with three special features: (i) it minimizes the negative environmental, economic and social impacts often associated with mass tourism; (ii) it delivers a net positive contribution to environmental conservation; and (iii) it improves the livelihoods of local people (Lindberg and Hawkins, 1993; Cater and Lowman, 1994; Barkin, 1996; Ceballos-Lascurain, 1996; Honey, 1999; Wearing and Neil, 1999). In other words, it is tourism that attempts to minimize negative impacts and make instead serious positive contributions to a number of today's environmental and social challenges.

Economically, this form of tourism can be a real boon to people in host destinations. In addition to raising foreign exchange and investment on a national level, ecotourism offers the potential of new jobs for local labour and new markets for locally produced goods and services. The cash and employment benefits from ecotourism, however, may actually be modest compared with its non-economic benefits. The latter can include revalorization of cultural traditions and beliefs, improved community organization and leadership, increased self-esteem and pride in the community, new skills and languages, and contact with an expanded network of people and potential sources of support, including international tourists and tour companies, private foundations, universities and researchers, and non-governmental organizations (Stronza, 2001; Landell-Mills and Porras, 2002).

Community-based ecotourism has an advantage with regard to ecotourism's conservation and development goals. In community-based ecotourism, a local community or group of communities has substantial involvement in, and control over, ecotourism's development and management, and a major proportion of the benefits remain within the community (Denman, 2001). In a community-based approach, local voices, values and knowledge are proactively channelled into strategies for managing resources (Brosius *et al.*, 1998). Many proponents argue that such participation is an essential element of sustainability, giving rise to a sense of ownership and empowerment in the community (Schevyens, 1999; Alexander, 2000; Stronza, 2005). Conversely, other authors see unequal relations of power among locals and visitors in tourism destinations as a potential source of environmental problems (e.g. Stonich, 2000; Gossling, 2003). The debate is currently not *whether* local communities should be involved in the development of tourism to their areas, but *how* they should be involved.

Meanwhile, conservationists are hopeful that the array of social and economic benefits from ecotourism will generate incentives for local residents to protect the landscapes and resources tourists pay to see. In this light, ecotourism is sometimes viewed as the quintessential 'integrated conservation and development project' (ICDP). It has the potential to make economic development work in the service of conservation in various ways. First, ecotourism can minimize or eliminate local economic dependence on activities that exploit natural resources directly and are therefore more damaging to biodiversity, such as commercial agriculture, hunting, logging, cattle ranching and gold mining (Langholz, 1999; Jones and Young, 2004). Second, ecotourism can generate visitor fees to help finance parks and protected areas (Groom *et al.*, 1991; Borges Hernándes *et al.*, Chapter 12, this volume). This is especially noteworthy in places that are rich in biodiversity but poor in revenues. Ecotourism can also help build the managerial and organizational capacity of local communities to manage natural resources (Borman, 1999; Gordillo Jordan *et al.*, Chapter 3, this volume). By establishing ecotourism operations in their own territories, local peoples may become better prepared to defend resources and even resist outside interests, such as timber or mining companies (Rodríguez, Chapter 10, this volume).

Finally, in addition to bringing benefits to local communities and supporting conservation, ecotourism also has the potential to raise public environmental awareness. Many ecotours include interpretative activities that help visitors learn about conservation and ecology as they are exploring new landscapes and communities (Orams, 1997; Kimmell, 1999; Thaites *et al.*, 2002). Many also present information on cultural history and human–environment interactions of a region, encouraging visitors to consider not only the beauty of the destination but also the environmental challenges it is facing (Bidwell Pearce and Ocampo-Raeder, Chapter 7, this volume). This mix of leisure, learning and discovery may help build new popular bases of support and advocacy for conservation (Kohl, Chapter 8, this volume).

Will It Really Take Us Where We Want To Go?

For its many promises, ecotourism has captured considerable attention. Most international financial institutions and development agencies have begun channelling significant amounts of economic and technical assistance to potential ecotourism destinations around the world (Epler Wood, Chapter 14, this volume). Much effort has been aimed at building local capacity for ecotourism so that communities can begin making tourism work for their own development goals. With similar optimism, a number of conservation organizations have begun sponsoring ecotourism projects in biodiversity 'hotspots' around the world (Christ *et al.*, 2004). Tropical countries have been particularly encouraged to invest in ecotourism as a possible solution to raising much-needed foreign exchange while also curbing environmental degradation. In fact, most countries with protected areas now have some form of national or regional marketing strategy to attract ecotourists (Ceballos-Lascurain, Chapter 13, this volume).

Ecotourism has also become a subject of significant study and policy debate (Hawkins and Lamoureux, 2001). In the international arena, for example, the United Nations declared 2002 the 'International Year of Ecotourism', marking it as a time to take collective stock of lessons learned. At that year's Ecotourism World Summit in Quebec, Canada, over a thousand delegates from 132 different countries, representing public, private and non-governmental organizations, academic institutions, national and international development agencies, as well as local and indigenous communities, gathered to discuss the pros and cons of ecotourism for peoples and ecosystems around the world. Now plans are taking shape for discussions of certification and accreditation on a global scale. Likewise, much attention is also being paid at national and regional levels. The scholarly literature is booming, a steady stream of workshops and training sessions is under way, and national policies on ecotourism are being written daily. A number of universities in the USA and abroad now offer courses and degree programmes in ecotourism.

Despite the optimism, there have been few careful appraisals of ecotourism. Few ecotourism projects to date have been audited, accredited or even evaluated in any systematic, objective way (Redford and Agrawal, 2006). Few studies of any depth and duration have been undertaken (Kiss, 2004), and untold numbers of operations and companies are calling themselves 'ecotourism' even when they may not conform to its definition (Honey, 2002; Kruger, 2005). Though ecotourism may well be making strides towards its environmental, social and economic promise, there remains high variance and plenty of room for scepticism.

Some critics argue that ecotourism is firmly 'locked into notions of green capitalism', so that concerns for profit will always outweigh those for conservation (Duffy, 2002, p. x). Others observe that, despite the rhetoric, ecotourism is hardly culturally sensitive. The problem, they say, is that ecotourism remains embedded in a neoliberal political and economic system, which precludes real respect for local customs, real opportunities for sustainable development or real empowerment for local communities (Mowforth and Munt, 1998; West and Carrier, 2004; Cater, 2006).

Meanwhile, other sceptics note that even the business side of ecotourism has come up short. By some accounts, ecotourism has created only a few jobs (Lindberg, 1994) and even then is increasing local dependency on a single income source, compelling local communities to shift away from more stable, diversified economies (Belsky, 1999). The industry is prone to boom–bust cycles and dramatic seasonal fluctuations, which can create great vulnerability, especially for subsistence producers (Epler Wood, 2002). Operations labelled 'ecotourism' have also been associated with increased social differentiation and a growing gap between the rich and the poor (Stonich, 2000). At the same time, leakage of profits is a persistent problem, and though tourists often pay heftily for their eco-expeditions, some tour operators have been reluctant to pass on the returns to local communities (Lindberg, 1991; Landell-Mills and Porras, 2002). In fact, analysis indicates that relatively few local communities have realized significant benefits, regardless of their proximity to tourism operations or protected areas (Bookbinder *et al.*, 1998).

Further scepticism arises from the fact that the links between ecotourism and conservation are tenuous. Some studies have shown that few people in host destinations actually gain enough economic benefits from ecotourism to provide sufficient incentives for conservation (Kellert *et al.*, 2000). Furthermore, in the great majority of protected areas, tourism revenues are not able to cover even basic management costs (Davenport *et al.*, 2002). But even if ecotourism were lucrative enough to offer economic incentives for conservation, there are signs of direct impacts from the industry that cause more harm than good. These include converting habitat for tourism activities, cutting trails and disturbing wildlife (Butynski and Kalina, 1998). Biologists have also found instances of disease transmitted to wildlife or subtle changes to wildlife health through disturbance of daily routines or increased stress levels (Isaacs, 2000; Ananthaswamy, 2004). Such changes may translate to lowered rates of survival and breeding.

These criticisms of ecotourism have emerged at a time when sustainable development and market-based approaches to conservation in general are being questioned (e.g. Kramer *et al.*, 1997; Brandon *et al.*, 1998; Oates, 1999; Terborgh, 1999). As successes of ICDPs have been few and far between, the barrage of critical literature has fuelled concern among conservationists over just this kind of endeavour (Chapin, 2004). Nevertheless, a number of prominent biologists continue to endorse ecotourism as a potentially effective tool for conservation (see Terborgh *et al.*, 2002, pp. 6–7; Daily and Ellison, 2003). Perhaps it is because some ecotourism projects are effective at linking business, economic benefits for locals and biodiversity conservation that ecotourism is a holdout among failed experiments in sustainable development. Though many other market-based approaches to conservation are being dismissed as wishful thinking, ecotourism warrants continued appraisal. The questions now are: how, when, where and under what conditions can ecotourism truly deliver on its promises?

Ecotourism and Conservation in the Americas

The volume assembled here presents views of scholars, practitioners, tour operators, educators and policy makers who are pioneers of ecotourism. Written in a style that combines reports from the field with detailed case studies and regional overviews, the authors share insights and lessons from on-the-ground efforts to make ecotourism an effective tool for conservation and development. Included are honest evaluations of both the pros and cons of ecotourism for local communities and ecosystems in places as far ranging as the Galapagos, the Peruvian Amazon, Cuba and the Rocky Mountain West. Together, the chapters tell the story of ecotourism not as an end result, but rather as a work in progress.

Why focus on the Americas? Although ecotourism has spread every-where, it is in the Americas that the idea got an early start (Honey, 1999), and today it is arguably the region with the greatest amount and diversity of ecotourism activity in the world. In assembling the book, we drew upon that scale and diversity of activity to gain cross-cutting coverage of the issues. The contributions are organized into seven main sections of the book, each of which contains 'couplets' of complementary chapters. We hope readers take the opportunity to read these chapters together, as they provide useful counterpoints and comparisons on several subjects, includ-ing community-based ecotourism, marine ecotourism and ecotourism in US settings.

Community-based ecotourism

We begin with a focus on community-based ecotourism. Interest in ecotourism is especially strong today on the part of indigenous communities because it offers a potential means to secure homelands, foster economic development and promote cultural survival. As Randy Borman explains, this was not the case in 1983 when a small group of individuals belonging to the Cofan ethnic group of north-eastern Ecuador began to take groups of paying visitors into the more remote forests of the Cofan ancestral territory. Although none of those individuals realized it, they were establishing themselves at the forefront of a process that would later be known as community-based ecotourism. In subsequent years, the Cofan experience became a leading example of how to go about conserving a cultural system and its multiple environments using ecotourism – rather than raw materials – as the link to Western markets. In recent years, however, the delicate nature of ecotourism has forced the Cofan to diversify from their initial success and to pursue additional routes to cultural survival. The Cofan case thus represents in microcosm both the potentials and pitfalls to 'bottom-up' ecotourism in indigenous communities.

Javier Gordillo and colleagues follow the Cofan case study with a description of the successes and challenges of a community-based ecotourism project in south-eastern Peru. The Posada Amazonas lodge is a joint venture between a private ecotourism company, Rainforest Expeditions, and a community of 150 indigenous and mestizo families, called the Native Community of Infierno. This 'from the field' account is especially illuminating for understanding how ecotourism can both deliver benefits for communities and ecosytems while also presenting new social and ecological challenges. The two partners signed a 20-year contract in 1996, agreeing to split profits and share in the operation and management of the ecolodge. Not only has the project proved successful in economic terms, providing an initial 5-year income of over US$600,000 to the community, but it has also spawned and promoted a range of conservation activities and other benefits. Some conservation effects are indirect, such as the tapered clearing of new forest by ecotourism employees. But some are direct and visible to all, including the protection of harpy eagle nests and a self-declared 'protected area' around the oxbow-lake habitat of some endangered giant otters of the region. This innovative project is far from perfect, yet by all indications it is delivering on ecotourism's conservation promise.

Ecotourism in marine environments

Next we turn the focus from rainforests to marine environments. Susan Stonich brings the critical and timely concern over climate change to the discussion of ecotourism, especially in marine environments. She lays out several of the unresolved social and environmental issues related to the growth of ecotourism (and tourism more generally) in and near marine protected areas (MPAs). Then she explores the answers to two questions: can ecotourism be a tool for conservation and support of MPAs, and can successful MPAs likewise enhance ecotourism and ecotourist experiences? Understanding the power of ecotourism and MPAs to alter coupled human and natural systems becomes even more important, as well as challenging, in the context of climate change. Coastal, near-shore marine and estuarine environments are especially vulnerable. She forecasts that climate change will present complex and unpredictable new challenges for people, communities and regions that are already dependent on tourism. Yet, there are still opportunities to create cooperative, flexible and adaptive arrangements to deal with this unpredictability through the integration of ecotourism and MPAs.

In 'Fishing for Solutions', William Durham argues that parks and protected areas themselves are doomed without the support and engagement of surrounding local people, who may be recruited to such cause through incentives like those from ecotourism. Durham bases his argument on the headline case of Galapagos, where a world-famous National Park has been repeatedly attacked and damaged in recent years by locals who feel themselves excluded from both the decisions and revenues of conservation. Durham reviews the historical development of the issue, showing that ecotourism has been both a major boon to conservation in Galapagos and also indirectly a threat, because locals have historically played so little a role in the conservation process. In this famous 'showcase' of conservation and biodiversity, the hope is now that fishermen can be re-trained for and perpetually sustained from a variety of new roles in ecotourism. The Galapagos case suggests that social instability is an inevitable problem for protected-area conservation that fails to provide decision- and benefit-sharing for local peoples – the very kinds of outcomes that ecotourism is designed to provide.

Ecotourism in the USA

In this section, our paired contributors note that most ecotourism initiatives in the Americas have occurred outside the USA, where climates are warmer, seasons longer, biodiversity greater and labour relatively inexpensive. William Bryan, a founder of Off the Beaten Path, an adventure travel company and tour operator in the Rocky Mountain West, explores the challenges and opportunities to developing ecotourism in the USA. Bryan makes a series of recommendations for more successful ecotourism in the USA, including elements of a profitable yet responsible business plan, and the essentials of building an environmentally sustainable facility with interesting, educational activities plus local community involvement. He argues that we need to accept the fact that responsible travel is a business first, and then work to make it sustainable. As one way to grow more successful ecotourism operations in the USA, he urges the creation of networks and organizations that can interact and build on each other's experiences.

Alison Bidwell Pearce and Constanza Ocampo-Raeder build on Bryan's chapter, addressing challenges in the marketplace to the development of ecotourism and responsible travel options in the USA and other 'developed' settings. Whereas Bryan highlighted structural challenges, this chapter points to obstacles that stem from preconceived notions within the travel industry and ecotourism community. The authors suggest that ecotourism efforts in the USA have often been categorically dismissed on superficial grounds related to geographic or socio-political setting, rather than on any thorough analysis of the social and environmental impacts of these operations. As a case in point, they examine the privately-owned Papoose Creek Lodge just outside Yellowstone National Park in the Madison Valley of south-west Montana. Their study of Papoose Creek reveals that such ventures do have the same laudable goals and intentions as those abroad, and that they are beginning to produce the same tangible benefits to conservation and local livelihoods. If the travel industry can get beyond geographic restrictions on the term, there are many local benefits to be gained from ecotourism in the USA and beyond.

Educating tourists

Our fifth section focuses on environmental education as a more global kind of benefit from ecotourism, but one that may have equally important implications for conservation. Authors address questions such as what do ecotourists actually learn and under what conditions are visitors more likely to absorb environmental lessons? Do the lessons learned truly translate into changed behaviour back home and thus enhanced efforts at biodiversity conservation? What are the ways in which that happens? An important lesson from this section is that the associated cultural dimensions of ecotourism – for example, learning from local and indigenous guides – adds greatly to the take-home value of travel-based learning.

In Chapter 8, Jon Kohl highlights the oft-neglected benefit of travel-based learning. Kohl distinguishes between interpretation and environmental education, and uses 'concept modelling' to explain how interpretation improves conservation in public-use areas. Interpretation is the more appropriate conservation strategy when dealing with ecotourists, says Kohl, because it improves visitor experience, delivers environmental messages, and helps set up a system of soliciting and tracking visitor contributions to conservation activities.

In Chapter 9, Julie Ivker Dubin looks at what ecotourists actually learn as a result of their responsible travel to natural areas. She draws upon data from a case study of middle- and high-school students who participated in a series of Children's Environmental Trust workshops in the Peruvian Amazon. Her study objectives were: (i) to determine the relative educational effectiveness of ecotourism in four realms, i.e. ecological literacy, cultural lessons, personal growth and advocacy/conservation; and (ii) to identify existing correlations between ecotourists who report they had a successful learning experience and their demographic characteristics. She reports that the incidental *cultural* aspects of ecotourism – from travel contact with individuals from culturally distinct backgrounds – have the greatest impact on ecotourists, probably from positive emotional reactions to meaningful human contact. The results of her study indicate that measures to help ecotourists prepare educationally for their travels will enhance their learning in all areas, whether biological or cultural.

Outcomes for communities

In this section, we consider the multiplicity of ways ecotourism alters social and political realities for people in host destinations. Arnaldo Rodríguez begins with comparative assessments of several ecotourism projects among indigenous populations in Ecuador, including the Achuar and the Huaorani. Against a historical background of indigenous exploitation and environmental degradation, Rodríguez explains how ecotourism in indigenous communities emerged as a hopeful alternative in Ecuador in the 1990s. He describes duality between a market economy and a gift economy as a factor that affects ecotourism's potential for success among indigenous communities. Another factor of equal importance is the difference between the principles governing a community and those that govern a business.

Fernanda Pêgas and I put the ecotourism 'equation' to the test and ask: do benefits for people equal benefits for conservation? A key premise of ecotourism is that economic returns from tourism can provide compelling incentives for people to protect the landscapes and resources that tourists pay to see. In some places, ecotourism has indeed served as an effective tool for biodiversity conservation; in others, it has thus far failed to achieve this goal. The factors that determine success remain unclear. Some studies suggest that failure follows when economic benefits from ecotourism have been too limited to build enduring conservation incentives in local communities. Other studies indicate ecotourism also fails when it does not include local community participation in decision making. This point builds on the lesson from Durham's analysis of ecotourism in the Galapagos. Here, we try to evaluate which factors lead communities to support ecotourism endeavours. Based on case studies from Brazil and Peru (including Posada Amazonas), we suggest that when communities share in both the benefits and decisions of an enterprise then the benefits to people of ecotourism are more likely to translate into tangible benefits to conservation.

National perspectives

The authors of this section describe national-level policies for ecotourism. Teresita Borges and colleagues present the case of ecotourism in Cuba where the regulations for ensuring responsibility and sustainability in tourism are mandated by the central government via a constitution that includes 'sustainable development' as a basic policy principle. In collaboration with the tourism sector, the Ministry of Science, Technology and Environment created a nationwide system for granting recognition to tourism operations showing concern for environmental sustainability. Implemented in 1999, their National Environmental Strategy set guidelines for tourism development and established an environmental regulatory body for the tourist sector. While it is still early to assess the success of the programme, the rate of growth in tourism is also higher in Cuba than in any other Caribbean nation. As a member of the Association of Caribbean States, Cuba has also publicly committed to working towards a 'Sustainable Tourism Zone' in the region.

In Chapter 13, Hector Ceballos-Lascurain offers brief descriptions of ecotourism projects in Peru, Ecuador, Costa Rica, Belize and Brazil. An architect by training, Ceballos-Lascurain devotes special attention to the design aspects of exemplary ecolodges in several countries. He emphasizes five main principles of ecodesign, including the idea that solutions grow from a sense of place, ecological accounting can help inform design and that successful ecolodge designers go out of their way to 'make nature visible' to visitors.

Guidelines and standards

In our closing section, we address the need for setting and maintaining standards in ecotourism. Here authors explore the pros and cons of certification and accreditation programmes for ecotourism. Though such an assessment must be an ongoing endeavour, there are good reasons to reward projects and companies that are already making positive contributions. Yet the challenges to certification are numerous. Which companies and projects should be spotlighted as effective ecotourism operations and according to what criteria? Who shall decide on criteria and carry out the assessments? How will certification gain operator buy-in and public recognition? These are crucial questions if ecotourism is to remain free of counterfeit 'greenwashing'.

In Chapter 14, Megan Epler Wood provides a framework for evaluating ecotourism projects from the perspective of international development donors. She documents the ways in which donors – including private foundations and bilateral and multilateral agencies – comprise one of the most influential sectors in the ecotourism development process. Donors are striving to develop clear and transparent guidelines for ecotourism project development, and standards for evaluation, to ensure that the ecotourism projects they fund worldwide meet 'triple bottom-line' standards for conservation, development and profitability. The chapter includes a review of the literature regarding standards for ecotourism development projects and a draft framework to use for conducting better evaluations of ecotourism projects in the future.

Martha Honey provides a global, historical context for the emergence of certification – not just in ecotourism – and explains why ecotourism is an especially difficult commodity to certify. Honey characterizes common components of certification programmes (voluntary enrolment, logo, fees, assessment), the pros and cons of different methodologies for creating sustainability in tourism (i.e. process- versus performance-based standards), and the different certification programmes that exist for conventional tourism, sustainable tourism and ecotourism. If ecotourism is to continue to fulfil its social and environmental promise, Honey asserts, it will need its own global accreditation system to 'certify the certifiers'.

The challenge ahead

In the final chapter, co-editor William Durham brings us back to an integrated assessment of ecotourism as it stands today. The chapter highlights five major conclusions from this volume.

1. Ecotourism cannot work everywhere and cannot solve all problems of conservation and development; it requires special natural attractions or draws, and even then, it should be but part of a bundle of complementary activities for conservation and development.
2. Community involvement in ecotourism is a predictor of success with regard to development as well as conservation; more than a matter of economic benefits alone, successful involvement entails decision making authority.
3. Ecotourism can be empowering for marginalized and disenfranchised people, and can help in their efforts to gain recognition, rights and resources.

4. Ongoing adaptive management (with feedback and corrective responses) is crucial to the long-term viability of ecotourism efforts.

5. Although tourists appreciate many different aspects of ecotourism (aesthetics, entertainment, communion with nature, etc.), what sustains successful ecotourism is its educational/interpretive value, and this is important to remember.

Durham's chapter concludes with the argument that ecotourism is unique among commercial activities in rural areas because, unlike so many other activities, ecotourism works best when it builds on local knowledge and authenticity. In at least this one domain, outsiders have a built-in disadvantage compared with locals. Carefully designed ecotourism initiatives do have the potential to contribute both to biodiversity conservation and to local community development.

References

Alexander, S.E. (2000) Resident attitudes towards conservation and black howler monkeys in Belize: the Community Baboon Sanctuary. *Environmental Conservation* 27, 341–350.

Ananthaswamy, A. (2004) Massive growth of ecotourism worries biologists. *New Scientist*; available at http://www.newscientist.com/article.ns?id=dn4733 (accessed February 2008).

Barkin, D. (1996) Ecotourism: a tool for sustainable development in an era of international integration? In: Miller, J.A. and Malek-Zadeh, E. (eds) *The Ecotourism Equation: Measuring the Impacts.* Yale University Press, New Haven, Connecticut, pp. 263–272.

Belsky, J.M. (1999) Misrepresenting communities: the politics of community-based rural ecotourism in Gales Point Manatee, Belize. *Rural Sociology* 64, 641–666.

Bookbinder, M.P., Dinerstein, E., Rijal, A., Cauley, H. and Rajouria, A. (1998) Ecotourism's support of biodiversity conservation. *Conservation Biology* 12, 1399–1404.

Borman, R. (1999) Cofan: story of the forest people and the outsiders. *Cultural Survival Quarterly* 23, 48–50.

Brandon, K., Redford, K.H. and Sanderson, S. (1998) *Parks in Peril: People, Politics, and Protected Areas.* Island Press, Washington, DC.

Brosius, J.P., Tsing, A.L. and Zerner, C. (1998) Representing communities: histories and politics of community-based natural resource management. *Society and Natural Resources* 11, 157–168.

Burns, P.M. (1999) *An Introduction to Tourism and Anthropology.* Routledge, London.

Butler, R. and Hinch, T. (eds) (1996) *Tourism and Indigenous Peoples.* International Thompson Business Press, London.

Butynski, T.M. and Kalina, J. (1998) Gorilla tourism: a critical look. In: Mildner-Gullan, J.M. and Mace, R. (eds) *Conservation of Biological Resources.* Blackwell, Oxford, pp. 294–313.

Cater, E. (2006) Ecotourism as a Western construct. *Journal of Ecotourism* 5, 23–29.

Cater, E. and Lowman, G. (eds) (1994) *Ecotourism: A Sustainable Option?* John Wiley and Sons, Chichester, UK.

Ceballos-Lascurain, H. (1996) *Tourism, Ecotourism, and Protected Areas: The State of Nature-based Tourism Around the World and Guidelines for its Development.* International Union for the Conservation of Nature and Natural Resources, Cambridge, UK.

Chambers, E. (2000) *Native Tours: The Anthropology of Travel and Tourism.* Waveland Press, Prospect Heights, Illinois.

Chapin, M. (2004) A challenge to conservationists. *World Watch* November/December, 17–31.

Christ, C., Hillel, O., Matus, S. and Sweeting, J. (2004) *Tourism and Biodiversity: Mapping Tourism's Global Footprint.* United Nations Environment Programme and Conservation International, Washington, DC.

Daily, G.C. and Ellison, K. (2003) *The New Economy of Nature: The Quest to Make Nature Profitable.* Island Press, Washington, DC.

Davenport, L., Brockelman, W.Y., Wright, P.C., Ruf, K. and Rubio del Valle, F.B. (2002) Ecotourism tools for parks. In: Terborgh, J., van Schaik, C., Davenport, L. and Rao, M. (eds) *Making Parks Work: Strategies for Preserving Tropical Nature.* Island Press, Washington, DC, pp. 279–306.

Denman, R. (2001) *Guidelines for Community-based Ecotourism Development.* World Wildlife Fund International, Gland, Switzerland.

Desmond, J. (1999) *Staging Tourism: Bodies on Display from Waikiki to Sea World.* University of Chicago Press, Chicago, Illinois.

Duffy, R. (2002) *A Trip Too Far: Ecotourism, Politics, & Exploitation.* Earthscan, London.

Eadington, W.R. and Smith, V.L. (eds) (1992) *Tourism Alternatives: Potentials and Problems in the Development of Tourism.* University of Pennsylvania Press, Philadelphia, Pennsylvania.

Epler Wood, M. (2002) *Ecotourism: Principles, Practices and Policies for Sustainability.* United Nations Environment Programme, Paris.

Giannecchini, J. (1993) Ecotourism: new partners, new relationships. *Conservation Biology* 7, 429–432.

Gossling, S. (ed.) (2003) *Tourism and Development in Tropical Islands: Political Ecology Perspectives.* Edward Elgar Publishing Ltd, Cheltenham, UK.

Greenwood, D.J. (1989) Culture by the pound: an anthropological perspective on tourism as cultural commoditization. In: Smith, V. (ed.) *Hosts and Guests: The Anthropology of Tourism*, 2nd edn. University of Pennsylvania Press, Philadelphia, Pennsylvania, pp. 171–185.

Groom, M.A., Podolsky, R.D. and Munn, C.A. (1991) Tourism as a sustained use of wildlife. In: Robinson, J.G. and Redford, K.H. (eds) *Neotropical Wildlife Use and Conservation.* University of Chicago Press, Chicago, Illinois, pp. 393–412.

Hawkins, D.E. and Lamoureux, K. (2001) Global growth and magnitude of ecotourism. In: Weaver, D. (ed.) *The Encyclopedia of Ecotourism.* CAB International, Wallingford, UK, pp. 63–72.

Honey, M. (1999) *Ecotourism and Sustainable Development: Who Owns Paradise?* Island Press, Washington, DC.

Honey, M. (2002) *Setting Standards: Certification in the Ecotourism Industry.* Island Press, Washington, DC.

Honey, M. and Rome, A. (2000) *Protecting Paradise: Certification Programs for Sustainable Tourism and Ecotourism.* Institute for Policy Studies, Washington, DC.

Isaacs, J.C. (2000) The limited potential of ecotourism to contribute to wildlife conservation. *Wildlife Society Bulletin* 28, 61–69.

Jones, C.B. and Young, J. (2004) Hunting restraint by creoles at the Community Baboon Sanctuary, Belize: a preliminary study. *Journal of Applied Animal Welfare Science* 7, 127–141.

Kellert, S.R., Mehta, J.N., Ebbin, S.A. and Lichtenfeld, L.L. (2000) Community natural resource management: promise, rhetoric and reality. *Society and Natural Resources* 13, 705–715.

Kimmell, J.R. (1999) Ecotourism as environmental learning. *Journal of Environmental Education* 30, 40–44.

Kiss, A. (2004) Is community-based ecotourism a good use of biodiversity conservation funds? *Trends in Ecology and Evolution* 19, 231–237.

Kramer, R.A., van Schaik, C.P. and Johnson, J. (eds) (1997) *Last Stand: Protected Areas and the Defense of Tropical Biodiversity*. Oxford University Press, New York, pp. 3–14.

Kruger, O. (2005) The role of ecotourism in conservation: panacea or Pandora's box? *Biodiversity and Conservation* 14, 579–600.

Landell-Mills, N. and Porras, L. (2002) *Silver Bullet or Fools' Gold? A Global Review of Markets for Forest Environmental Services and Their Impact on the Poor*. International Institute for Environment and Development, London.

Lanfant, M., Allcock, J.B. and Bruner, E.M. (eds) (1995) *International Tourism: Identity and Change*. Sage, London.

Langholz, J. (1999) Exploring the effects of alternative income opportunities on rainforest use: insights from Guatemala's Maya Biosphere Reserve. *Society and Natural Resources* 12, 139–149.

Lindberg, K. (1991) *Economic Policies for Maximizing Nature Tourism's Contribution to Sustainable Development*. World Resources Institute, Washington, DC.

Lindberg, K. (1994) *An Analysis of Ecotourism's Economic Contribution to Conservation and Development in Belize: A Report*. World Wildlife Fund, Washington, DC.

Lindberg, K. and Hawkins, D.E. (eds) (1993) *Ecotourism: A Guide for Planners and Managers*. Ecotourism Society, North Bennington, Vermont.

Mowforth, M. and Munt, I. (1998) *Tourism and Sustainability: New Tourism in the Third World*. Routledge, London.

Oates, J.F. (1999) *Myth and Reality in the Rainforest: How Conservation Strategies are Failing in West Africa*. University of California Press, Berkeley, California.

Orams, M.B. (1997) The effectiveness of environmental education: can we turn tourists into 'greenies'? *Progress in Tourism and Hospitality Research* 3, 295–306.

Redford, K. and Agrawal, A. (2006) *Poverty, Development, and Biodiversity Conservation: Shooting in the Dark?* Working Paper No. 26. Wildlife Conservation Society, New York.

Scheyvens, R. (1999) Ecotourism and the empowerment of local communities. *Tourism Management* 20, 245–249.

Stonich, S. (1998) The political ecology of tourism. *Annals of Tourism Research* 25, 25–54.

Stonich, S. (2000) *The Other Side of Paradise: Tourism, Conservation, and Development in the Bay Islands*. Cognizant Communication Corporation, New York.

Stronza, A. (2001) The anthropology of tourism: forging new ground for ecotourism and other alternatives. *Annual Review of Anthropology* 30, 261–283.

Stronza, A. (2005) Hosts and hosts: the anthropology of community-based ecotourism in the Peruvian Amazon. *National Association for Practice of Anthropology Bulletin* 23, 170–190.

Terborgh, J. (1999) *Requiem for Nature*. Island Press, Washington, DC.

Terborgh, J., van Schaik, C., Davenport, L. and Rao, M. (eds) (2002) *Making Parks Work: Strategies for Preserving Tropical Nature*. Island Press, Washington, DC.

TIES (2000) *Ecotourism Statistical Fact Sheet*. The International Ecotourism Society, Burlington, Vermont.

Thaites, R, Lipscombe, N. and Smith, E. (2002) Providing education in a growth industry: issues in ecotourism education and employment in Australia. *Journal of Teaching in Travel & Tourism* 2, 81–97.

Wearing, S. and Neil, J. (1999) *Ecotourism: Impacts, Potentials, and Possibilities*. Butterworth Heinemann, Oxford, UK.

West, P. and Carrier, J.G. (2004) Ecotourism and authenticity: getting away from it all? *Current Anthropology* 45, 483–491.

WTO (2004) Tourism 2020 Vision. World Tourism Organization, Madrid; available at http://unwto.org/facts/eng/vision.htm (accessed August 2007).

Part II

Community-based Ecotourism

———————————

2 Ecotourism and Conservation: the Cofan Experience

R. Borman

Fundación para la Sobrevivencia del Pueblo Cofan, Carcelén Alto, Quito, Ecuador

Introduction

In 1978, I was in a quandary. I had already spent 4 years fighting to achieve recognition for Cofan land rights at my home village of Doreno. I was deeply involved in the continuing process of establishing our legal rights as a community, and organizing our village to be able to resist the relentless colonization and destruction of our forest environment that had begun with the arrival of the oil companies in 1964. I was marginally aware of what was happening to our culture – the result of hundreds of years of living in a pristine physical environment and rich social and cultural environments – but along with most of my peers, I was far more concerned with surviving until tomorrow. Where were we going to get the money to survive? The mainstay of our traditional economy had been fine craftwork – feather crowns and necklaces, hammocks and bags made from twisted palm fibres, and other items – that were traded or sold to other cultural groups or to interested outsiders. However, while this represented enough to buy salt and fishhooks, I needed some form of income that would allow us to carry our organizational work and the protection of our rights to the capital city of Quito and beyond.

We were already involved with visitors. They were mostly backpackers, doing the 'see South America on a dollar a day' routine, but a bit of talk and a lot of interest led from one thing to another. A few friends and I were taking groups of these backpackers along on our hunting and fishing trips to more remote areas of the forest away from the village. They paid for the gas to get to areas we otherwise couldn't have accessed, and we would come back with food for weeks. It seemed a good deal, but other than the extra gas money, there was no real pay coming out of it.

But not all of the people who were coming in wanted to just go along on a hunting trip. Some wanted something different: they wanted to not just hunt the animals with us, but to see, experience and learn some of what we knew about the forests. We decided to see if these people would pay us for taking them, over and above the cost of the motorboat. They would. And ecotourism, Cofan style, was born.

The Cofan Ecotourism Model

During the following years, we went through a number of changes. We parleyed our economic advantages into new lands, a new community named Zabalo far from the region affected by the outside world, and a new way of life. We fought oil companies to a standstill, and began innovative conservation programmes. And we continued to refine what was now known as 'ecotourism'. As we did so, we slowly began to see a model emerging. This model was based on three principles that I established early in our experience, in many ways less from foresight than from practicality, and was later to incorporate – or more accurately, be incorporated by – one more highly significant principle.

The first principle was that in all of our dealings with visitors we would emphasize our 'natural' environment, rather than our social or spiritual environment. This meant no 'dressing up for the tourist', no fake 'ceremonies' or 'dances', no silly 'visits to a Cofan home'. Instead, it meant we would show the tourist our forests, our rivers, our animals, our medicinal plants. We would use our considerable knowledge of these to make the trip an exciting nature experience. And if during the trip we became friends with the visitors, we might take them into our homes or allow them into some of our social activities – but as friends, not as tourists. The emphasis would remain solidly on a natural history experience.

The second principle was that we would hire only 'insiders'. Especially at first, when our Cofan ideas of cooking conflicted sharply with the palates and gastrointestinal needs of our tourists, the temptation to hire outsider cooks was strong. And the development not only of cooks but of cross-cultural skills as guides and administrators was also a long and difficult process. As we began working increasingly with foreign tourist agencies, we received some very sharp letters concerning some of our accommodations and our performances. But throughout, our group remained solidly Cofan, and we learned and we learned. The vast majority of our visitors left with solid memories, a deeper appreciation of the Amazonian rainforest, and a deep appreciation for our help in experiencing it. And not really surprisingly, by the end of a tour, the vast majority also realized that they had been part of a far more profound cultural experience than any of the 'come see the natives' tours could have ever provided.

The third principle was that we would commit to a completely different sort of division of received resources than that being presented by the local form of Western culture with which we were familiar. This meant that our division of the economic resources we received would be based upon real knowledge, not acceptable local pay scales, and would also reflect our responsibility as a subgroup within the larger social context of our village and people.

As a member of the Cofan culture, I was deeply aware that the Cofan culture's body of knowledge was fully as intricate, fully as deep, as that of any field of knowledge in the Western world. Thus, the older men who had mentored me during my growing up were fully as intelligent, and were handling fully as much information, as any of the Western world's scientists and teachers from whom I had learned my Western skills. Thus, they deserved a much higher return for their knowledge than was available to them within the present economic context of our Cofan world. With tourism money, this became possible, and in the process, we established the continuance of our Cofan form of knowledge as a viable path for young people within the community to pursue (Fig. 2.1).

By the same token, the new skills we were learning as we dealt with the multitude of details that went into taking care of the physical needs of our visitors were worthy of higher levels of pay. But how to justify giving everybody similar wages? We needed to build infrastructure, and within a very short time we found ourselves working as a team. Wages ceased to be a way of paying for day labour, and began to be viewed as a communal

Fig. 2.1. Cofan children. (Photo: Randy Borman.)

reward not only for the work we were doing on the trip but also for the other work we were accomplishing together as a group as we built the houses, remodelled the boats and cut the trails for our visitors. It was only a short jump for me, as the founder and key person in our little venture, to begin to use the extra economic profits we were receiving to buy items that were of value to all of us who were involved in the tourism.

But this was not yet truly 'community' tourism. Community-based, yes, but the community as a whole was benefiting only in fringe ways. One of these was the sale of handicrafts. Another was secondary wages paid by members of our 'tour company' for helping out with fields or other small-scale jobs. But the community at large was not necessarily in the loop. We needed some way of cutting in the community as a whole, not as individual members. This we found in the development and management of our physical infrastructure of cabins. This part of the model resulted in a way all members of the community could participate, and the community was able to raise substantial amounts of funding for our parallel activities in trying to legalize lands and hold together as an organization.

The fourth principle involved concepts none of us had really thought too much about when we first began, but which developed in a surprisingly smooth manner during the following years. This principle is simply that if we are going to continue as a culture, we need to actively protect and conserve our environment. Ecotourism was an important developmental tool in bringing this principle into the forefront of our outlook as a people, but the lesson for us was far broader.

It had never really been necessary for us as a people to conserve or protect our physical environment. Through the centuries, populations grew or diminished, technology changed, aspects of the culture adapted to new social, spiritual and physical dynamics. But never had the continuance of what we termed simply the Forest – the sum total of pristine rivers, towering mountains, vast oceans of trees, interminable swamps, thousands of marvellous species of birds, fish, reptiles, mammals, and more – been actively called into question. It was always there, always central, always giving. We had always made our living from It. The idea of owning It, protecting It, conserving It, had never occurred to us. Now, suddenly, we recognized that this was absolutely necessary if we were to survive as a people.

In our case, the catalyst for this developing awareness was tourism. Tourism caused us to begin to look at the Forest as our ultimate resource. So much of our relationship with the Forest was so natural and so deeply ingrained that we had never really been aware of Its importance to us. But as we presented the rainforest to our clients, we began to realize the degree to which this Forest truly was the root of our culture and that, without It, we were nothing. All of our knowledge would be gone, all of the things we needed for daily life would be gone.

Our first 'conservation' experiences were sort of in reverse. At first, we continued to hunt, but began changing our methods and the animals hunted. We learned the hard way that certain animals and methods were 'ok' and others were not, regardless of things like relative abundance or the place of a particular creature on the endangered species list. For example, we found that monkeys were definitely 'out', no matter how good they tasted or how abundant they were. It was hard at first for a bunch of veteran hunters to watch a troop of fat woolly monkeys peering down at us (imagine yourself in the supermarket, showing foreign friends around, to find your favourite food on sale for a tenth of the normal price but being unable to take advantage of the sale because of their prejudices). But slowly, we learned to appreciate viewing them just as much as we appreciated their meat on the table. With macaws, it was a classic case of 'a bird in the bush is worth two in the hand'. We found that even the toucan, crow-like in its ubiquity, was too 'pretty' to be hunted. On the other hand, most tourists could cope with deer or wild peccary being hunted, and any of the assorted turkey-like or chicken-like birds seemed to be ok.

Meanwhile, we began to actively wrestle with how to protect species that were obviously of high touristic value, to ensure their presence when visitors came. We soon found ourselves developing usage regulations for these at a community level, and we began to experience the excitement of the return and the taming of many of these species. (We continue even to this day to offer certain meat and fish that we consider to be in no danger of extinction to the tourist, as an alternative to meat involving the clearing of rainforests and fish captured in environmentally unsound manners.)

First, then, we dealt with what not to shoot for the audience; and later, what to protect and how to do it. We were working our way into something completely new, called management. We were not only making a living from our environment, we were now managing that environment. And our management was directed towards conserving it. Suddenly, our sense of ownership began to come into play and with it a complex realization of our ancestral use patterns. The concept of ancestral territorial rights began to take on meaning.

All of this took a little over a decade to come together. We started our first non-tourist oriented conservation regulations ten years after our first tourism programme and our first proactive conservation programmes thirteen years from that first trip. The evolution of our value structure was based on a number of influences besides ecotourism, but ecotourism provided both the financial incentives to develop our cultural and environmental awareness and the economic power that we were able to translate into real-life solutions to our conservation needs.

The Shattering of a Successful Model

We all tend to develop a smug attitude when all is going well. By the early 1990s, all was going well for the Cofans. We had a new community in an area called Zabalo (Fig. 2.2) and had gained control of a far larger territory there. We had successfully resisted the pressures of the colonists and the oil companies who were continuing their expansion, and our forests were intact, pristine and beautiful. We had developed relationships with not only our previous travel agency contacts but also with the most powerful Ecuadorean tour company, and were offering a variety of services to thousands of tourists a year. We had recently developed a new trekking programme, along with a new model for combining the commercialization powers of outside travel agencies with the local skills we had built over the years. Money was rolling in and it seemed our ecotourism model was a total success. We were managing the Forest and we were earning a living at the same time, in spades.

But then trouble began. A dispute over territory far away on the southern border of Ecuador – time-wise, more distant from us at Zabalo than even San Francisco – had destroyed relations between Ecuador and Peru, and a war had begun. And suddenly, we became painfully aware of a new side of the ecotourism model. This side of the model was its extreme fragility in the face of any perceived – not necessarily real, but perceived – danger near the destination. It was simple and easy to understand: you don't go where you might get shot at unless you have to and you certainly don't go there as a paying guest on your vacation time. But it was intensely frustrating. We had worked so hard to protect our forests, build our interesting species populations and develop adequate infrastructure to ensure that our tourists had a wonderful experience. Suddenly, through absolutely no fault of our own, the tourists ceased to come. What made it even more frustrating was that the threat was only a

Fig. 2.2. Cofan community. (Photo: Randy Borman.)

perceived one: all of the fighting was going on at the opposite end of the earth from us as far as we were concerned. And what was far more chilling was that if people didn't come to us, they would go elsewhere – and it would take years to redevelop a clientele in a business that relies heavily on the word-of-mouth advertising of satisfied customers.

Unfortunately, the war with Peru, in 1995, was only a foretaste of another similar but far more devastating blow that would come a few years later. We rebuilt following that first war, and slowly regained our feet and business as we began to use the new information tools available to us on the Internet and other methods. But our province in Ecuador now appeared on the travel advisory list of the US State Department, and it was only a short time until the escalation of the USA's War on Drugs was to change even our actual security situation.

In the last year of President Bill Clinton's administration, the Plan Colombia was signed into effect. This controversial programme destabilized the border region of Colombia, our neighbour to the north, resulting in a sharp increase in the violence in Colombia and an influx of Colombian refugees. Unfortunately, not only refugees spilled across our border. Kidnappings of oil workers in Ecuador by Colombian-based professional kidnapping bands and a general increase in delinquency near Lago Agrio – the gateway city for the region – inevitably pushed our province into the 'travel warning' class, and large-scale operations such as that of Metropolitan Touring's Flotel – an integral part of our community efforts – were suddenly very vulnerable. Tourism dropped, and finally the Flotel was forced out of the business. Clients for our trips were far fewer and more wary, not so much about our area, but about getting to our area. We needed to start looking for some real alternatives.

A New Challenge

The new millennium for the Cofan community began on a note of challenge. Where do we go from here? Our management model for our lands relies heavily on ecotourism for its economic justification. Is the model still valid with a highly reduced influx of visitors? The security situation in Lago Agrio is more and more difficult to predict. Should we still continue to risk bringing people in via this route? The economic situation in all of our Cofan villages, not just Zabalo, has gone from bad to worse. What cultural and environmental alternatives can we offer them? Finally, is it really worth the trouble? What is the future?

The first step was already in place. In 1998, we created a not-for-profit organization with branches in both the USA and Ecuador, named Cofan Survival Fund and Fundación Sobrevivencia Cofan, respectively. This new organization has as its primary goal the survival of the Cofan people: the culture, the language, the rainforest environment that defines us. Into it we incorporated what we had already begun at Zabalo in terms of conservation initiatives and non-tourism related activities. Under its umbrella, we had already begun to seek outside grants and generalized help to further develop especially our land legalization and management programmes. Now, as we faced the severe reduction in our primary source of income as both a community and a people, we began to use this organization to put together a tri-part programme for our continued survival.

The first part embodies essentially our short-term goals. For Zabalo, this means revitalization of our tourism, and the only way we can see to do this is by offering our clients a way to bypass the increasingly dangerous region around Lago Agrio. The solution? To put in an airstrip, aimed at providing direct access from Quito to Zabalo. We are now in the process of finding the necessary financial assistance to complete this strip. This will provide not only danger-free access to Zabalo, but also a major incentive for the revitalization of the tourist industry in the lower part of the Cuyabeno Wildlife Reserve, and will help not only us but the other non-Cofan communities in the region. Also involved in our short-term planning is the internationalizing of our handicrafts sales. With the World Wide Web, and interested and strategically located volunteers, this expands our market possibilities enough that handicraft sales may eventually become the primary economic resource for our Cofan villages.

Our mid-term planning is based on accessing increased funding for the management and scientific monitoring of our now sizeable land base. At the moment, most of this funding looks to come from internationally oriented conservation organizations. It is hoped that, as the world increasingly realizes the importance of intact rainforest for everything from climate control to carbon sequestering, we will eventually begin to receive direct income for this important work. Basically, what is involved in management and monitoring is training community members to do year-around transect or trail analysis, with varying lists of species and conditions as subjects. This also provides us with a full-time 'park guard' corps that serves as an early warning system for incursions from colonists, lumber companies, oil companies, commercial hunters and other *personae non grata*. In our mid-term planning, we also include our species repopulations programmes which are not only valuable conservation initiatives, but also major sources of community and individual income.

Our long-term planning is based around education. We are actively trying to educate small groups of Cofan young people in the best possible schools in Quito. We operate a 'Cofan dorm' to allow the students a solid and familiar Cofan cultural base from which to go to school, but the theory is to educate a cadre of thoroughly tri-lingual and tri-cultural leaders to take the reigns in the future. We want to provide our own tour companies, our own biologists, our own management planners, our own indigenous political leaders. We want to cease to be the pawns of often well-meaning, but always outsider, organizations and institutions. We want to take our place as Cofans not only at the local level, but at all levels of management of our culture, its lands and its heritage. Thus, and only thus, will we be able to continue our culture's relationship with our Forest for the next centuries, even as we have for the past centuries.

Notes

The basic format for our Cofan ecotourism is, and remains:

- Cofan guides, with appropriate pay.
- Cofan cooks and crew, with appropriate pay.
- Community intervention in activities that can incorporate all members of the Cofan community.
- Community-wide perceived benefits via artisanal sales.

For institutions interested in helping communities begin ecotourism as an economic and conservation tool:

- On-site training of guides and cooks is valid.

But, of far more importance is to:

- Establish a good commercialization scheme for the newly formed group.
- Establish a good communication system for the newly formed group.

Without these two basics, the project will fail.

Of only slightly less importance is helping the community through the maze of legalizing their operation. Here the big questions will be:

- Is the community interested in ecotourism as a full-time or a part-time job?
- Will ecotourism be the primary source of income or a rather secondary one?
- Is the community capable of operating as a community, or would it be much more viable to identify groups of individuals and build 'mini-companies'? What areas can you identify in which all of the community can really participate?

Cofan 'vital statistics', alluded to above but not specified, are as follows:

- Population (in Ecuador): 1200.
- Number of communities: 10.
- Total land area: legalized, 430,000 ha; under control but not legalized, approximately 80,000 ha.
- Total number of oil fields within the above-mentioned area: 5.
- Total number of barrels of oil taken out of Cofan lands by the year 2000: approximately 2,000,000.
- Total amount of payment in any form received for oil activities: four spoons, approximately 50 meals of rice and sardines.

3 An Ecotourism Partnership in the Peruvian Amazon: the Case of Posada Amazonas

J.F. Gordillo Jordan[1], C. Hunt[2] and A. Stronza[2]

[1]Posada Amazonas Rainforest Expeditions, Puerto Maldonado, Madre de Dios, Peru; [2]Department of Recreation, Park and Tourism Sciences, Texas A&M University, College Station, Texas, USA

Introduction

From the moment the term was coined (Ceballos-Lascurain, 1987), ecotourism was deemed to be an integration of conservation and local development. It is widely recognized as well that, in order to provide a memorable and authentic experience, ecotourism requires relatively intact natural areas, many of which are found in the poorest and most remote regions of the world (Christ *et al.*, 2003). None the less, ecotourism has demonstrated the capacity to bring together demand with the offer in such a way that win–win situations sometimes occur between the stakeholders involved: the environment, communities, entrepreneurs/ operators and visitors.

One example is Posada Amazonas, a 30 double-bedroom lodge located along the Tambopata River in south-eastern Peru, in the biodiversity 'hotspot' of the Tropical Andes (Myers *et al.*, 2000). The lodge brings together the native community of Infierno and a private company, Rainforest Expeditions, to achieve a common goal: to prove that local communities can generate enough income through ecotourism to promote natural resource stewardship and conservation. By pursuing sustainable local development through the marketing of wildlife and nature, the long-term goals of both the community and the private company can be met.

Two Partners, Two Ways of Thinking

The community

The native community of Infierno was founded in 1976 by 80 families of the Ese'eja, Andean and Ribereño ethnic groups. The first group are the original inhabitants of the Tambopata River, while the Andean and Ribereño groups migrated to the region from other parts of Peru and the wider Amazon. Their major activities are slash-and-burn agriculture, hunting and fishing, Brazil nuts and palm fruits collection, timber and, more recently, tourism, handcrafting and fish farming. As of 2007 the population of Infierno is approximately 600. Their community infrastructure includes a kindergarten, primary and secondary schools, a fresh water tank, and connectivity via an unpaved 19 km road to Puerto Maldonado, the region's capital (Fig. 3.1).

In the mid-1980s the Tambopata National Reserve was created. In the process part of the Infierno's territory was included by mistake. The community disputed the error and, following the recommendations of local environmental and indigenous rights non-governmental organizations (NGOs), the Peruvian Authority for Natural Resources (INRENA) agreed to the devolution of the land with one condition: the community should declare the returned land as a reserve. Infierno agreed, and in 1987 established a Communal Reserve of approximately 3000 ha, a full 30% of its titled territory. Within the reserve, all resource extraction (hunting, logging, fishing, etc.) is banned. In addition to this community reserve, the community also created an elaborate medicinal garden that same year. The Ñape Ethno-botanical Center is a place devoted to traditional medicine.

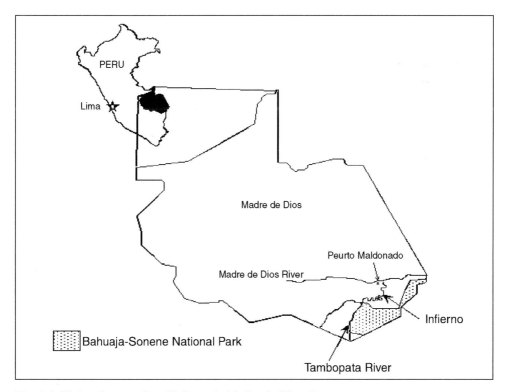

Fig. 3.1. Native Community of Infierno in Madre de Dios, Peru.

Ñape serves not only Infierno but also many other communities in Madre de
Dios.

Until 1993 Infierno residents managed to avoid tourism development
in their community. They watched tourism boats go up and down river,
crossing their territory, and wondered whether tourism could be a good
alternative for them. Still, the memory of a previous bad experience with
a tour operator who promised to pay for recreational use of their land, yet
never did, made them very cautious of tourism and of outsiders in general
at that point. As a result, Infierno rejected Rainforest Expeditions' first
attempt to collaborate with them.

The company

Rainforest Expeditions is a Peruvian tour operator established in 1989,
founded by Eduardo Nycander and Kurt Holle. It initially oriented its efforts
towards developing a research station devoted to the large Amazon macaws
along the Tambopata River, 8 h by boat upriver from Puerto Maldonado. In
1992, the Tambopata Research Center was opened to tourists with a goal of
using tourism revenues to continue funding the research endeavours.
However, the long boat ride usually forced them to stay overnight en route,
either camping on a beach along the river or spending the night in a
competitor's lodge. They needed a place for an overnight stay. By that time,
some of Infierno's community members had been hired to work as research
assistants. This helped establish relationships within the community that
would be effective in helping forge collaboration between the two future
partners.

An Innovative Partnership

After a first attempt failed in 1993, an Ese'eja leader from Infierno approached
Nycander in 1995 to propose the idea of building a lodge in the community.
For Rainforest Expeditions, the prospect was quite exciting. They knew
Infierno still had primary forest, particularly in the Communal Reserve, and
that, along with the presence of typical Amazonian biodiversity, harpy eagles
were currently nesting there and giant otters were easily seen in the oxbow
lake nearby. These charismatic mega-fauna provided the perfect 'franchise
species' for ecotourism development. Moreover, Infierno was within 2 h of
Puerto Maldonado – the major gate to the Madre de Dios Region where flights
arrive daily from Cusco, one of the most popular destinations in all of South
America. However, coming to an agreement with the community was not
easy. Dissemination of information about the project and close communication with families in the community was needed. Community
members, Rainforest Expeditions' owners and local offices of Conservation
International (CI) worked hard through group meetings and with individual
households to discuss the potential benefits of a partnership.

The contract

Finally, in May 1996, Infierno and Rainforest Expeditions signed a 20-year agreement for Posada Amazonas Lodge (PAL). This contract held Rainforest Expeditions responsible for funding, building and operating the new lodge. However, profits would be split 60/40, favouring the community. The agreement also stated that transfer of ownership of Posada Amazonas from Rainforest Expeditions to the community would take place after the initial 20 years of operation. At that point, the community may choose to continue working with Rainforest Expeditions, collaborate with another partner or operate the lodge entirely on its own. In the meantime, the community is bound by contract to work exclusively with Rainforest Expeditions in order to avoid a disordered spring-up of other projects that could damage tourism development at Posada Amazonas and local resource-carrying capacities. The partners also agreed that the lodge would be located in the Communal Reserve, and the community would continue to enforce restrictions on resource extraction in that area.

After spending nearly a year looking for funds, construction on the new lodge started in 1997. It was then that the magnitude of the situation and the construction ahead began to set in for Rainforest Expeditions and Infierno: obtaining government permissions for the community to gather materials, such as wood and palm-tree roofs; organizing work teams, which was considered a non-paid, matching contribution of the community according to the grant obtained; and directing the construction of buildings far bigger than anything that existed in the community. Despite such large-scale effort, the lodge was carefully designed to offer the visitor the maximum opportunity to connect with the forest. For this reason the only areas of rainforest cleared were precise footprints of the buildings that formed the lodge. The rest of the primary forest was left intact; in fact, tourist rooms have only three walls, the fourth side being open to the forest.

In April 1998, the first tourist group arrived at Posada Amazonas. Since then, the lodge has become internationally known and runs at capacity year-round. The number of visitors has grown annually, recently totalling more than 7000 a year. The partnership between Infierno and Rainforest Expeditions originally emerged as the result of two intentions coming together: the community pursued collaboration with the company as a way to achieve economic development; the company saw collaboration as a way to expand its other business operation 8 h upriver. While these goals have been achieved, Posada Amazonas has come to mean much more to both partners.

Profit Sharing

The Peruvian–Canadian Fund agreed to fund Rainforest Expeditions US$350,000 to build the lodge and do the initial training. While the majority was granted, US$110,000 was deemed a loan. This amount was repaid continuously from 1998 to 2000. In every one of these initial years, Rainforest Expeditions' owners visited the community and explained the financial situation. The end message was no profits to share yet. Finally, in 2001, the situation changed and profits were available to share between partners. It was only then that the project ensured its permanence in Infierno. *Comuneros* wanted a return on their investment, some economic benefits after 5 years of involvement in the project. At first the profits were not high, as each family received little more than US$100 for the entire year. Even so, the message was clear: respecting the Communal Reserve was worthwhile; respecting certain wildlife was worthwhile; the partner, Rainforest Expeditions, was meeting its commitment. Tourism could in fact be a good option.

As of 2006, the community of Infierno has received more than US$500,000 in profit from Posada Amazonas. From that portion, around 70–80% has been split among 150 families for their personal use. The remaining revenues were used to improve Infierno's infrastructure with works such as a secondary school, a computer facility, additional road access alongside the community, and a potable water well and tank system. Additionally, social support in the form of a health emergency fund, care for the elderly and higher education loans has been made possible.

Institutional Support

Offering natural resources to visitors as the primary attraction of a tourism operation requires a profound knowledge about those resources. In this regard, Rainforest Expeditions has been working closely with several institutions that provide useful information about the best way to show and interpret a natural resource. These include the Frankfurt Zoological Society (FZS), several US universities (Stanford, Texas A&M, University of Michigan) and CI, among others. FZS collaborated with the ecotourism operation to establish codes of conduct for interacting with the otters in the Tres Chimbadas oxbow lake. The code prioritizes reproductive nests and foraging behaviours of the otters, keeping them inside a zone comprising half the lake area which remains untouchable to both community members and tourists alike. CI has collaborated with the community since 1996 on a wildlife monitoring programme that tracks levels of pressure on wildlife in Infierno due to hunting and tourism. Since 2005, community members have served independently as the wildlife monitors, gathering the data which CI analyses. Six *comuneros* have undergone this training, taking turns in pairs to collect data on the otters every six months.

The support from universities has come in various forms. One is a long-standing field research programme with Stanford University, which enables six student scholars every year to conduct research on topics in conservation biology, sustainability and ecotourism. Individual scholars too have carried out doctoral dissertations and long-term field research on the impacts of ecotourism (Stronza, 2000), harpy eagles (Piana, 2001) and resource management strategies of the Ese'eja (Ocampo-Raeder, 2006). The results of these and other studies in Infierno have influenced various initiatives for conservation and development. One example was a comparative study and series of workshops between local leaders of Posada Amazonas and two other community-based ecotourism partnerships – the Chalalan ecolodge in Bolivia and the Kapawi lodge in Ecuador. The 'Learning Host to Host Project', funded by the Critical Ecosystem Partnership Fund, enabled community members to see and learn for themselves how local residents in other communities were managing ecotourism (Stronza, 2004). Another result of research is the 'Macaw Project' at the Tambopata Research Center. Donald Brightsmith, a renowned parrot researcher, has gathered valuable information about macaw and parrot behaviour, nesting alternatives and customs regarding the daily congregations on the clay bluffs along the Tambopata River (Brightsmith, 2005). As researchers typically publish their work, these linkages constitute additional avenues for marketing Posada Amazonas to a specialized public with relatively little effort.

Building Capacity in the Community

By the time the transfer of ownership is due to take place in 2016, Rainforest Expeditions would have to have developed within the community the abilities needed to manage the entire operation. The contract stipulated that local labour from the community be hired whenever properly trained. For this reason it was necessary to develop capacity in the community. This process follows four stages, each increasing in difficulty: (i) training to fulfil operational positions at the lodge, such as waiters, housekeepers, boat drivers and cook assistants – this is crucial for enabling community members with no prior experience in tourism to start working at the lodge; (ii) more elaborate training to fill technical positions, such as bilingual guides (Spanish–English), maintenance chief, chefs and bartenders; (iii) accruing experience for community members to serve as lodge administrator and fill logistical positions at Puerto Maldonado office; and (iv) developing capacities for serving in the upper-level management positions in finance, human resources, operations and marketing. Every year a training course is held in the community to identify the best candidates. Those selected to work at Posada Amazonas are placed on a 2-year staff rotation in order to give the same opportunity of working at the lodge to all families of the community and also to develop experience in multiple aspects of lodge operation to those being groomed for higher-level positions.

Community guides

Every year, all community members interested in becoming guides participate first in a short training course about biology, conservation, sustainability issues and additional interpretation concepts. The top four performers in each course qualify to participate in a longer course that Rainforest Expeditions organizes every year. This 3-week guide course is an intensive programme that covers all of the knowledge an environmental interpreter should know in order to provide excellent service as a tourist guide in the Amazon rainforest. Along with the four selected Infierno members, participants are typically university trained biologists, foresters or environmental engineers. The best two community members are selected to work in the next guiding season. More than 60 *comuneros* have participated in the short course and 20 have attended the long one, nine of them proceeding to work as bilingual guides. In addition to the guide courses, ongoing training continues in the following areas: staff positions at PAL, basic accounting, sales and bookings, handicrafts, computer use, general maintenance, cooking, English, wildlife monitoring and communication, leadership and business concepts, park rangers.

Community guides quickly become more acquainted with tourists' preferences and behaviours because they experience it every day. Almost all of them dedicate themselves only to guiding because they find it very satisfying and it pays at least three times as much as traditional farming-related activities. The US$6000–8000 that guides earn annually is literally a fortune in Infierno, making them some of the wealthiest community members. Moreover, many of them have quit hunting in their spare time, choosing instead to use the same skills to identify and alert tourists to the presence of wildlife. One community member in particular has developed quite a reputation as world-class birdwatching guide. Such particularly gifted community guides now have the potential to become Peru-wide tour conductors.

Control committee

While profits are split 60/40, decision making would ideally be taken 50/50. A community 'Control Committee' (CC) was created to directly address issues connected to the lodge, including but not limited to those related to future investments, operational problems, sales, budgets, human resources and training, and service quality. The CC consists of ten members elected in a Communal Assembly, the primary governing body of Infierno to which the CC regularly reports. The CC meets every month at Posada Amazonas with Rainforest Expeditions representatives, among them the lodge manager, the project coordinator, the human resources manager, and often the owners of Rainforest Expeditions themselves. Meetings provide an opportunity for the CC members to discuss all tourism-related issues mentioned above and to increase their confidence in expressing and explaining their opinions. Since the beginning of the project, more than 40 *comuneros* have served as members of the CC.

Since the contract created it in 1996, the CC's presence in the project has grown continuously in significance. Through periodic changes in membership, the committee affords its members exposure to business concepts essential to the successful, independent operation of the lodge. This type of experience is otherwise not readily available in the community. Perhaps more importantly, however, they have learned that their opinions are of fundamental importance to the project, and they now freely express them during meetings and assemblies.

Empowerment Through Ecotourism

As tourism has grown in importance in the community, the CC has increased its influence in Infierno's everyday life. CC members have become more able and willing to express opinions in Communal Assemblies. They are now meaningful participants in the difficult decision-making process regarding all future community developments. Budgeting from the profits is one such heavily discussed theme. Every year the CC presents a proposal to reinvest a portion of the profits in projects for communal good to the entire Communal Assembly. As a result of their exposure to the tourism activity and the regular contact with Rainforest Expeditions representatives, CC members learn new concepts and values about business management and conservation, and these are transferred to the community at each Communal Assembly. It is a slow but steady process.

Moreover, the CC has undertaken many tough initiatives related to tourism development in the community over the last year, including a renegotiation of the original contract with Rainforest Expeditions and the possibility of increasing the number of lodges operating in the community. This latter undertaking is based on the fact that after 10 years of the exclusive contract, the community is savvier about the tourism industry and understands that visitor numbers can potentially increase without posing a threat to Posada Amazonas' success. In fact, in 2005, Rainforest Expeditions opened a new lodge, Refugio Amazonas, 2.5 h upriver from Posada, with relatively good success to date. As such, the CC requested the elimination of the exclusivity clause so that they can start their own tourism developments, possibly with other companies. Rainforest Expeditions agreed, recommending that Infierno prepare a territory-use plan and a tourism plan for the entire community. These plans continue to be discussed.

A Vehicle for Conservation

While the Posada Amazonas project has involved decisions related to conservation since the beginning, economic development edged out conservation as the primary goal of the partners at the outset. Now, owing to its growing capacity, intimate involvement in conservation-related activities and a heightened awareness of the tangible results that conservation behaviour can offer (e.g. revenues and capacities), the CC has directed the community to tackle difficult conservation situations in the region, none more ominous than the recent development of the inter-oceanic highway connecting the Amazon rainforest with the Pacific Coast.

Inter-oceanic highway

In 2004, the Peruvian Government announced the construction of a highway, or rather the pavement of an existing road, linking Brazil and the Atlantic Coast with the Peruvian rainforest town of Puerto Maldonado, the commercially important highland cities of Cusco and Puno, and eventually the Pacific Ocean. The highway totals 2586 km and requires an investment of US$892 million, backed by both the Peruvian and Brazilian governments, funded in its majority by the latter with an eye towards future exports from the region to the Asian Pacific (Balvín and Patrón, 2006; Dourojeanni, 2006). Many have cried out in opposition to this accelerated development as it places Peru, and especially the department of Madre de Dios, in a poor situation: lots of land without official titles; undetermined land-use regulations; little capacity to control for positive use of the highway; and no apparent production to compete with Brazil (Brandon *et al.*, 2005). Already, increasing immigration from Cusco and Puno to rainforest areas is causing deforestation, typically through a change in land use from primary or secondary forest to agriculture (Dourojeanni, 2006).

Ecotourism concession

This precarious situation has elevated the CC's interest in securing its own land and tourism resources. One of those resources is the Tres Chimbadas oxbow lake, located 5 min upriver from Posada Amazonas. Just outside community land, this lake is home for a family of giant river otters, important indicator species of the health of the freshwater ecosystem. The Tres Chimbadas Lake is located a perilous 7 km away from the inter-oceanic highway.

Prior to the Government announcement, Infierno recognized this impending threat and in October 2003 presented an application for a 1700 ha piece of land under the form of an Ecotourism Concession to protect the territories surrounding the lake. The process took almost 3 years, but at last the concession was granted to the community. It is the intention of the community to construct another lodge within this concession and build on the success of Posada Amazonas, which now has a waiting list for visitors. During this application process, Rainforest Expeditions connected Infierno with the Peruvian Society for Environmental Law (SPDA), an NGO devoted, in part, to supporting private conservation initiatives. For the CC, this reiterated the importance of alliances when pursuing complicated objectives.

However, the concession awarded did not include the Tres Chimbadas Lake itself. Because of unspecific legislation allowing several dependencies of INRENA to have different positions, an outsider was granted the concession to fish the lake. Infierno united with Rainforest Expeditions, other tour operators, SPDA and the FZS to challenge the concession. After many months of continuous meetings, INRENA agreed to revoke the concession. At the present time, Infierno, led by the CC, is forming an association with other tour operators to apply for their own concession to the lake in order to ensure its conservation. While the community will be required to pay for this concession, it will allow them to develop birding trails, access to clay licks, and other indirect uses in the area of the oxbow lake.

Cocococha Lake recreational license

Along with Tres Chimbadas Lake, the Cocococha Lake presents an opportunity to observe giant river otters. However, Cocococha is located within the Tambopata National Reserve, adjacent to Infierno land. Taking a proactive stance, the CC is attempting to secure access to this resource as a backup plan in case all efforts to protect Tres Chimbadas fail. To achieve this, Infierno has applied for a recreational license which will grant permission to take Posada Amazonas tourists on a 2-h walk to the lake.

Promotion of alternative agricultural tendencies

In Infierno, the common agriculture practice is slash and burn. This approach provides nutrients to the soil but only for the first year. Each *comunero* has 30 ha of land. In the majority of cases, 4–5 ha are used for farming and the rest is left as primary or secondary forest. From the year 2000 on, some *comuneros* started to use nitrogen-fixing plants to restore soil fertility and to minimize slash and burn. The coverage, called *mucuna* and *kudzu*, provides nitrogen during the whole year, requiring less investment of labour to have the farm ready to start another crop. Another new technique being promoted within the community, agroforestry, is an approach to farming that integrates short-, medium- and long-term crop plants with fruit- and nut-bearing trees. An agroforestry approach has the potential to increase the overall profitability of the farm.

Incorporating sustainability

Aguaje is a palm tree whose fruit is precious for Amazon people in general. It grows in swampy soils and its season corresponds with the rains between January and March. Traditionally, harvesting involves cutting the tree down to reach the fruits. In 2006, thanks to a grant from The Netherlands' embassy in Bolivia through World Wide Fund for Nature, a sustainable aguaje harvest committee was formed in the community. The *aguajeros* were very conscious of the need to protect the *aguajales* because every year they needed to walk further and further into the forest to find the aguaje palm trees. The committee implemented a new approach to harvesting aguaje through the use of climbing equipment. CI provided technical assistance and helped organize the *aguajeros* for the coming season. With no complete season totally registered yet, it is too soon to call this project a success. It may still be necessary to provide a market incentive to fully convince the committee about the profitability of sustainable harvest. However, it is certainly another indication of the community's shift in attitudes towards more sustainable approaches.

Perception of resources

In the past, Infierno members hunted certain species for prized feathers or animal skins. It has been a hard task to convince them that a macaw is worth more flying overhead than in a soup or decorating a dress. The same is true with harpy eagles, a highly endangered species that was traditionally hunted for its feathers. When an active harpy nest is found on a community member's property, the owner receives an amount of money for every tourist given the opportunity of viewing it from a distance. This ensures careful stewardship of the nest until the chicks have flown. This maturation process can take up to 8 months and, with a harpy eagle sighting being highly desirable among tourists, this represents a good earning opportunity for a *comunero*. Similarly, the giant otters in the oxbow lakes of Tres Chimbadas and Cocococha were sometimes hunted for their pelts but more often because community members considered them competitors for the lake fish they also eat. Together with the CC, regulations were set that include certain hours when fishing is permitted and restrictions on the type of equipment utilized to fish at the lake.

Satellite Projects

Even with the sharing of economic benefits it was always clear that Posada Amazonas would not cover all families' needs on a year-round basis. In view of all of the supplies and purchases required to operate Posada Amazonas and Rainforest Expeditions' other lodges in the region, it was therefore necessary to develop other business ventures so that Infierno could take advantage of the tourist demand, economic power and secure markets available through these projects.

Handicrafts project

As an additional part of the original contract, the two partners decided that products would be bought locally from the community as long as they met quality requirements and market price. An arts and crafts endeavour was the first to be established. Thanks to a World Bank grant of US$50,000 in 2000, community artisans built and equipped a workshop in the community and received training to use machines and prepare handicrafts. The products consist primarily of wooden carvings, jewellery composed of rainforest seeds, vine weaving and *yanchama* (traditional tree bark used for dressing). A small store was established at Posada Amazonas to create a secure market for the handicrafts and also to allow tourists to purchase items at the lodge rather than enter the community and disturb *comunero* life. Considering the number of tourists at PAL each year (around 7000), sales are still somewhat low (US$4600/year). However, there are 14 artisans whose ages range between 25 and 60 years, with an average age of 50. In the majority of cases, artisans devote time to making handicrafts only after meeting their needs for farming, hunting and fishing. It is often very difficult for them to shift the proportion of time dedicated to these traditional activities towards handicrafts until they recognize that the increased profitability can subsidize them. By devoting time to the modestly lucrative artisan activities, *comuneros*, particularly those advanced in age, are able to continue to provide income to the household unit and in some cases may even earn enough to hire younger individuals to assist with taking care of the family farm.

Ñape Center

Ñape is the ethno-botanical centre of the community. It was founded in 1987 to provide traditional health services to the communities of Madre de Dios. Until 2000, it was funded by an NGO which later had to end support for internal institutional reasons. At that time, the managers of Ñape Center approached Rainforest Expeditions and the CC with the goal of selling ethno-botanical tours to lodge visitors and focusing on medicinal properties of various rainforest plants. Since then, Ñape has received approximately 4000 visitors annually, generating US$12,000 each year. Ñape Center continues to expand and make preparations for the future. The plans include the construction of a laboratory, improved infrastructure for new health services to be offered to tourists, including a sauna, enhanced facilities for mystic tourism involving Ayahuasca sessions with local shamans, direct sale of natural medicines, and production of dyes and soaps to be utilized at Posada Amazonas and other Rainforest Expeditions' lodges (Fig. 3.2).

Fig. 3.2. Indigenous leaders on botanical walk in Posada Amazonas. (Photo: Amanda Stronza.)

Tourist port

Built in 2000 in order to save around US$10,000 per year in fuel expenses, the tourist port in Infierno consists basically of an access road linking the main Puerto Maldonado–Infierno highway with the Tambopata River. Initial investment was US$12,000, half of which was donated and half loaned by Rainforest Expeditions to a group of eight community members who agreed to take care of work and manage the port. Once the group paid off the loan, income from the port would pass to the community for another project. So far, Ecorosco SRL, an officially recognized enterprise formed by those eight *comuneros*, has been able to repay US$5000, maintain the road and port in good shape, and sell its services to other tourism companies at a rate of approximately US$0.50 per tourist. Annual income from the port is currently around US$10,000.

Fish farm

Motivated by a personal interest, one of the families in Infierno decided to invest its profit share along with other personal savings to build and operate a *piscigranja*, or fish farm. The farm will raise Amazon species, such as gamitana, pacotana and paco. As of 2006, the family has managed to supply Posada Amazonas with 10–20 kg of fish per week for nearly 6 continuous months. In 2007, they seeded 4500 more fish, which will be ready to sell in another 6 months. Current annual income from this project is around US$5000.

Juice factory

In 2000, CI developed a juice facility with the goal of testing whether the sustainable harvest of forest fruits could be a lucrative business for local residents. Unforeseen difficulties saw the plant close a year later. CI intended to transfer technology and know-how to the best available option. In 2004, supported by Rainforest Expeditions, the members of Infierno decided to solicit the transfer. After several months of negotiations, CI agreed to transfer the machinery and know-how to Infierno on the condition that the community and Rainforest Expeditions use Posada Amazonas revenues to fund two wildlife monitors who would continue to gather information about wildlife numbers in the community and the effects of hunting.

Having acquired the equipment and know-how required to produce juice, Infierno then needed a good facility with regular water and electricity services. In July 2005, Industrias Alimenticias Amazónicas EIRL (INALA), a small company in Puerto Maldonado, offered themselves as a partner. Within a few months, an agreement between Infierno and INALA was signed. Formal production of bottled juice and marmalade products started in March 2006, with Posada Amazonas again providing a secure market. At present (2008), this continues to be a small-scale project, staffed primarily by Rainforest Expeditions or INALA staff and involving only a small handful of local producers. Expanding distribution may further increase the economic impact of this facility on the community.

Some Thorns in the Rose

People receiving some kind of economic benefit from the ecotourism project have begun to change their attitude towards some species and the need to protect them. However, the majority of community members still work on their farms, do not participate in conservation efforts, watch without interest as tourists arrive each day and do not receive many direct benefits from the project. Owing to the logistical complexities of monitoring and guarding resources within the rainforest, many know they can easily get away with exploitive behaviours. In such remote and underdeveloped areas, even a 50% increase in income is not enough to elevate many families out of extreme poverty, and in such circumstances, conservation of natural resources is at direct odds with self-preservation. Therefore, despite all the positive changes for conservation and development described earlier, there continue to be many challenges that Posada Amazonas faces.

Trust

One might think that after 11 years of knowing each other, Rainforest Expeditions and the Native Community of Infierno would have developed full trust in each other as partners. However, this is not always the case. While the relationship between both parties has developed in a generally positive direction, there have been tensions between the two that at times nearly led to the demise of the project. So far, the problems have been overcome because the project is important for both partners. The only way to allow trust to reign is to communicate, communicate, communicate. As Kurt Holle, Rainforest Expeditions' co-founder, once said: 'Things get never tired of being clarified'.

Trust is also a challenge within the community. As mentioned at the outset, Infierno is a heterogeneous community formed not just from indigenous Ese'Eja rainforest families but also from the descendents of transplanted Ribereños and colonists from the Andean highlands. These groups often have colliding interests, agendas and *modus operandi*. Trust between the two partners, and within ethnic groups and families in Infierno, will continue to represent a challenge.

Unwillingness to assume responsibility

There are sometimes erratic decisions at the communal level that indirectly affect the normal course of project operations. For instance, the CC carries the responsibility for imposing sanctions on someone who has broken project regulations. Unfortunately, CC members often times choose the Pontius Pilate approach of 'washing their hands', leaving such difficult decisions to the overall Communal Assembly. In other situations, CC members will make difficult decisions among themselves about a certain issue and yet, when presenting the decision to the entire Assembly, have difficulty sharing their position, explaining their votes before the entire hall, or supporting sanctions against close friends or family members. Although the CC was created to make decisions about tourism issues, its representatives often prefer to pass the issue to the larger Assembly. In that context, the 'squeaky wheel gets the oil' where the most vociferous or feared individuals drive the vote. This imbalance subverts the whole purpose of having a CC for making strategic decisions about the ecotourism project.

Lack of development specialist

Members of Infierno participated in the Trueque Amazonica/'Learning Host to Host Project' in 2002–2003, which brought together members of various community-based ecotourism projects in South America. This exchange made clear the need to use each partner to the best of their capabilities. For instance, the Native Community of Infierno offers natural and cultural resources while Rainforest Expeditions brings its market and operations know-how. However, the exchange also highlighted the importance of a third party devoted to community development who serves as a translator/negotiator between the other two parties. Ideally, these three parties manifest in community-based tourism projects through the involvement of a community, a tourism company and an NGO. While Posada Amazonas is not supported by an NGO per se, that role is performed by a Community Project Office and the Community Project Coordinator. Despite an impressive history of grant acquisition, workshops, training and development consultation for the community, this office continues to lack human and financial resources needed to cover many of Infierno's needs.

Paradigm shifts

Because their rainforest environment features such an abundance and diversity of plant and animal resources, *comuneros* in Infierno sometimes ignore the need for long-term planning. Most of their basic food and water needs are easily satisfied. This makes it difficult to convince them of the need to plan and prepare for long- or even medium-term benefits. Such a shift in thinking is slowly happening across these ten initial years of the project. Maybe with a development NGO as a partner, this change could have been facilitated many years earlier.

Relationships with research institutions in Puerto Maldonado, like the Peruvian Institute for Amazon Studies, allow information sharing between scientists and *comuneros*. Such relationships have been crucial to the development of the aforementioned satellite projects. Yet problems persist. Good organization in a traditional forest community involves the idea that everyone does more or less the same work and therefore receives more or less the same benefit from it. However, these new endeavours involve a paradigm shift towards more capitalistic notions of organization that reward accordingly those who specialize and contribute more. While such a shift may increase production and sales, it may come at the expense of the community's social order.

Ownership

While knowledge of its ownership of Posada Amazonas has done much to empower the community of Infierno, it may have come with some negative consequences. Having been the benefactor of many collaborations, a 'what's in it for us?' ownership attitude has come to reign in the community that at times seems to have less to do with pride in the project than with exacting overly favourable benefit from, or even abusing, potential partners such as Rainforest Expeditions, NGOs and researchers.

While being able to act in one's own best interest is the goal of empowerment, a flippant attitude towards potential partners combined with short-term thinking may cause Infierno to lose out on future opportunities of the kind that have been responsible for its success to date. This then begs the question of whether or not simply paying dividends for land use in future ecotourism development would produce the same outcomes for conservation and development that have been seen in Infierno through the current ownership-oriented contract.

Hidden costs and lost opportunities

Making decisions and advising the community on development issues require additional costs that typical tourism companies do not often provide for. The expenses of a dedicated Community Project Office and corresponding Coordinator's salary, transportation between the Rainforest Expeditions' office in Puerto Maldonado and Infierno, and even small costs such as meals for CC and Rainforest Expeditions members during each meeting, are important details easily overlooked. Even anticipated training expenditures, already high due to constant staff rotation, have exceeded projections.

One reason for this is an unforeseen consequence of the initial contract itself. Designed to promote community involvement, the contract for Posada Amazonas includes a mandatory rotation among staff, the intent being to develop expertise in the various positions required to operate an ecolodge. However, once trained, many members prefer to stay at one particular position. This has led to an exodus of trained, experienced staff to other lodges that do not have a rotation requirement. Posada Amazonas is then required to recruit from a smaller pool of potential staff, is often forced to involve more youths who have demonstrated less responsibility towards their jobs, and must spend additional revenues on training.

Finally, hindsight has revealed some missed opportunities for ecotourism partners. While Infierno has benefited from investments in its educational system, Rainforest Expeditions now recognizes the lost opportunity of not investing more in education at the outset. As noted with respect to staff rotation, Posada Amazonas relies more on the youth of the community each day, and a generation has already been lost to a poor public school system that does little to foster a conservation ethic.

Conclusions and Expectations About the Future

Ecotourism can effectively be used as a tool to achieve economic development and this can bring a connected benefit of environmental conservation. In many ways, Posada Amazonas proves this ideal. However, as described here, the true integration of conservation and development through ecotourism has been a challenging and time-consuming process. Posada Amazonas has also benefited from certain advantages at the outset. For example, the community of Infierno already had 30% of its land set aside as a Communal Reserve. How many countries or regions have that amount of territory turned into protected areas? Peru as a whole only has 13% of its land under some form of protection (www.peru.info).

There are also important consequences of tourism revenues entering the community that may be at odds with a conservation ethic. How can we judge a community member for buying a chainsaw, or a television, or a boat motor, to make his or her daily life easier? While Infierno decided 20 years ago to protect a large portion of its land, it still has the right to use the rest in any way it wants. Yet as long as the ultimate decision-making authority of the community is respected, cannot we, as outsiders who have links with other realities, offer suggestions and help communities to make informed decisions? We need to collaborate by presenting different and successful alternatives, always keeping in mind as a mandatory requirement to show first and foremost the economic benefits and time investment involved. An important lesson from Posada Amazonas is that many conservation initiatives undertaken by Infierno were initially driven by economic motives rather than conservation ones.

As the end of the 20-year contract nears, Posada Amazonas stands at a crossroads: a savvier set of community partners who yearn for its independence yet still lack vital expertise, and a business partner that hopes to continue to earn profits while also fulfilling its commitment to integrated conservation and development. The case of Posada Amazonas will no doubt continue to be one of interest for ecotourism practitioners and researchers for years to come.

References

Balvín D.D. and Patrón A.P. (2006) *Carretera Interoceánico Sur: Consideraciones para su aprovechamiento sostenible.* Amigos de la Tierra and Asociación Civil Labor, Lima.

Brandon, K., da Fonseca, G., Rylands, A. and Cardosa da Silva, J. (2005) Challenges and opportunities in Brazilian conservation. *Conservation Biology* 13, 595–600.

Brightsmith, D. (2005) Competition, predation, and nest niche shifts among tropical cavity nesters: ecological evidence. *Journal of Avian Biology* 36, 74–83.

Ceballos-Lascurain, H. (1987) The future of ecotourism. *Mexico Journal* January, 13–14.

Christ, C., Hillel, O., Matus, S. and Sweeting, J. (2003) *Tourism and Biodiversity: Mapping Tourism's Global Footprint.* United Nations Environment Programme and Conservation International, Washington, DC.

Dourojeanni, M. (2006) Impactos socioambientales probables de la carretera transoceánica (Río Branco–Puerto Maldonado–Ilo) y la capacidad de repuesta del Perú. Boletín CF+S 19 – (EN)CLAVES INSOSTENTIBLES: tráfico, género, gestión, y toma de decisiones. Instituto Juan de Herrera, Madrid; available at http://habitat.aq.upm.es/boletin/n19/amdou.html (accessed August 2007).

Myers, N., Mittermeier, R.A., Mittermeier, C.G., da Fonseca, G.A.B. and Kent, J. (2000) Biodiversity hotspots for conservation priorities. *Nature* 403, 853–858.

Ocampo Raeder, C. (2006) Ese'eja signatures: a systematic assessment of the effects of indigenous resource management practices on an Amazonian forest. PhD dissertation, Stanford University, Stanford, California.

Piana, R. (2001) Traditional forest use and ecotourism at the Infierno Native Community: two different income generating activities and their impact on local people's economies. Master's thesis, Royal Veterinary and Agricultural University, Copenhagen; available at http://www.perunature.com/pdfs/rp_traditional_forest.pdf (accessed February 2008).

Stronza, A. (2000) Because it is ours: community-based tourism in the Peruvian Amazon. PhD dissertation, University of Florida, Gainesville, Florida.

Stronza, A. (2004) *Trueque Amazónico: Lessons in Community-Based Ecotourism*. Critical Ecosystem Partnership Fund, Washington, DC.

Part III

Ecotourism in Marine Environments

4 Ecotourism and Marine Protected Areas in a Time of Climate Change

S.C. STONICH

Departments of Anthropology, Environmental Studies, Geography, and Interdepartmental Graduate Program in Marine Science, University of California, Santa Barbara, California, USA

Introduction

The chapters in this volume are concerned with the opportunities and challenges of ecotourism as a means of enhancing both environmental conservation and economic development, especially at the local level. While many of the chapters also are concerned with the complex relationships between ecotourism and protected areas, most chapters (with the exception of Chapter 5 by Durham on the Galapagos) concentrate on terrestrial protected areas. The present chapter expands the terrestrial focus to include marine and coastal environments and marine protected areas (MPAs), which have emerged as a major conservation strategy for coastal and marine environments in the last several decades. As many of the chapters in this volume show, ecotourism has profound consequences on local peoples, places and environments; however, so do protected areas, including MPAs. Moreover, when tourism and/or ecotourism grow in tandem with MPAs in the context of accelerated climate change, the consequences may be truly profound.

The present chapter attempts to point out several of the major issues related to the growth of ecotourism/tourism and MPAs in an era of climate change. It begins with a brief summary of the rapid growth of MPAs, the potentially confusing diversity of categories, forms, types, goals and objectives of MPAs, and a few of the many unresolved social and environmental issues related to MPAs. It goes on to lay out the symbiotic relationship between ecotourism and MPAs. It asks a two-part question: can ecotourism be a tool for conservation and support of MPAs and can successful MPAs likewise enhance ecotourism and the ecotourist experience? Understanding the tremendous power of ecotourism and MPAs to significantly change integrated human and natural systems becomes even more important, as well as challenging, in the context of climate change, especially in coastal, near-shore marine and estuarine environments where the effects of climate change are already being felt so deeply (IPCC, 2007). According to the International Union for the Conservation of Nature and Natural Resources' (IUCN) World Commission on Protected Areas (WCPA), global climate change may be the most important environmental issue affecting protected areas and tourism in the 21st century (Eagles, 2007).

Marine Protected Areas

Marine protected areas are a relatively new approach to marine conservation and fisheries management. They are viewed by many marine scientists, multilateral and bilateral donors, private foundations and environmental non-governmental organizations (NGOs) as a critical means of conserving marine biodiversity and rebuilding depleted fish stocks. Currently a plethora of diverse MPAs have been established in virtually every country with coastal and marine areas, in extremely varied social, political and biological contexts (NRC, 2001).

One of the most commonly quoted definitions for MPAs is that provided by the IUCN:

> Any area of intertidal or subtidal terrain, together with its overlying water and associated flora, fauna, historical and cultural features, which have been reserved by law or other effective means to protect part or all of the enclosed environment (Resolution 17.38 of the IUCN General Assembly [1988] and Resolution 19.46 [1994]).

Although the potential conservation benefits of MPAs have been touted by conservationists and scientists since the 1970s, only since the mid-1980s have MPAs been established extensively worldwide. According to the IUCN, in 1970, 118 MPAs had been established in 27 nations with 100 others in the planning stage (NRC, 2001). By 1985, 430 MPAs had been created in 69 countries with an additional 298 proposed (Silva and Desilvestre, 1986). By 1994, the IUCN identified 1306 existing MPAs with hundreds of other proposed sites (Kelleher et al., 1995). By 2005, according to the IUCN WCPA, around 4500 MPAs had been established globally and several thousand more were in the process of being created (IUCN-WCPA, 2007). Four of the 20 largest nationally designated protected areas worldwide are some type of marine protected area or reserve: the Great Barrier Reef Marine Park and Macquarie Island in Australia, the North-western Hawaiian Islands Coral Reef Ecosystem Reserve in the USA, and the Galapagos Marine Reserve in Ecuador.

Despite their proliferation in recent years, MPAs constitute less than 1% of the total number of protected areas globally. Moreover, while terrestrial protected areas now cover over 12% of the earth's land surface, MPAs represent only about 0.5% of the total ocean surface and about 1% of the coastal shelf area (Chape et al., 2005). This likely is an underestimate of the actual number and extent of MPAs for several reasons. Most importantly, the

IUCN WCPA list includes only protected areas that are recognized at national level and hence does not include an unknown number of local, community and/or regional MPAs (West *et al.*, 2006). However, the IUCN for several years has maintained that the number and coverage of MPAs is woefully inadequate. Currently, an estimated 675 MPAs have been established in Latin America (including Central America, South America and the Caribbean) constituting approximately 16% of the total number of protected areas in the region, much higher than the global average; about half (370) are located in the Caribbean, about 200 in South America and a little more than 100 in Central America (IUCN-WCPA, 2007).

Heightened support for MPAs emerged in light of growing concern over declining yields in global fisheries and widespread degradation of marine habitats (including coral reefs) that highlighted the inadequacies of conventional marine management strategies (NRC, 2001). MPAs now are widely seen as promising components of a comprehensive, ecosystem approach for conserving marine and coastal environments. Over the last two decades, not only have MPAs increased in number but also in types, forms, scales and functions – leading to some conceptual, definitional and operational confusion. A recent cover story in the *MPA News* (International News and Analysis on Marine Protected Areas), entitled 'Do We Really Need 50 Ways to Say "Marine Protected Area"?' (*MPA News*, 2007), pointed to a background paper prepared for a recent IUCN WCPA Summit in which more than 50 terms were used to classify various marine and coastal protected areas. Despite this proliferation of named categories, a much smaller number of classificatory terms are common. These include: (i) Marine Protected Areas (MPAs), the most general, inclusive category, defined as a geographical area with discrete boundaries that has been designated to enhance the conservation of marine reserves; (ii) Marine Reserves (MRs), 'closed' or 'no take zones', a demarcated area in which some or all of the biological resources are protected from removal, disturbance and other activities; and (iii) Multiple-Use MPAs, an approach often employed over large (eco)regions that allows for integrated management of complete marine ecosystems usually through some kind of a zoning process (NRC, 2001).

In addition to categorical types, MPAs also are quite diverse in terms of goals, functions and objectives, which contribute to their flexibility and versatility (a potential opportunity) while also presenting challenges to their design, implementation and management (a challenge). In their global review of MPAs, the US National Research Council (NRC) identified the following multiple goals of MPAs in order of importance (NRC, 2001).

1. Conservation of marine biodiversity and habitats.
2. Improvement of fisheries management.
3. Increased scientific knowledge.
4. Expanded educational opportunities.
5. Enhanced tourism and recreational activities
6. Protection of cultural heritage.

While tourism and recreational opportunities appear on the NRC list they are not the prime objectives of MPAs, akin to biological conservation and fisheries management. Neither, it should be noted, are goals of sustaining or improving local lives, livelihoods and communities included in the NRC list of major objectives. Other analyses of the goals of MPAs as presented in peer-reviewed journals similarly conclude that conservation and scientific goals are paramount and further that the objectives and goals of MPAs generally are set by the environmental conservation and scientific communities and by national governments (Jones, 1994, 2001; Agardy, 1997, 2001, 2005; Christie *et al.*, 2003b).

Although maintaining local peoples and places frequently are not the primary goals of MPAs when reviewed worldwide, many so-called 'community-based MPAs' with precisely those objectives have been established in various parts of the world, and in fact have been the major MPA strategy in the Philippines and the US Pacific North-west (Christie *et al.*, 2003a). Consequently, another way to think about categorizing MPAs is in terms of whether they are based on the powerful 'park' model central to the NRC analysis, i.e. a top-down approach in which a national government, usually with international support, declares a designated area as an MPA with the primary objective of conserving biodiversity and enhancing fish stocks, and decrees regulations regarding access to and use of resources within the park; or a 'community-based' model in which local people and communities assume management, oversight and enforcement responsibilities in order to improve and/or sustain local livelihoods and communities, as well as to conserve coastal and/or marine resources (Christie *et al.*, 2003a). Although many MPAs have been established using each model, the considerable early enthusiasm regarding community-based approaches has ebbed, largely based on biological science arguments regarding the optimal size and scale of 'effective' MPAs. This argument favours larger 'park' models (e.g. ecoregional models) over generally spatially smaller 'community-based' models (Agardy *et al.*, 2003). It should be noted that, although based on a 'scientific' argument, the 'park' model also is much simpler (and easier) to design and implement than community-based models.

Readers of this volume will notice striking similarities between the key goals and objectives of community-based MPAs and those generally specified for ecotourism including: sustaining and/or improving the well-being of local people, conserving the environment, respecting local culture, providing economic alternatives for local people, building environmental awareness, and supporting democratic movements and human rights (Brandon, 1996; Honey, 1999). While many of these goals are shared by the 'park' and 'community-based' models of MPAs, as summarized by the NRC and listed above, critically missing from the NRC characterization is any mention of community control or the improvement of local well-being – central features of both community-based MPAs and most generally accepted conceptualizations of ecotourism. Perhaps this is understandable because ecotourism and community-based MPAs both emerged as alternative models to overarching and powerful top-down approaches to tourism development and to MPAs, respectively. Likewise, both ecotourism and community-based conservation efforts (marine and terrestrial) continue to be part of contentious debates with these very powerful approaches to development and conservation.

Unresolved Issues Regarding Marine Protected Areas

In addition to fundamental differences regarding the starting point, the choice of a 'park' or a 'community-based' model for MPAs, several other significant issues related to MPAs remain unresolved (Agardy *et al.*, 2003). One of the most important of these is how to conceptualize and measure the 'success' or 'effectiveness' of MPAs. Until recently, most such assessments were based primarily on biological criteria despite increased recognition that social and political issues – such as broad participation in management, shared economic benefits and incorporated mechanisms to resolve inevitable conflicts – are crucial to long-term MPA success (Agardy, 2000; Agardy *et al.*, 2003; Christie *et al.*, 2005).

The neglect of the human dimensions of MPAs, both in terms of driving forces and the impacts of MPAs on human–natural systems, has been the missing dimension in many attempts to design, implement, manage and evaluate MPAs until recently. However, a growing number of social science scholars, along with donors, policy makers, conservationists, resource users and their biological science colleagues, have been attempting to develop interdisciplinary research agendas for MPAs that confront social and political realities and integrate social and biological dimensions in a more balanced and realistic way (Lyons and Wahle, 2002; Christie *et al.*, 2003b, 2005; Friedlander *et al.*, 2003; Christie, 2005). Such balanced, interdisciplinary, participatory agendas may contribute significantly to the long-term effectiveness and success of MPAs.

(Eco)tourism and (Marine) Protected Areas

Establishing the fundamental geographic connections between tourism, environmental conservation and protected areas became a major initiative of the United Nations Environment Programme (UNEP) and Conservation International (CI) in their joint 2-year project in the early 2000s, 'Tourism and Biodiversity: Mapping Tourism's Global Footprint' (Christ *et al.*, 2003). This project attempted to demonstrate the spatial/geopolitical relationship between nature-based/ecotourism and biological hotspots/wilderness areas. The project used remotely sensed data and geographic information systems to overlay areas of tourism development and growth with previously identified biological hotspots (many of which were terrestrial and marine protected areas) and areas of 'low human development' (i.e. areas characterized by widespread human vulnerabilities). One of the major findings of this project was that in many biodiversity-rich countries of the south, including some of the world's poorest countries, tourism already was a major sector of the economy and was increasing rapidly. Further, in a number of developing countries with biodiversity hotspots (including Belize, Costa Rica, Honduras and Nicaragua) biodiversity was the major tourist attraction. Finally, the study found that expert forecasts predicted that tourism would increase in importance in biodiversity hotspot countries throughout the decade and thus recommended enhanced planning to avoid or mitigate negative impacts on biodiversity.

The predictions of the UNEP–CI study regarding the growth of tourism were realized in much of Latin America through the remainder of the decade – particularly in Central America, South America and Mexico, as well as in some countries in the Caribbean. Between 2000 and 2005, the average annual growth rate in tourist arrivals to the Americas (including the USA and Canada) was only 0.8% (due largely to the significant decrease in tourist arrivals to the USA after September 11, 2001), significantly lower than the global average annual growth rate of 3.3% during the same period (UNWTO, 2007). In contrast, the average annual growth rate in Central America between 2000 and 2005 was 8.5% and in South America 3.6%, surpassing the global rate for the same period. During the mid-2000s, tourist arrivals to Central and South America have accelerated markedly, by double digits in most countries in most years. In 2004 and 2005, international tourist arrivals to Central America grew by 17.8% and 16% respectively, considerably exceeding the global growth rates, which were 10% and 5.5% for the same periods. The 16% growth in tourist arrivals to Central America in 2005 made it the fastest-growing sub-region in the world despite the massive flooding, landslides and human fatalities from Hurricane Stan, which struck the region in late September and early October (UNWTO, 2007). One has only to skim the government-sponsored tourism sites for the Central American countries to see their overwhelming promotion of ecotourism and other nature-based tourist activities.

Trends are similar for South America, especially since 2004: the percentage of international tourist arrivals to South America increased by 17.2% in 2004 and 12.2% in 2005, making South America along with Central America the fastest-growing tourism sub-regions in the Americas. Argentina, Brazil, Chile, Colombia, Paraguay, Peru and Suriname all reported growth rates in the range of 10–20% in 2005 (UNWTO, 2007). Although the international tourism industry is more diversified in South America and less dependent on traditional forms of ecotourism than in Central America, nature-based tourism of all sorts is an important segment of the tourism sector in the region.

Although growth rates for the entire Caribbean region have stabilized or declined, several countries have seen a significant increase in tourist arrivals in recent years. Despite the fact that the average annual growth rate of international tourist arrivals to the Caribbean was only 2.0% between 2000 and 2005, that rate increased to 5.9% in 2004 and 4.3% in 2005. Several Caribbean countries countered this trend: in 2005, tourist arrivals to

Anguilla grew by 15%, Cuba 12%, the British Virgin Islands 11%, the Dominican Republic 7% and Saint Lucia 6.5% (UNWTO, 2007). Ecotourism, in its most common conceptualizations, is a marginal component of the Caribbean tourism industry and is best illustrated by so-called 'diversionary activities' associated with sustainable tourism enterprises (including beach resorts) such as diving, snorkelling, hiking and others (Weaver, 2004). Weaver sees an opportunity in such partnerships between sustainable mass tourism firms and alternative tourism providers to promote effective ecotourism in the Caribbean (Weaver, 2004). It is important to note that the Latin American sub-region with the greatest number of MPAs (i.e. the Caribbean) also is the least engaged in ecotourism at the moment.

Given what to many is the obvious connection between protected areas and ecotourism (and other types of nature-based tourism), it is surprising that it took the international protected area community as long as it did to face this actuality directly. In 2003, more than 3000 delegates met in South Africa for the Fifth World Parks Congress which is held every 10 years by the WCPA of the IUCN. Yet, tourism was not a major workshop stream at this important international meeting despite requests to the organizing committee to make tourism a major theme. Tourism was, however, the focus of many keynote and plenary sessions, side events and concurrent sessions, as well as the central organizing concept around the publication of *Tourism and Protected Areas: Benefits Beyond Boundaries*, one of the major publications from this meeting (Bushell *et al.*, 2007). One of the main themes of this book is how to make ecotourism (and other nature-based tourism) a tool for conservation and support of protected areas, including (but not limited to) providing financial support for conservation (Bushell and McCool, 2007).

While the WCPA may have taken its time before adequately confronting the interconnections between ecotourism and protected areas, a growing number of scholars have been engaged in such efforts for several years. A number of studies have critically examined the relationship between (eco)tourism and protected areas including MPAs (Trist, 1999; Weaver, 1999, 2004; Young, 1999a,b, 2001; Sandersen and Koester, 2000; Farrell and Marion, 2001; de los Monteros, 2002; Abel, 2003; Stonich, 2003; Carrier and Macleod, 2005; Kruger, 2005; Moreno, 2005; West *et al.*, 2006; Cardenas-Torres *et al.*, 2007).

In *Current Anthropology*, West and Carrier (2004) situate ecotourism in tropical developing countries in its larger, transnational, political–economic context – i.e. neoliberal globalization – in two very different environmental, social, cultural and political contexts: Jamaica and Papua New Guinea. They conclude that, despite rhetorical emphasis on more participatory and community-based ecotourism and conservation efforts in both cases, community and environmental concerns were subordinated to financial ones that were aimed principally at increasing the number of ecotourists and tourist revenues.

West and Carrier's conclusions echo the findings from my own long-term work in the Bay Islands, off the north coast of Honduras, in which I specifically examined the growth of ecotourism/tourism and MPAs as an example of the simultaneous integration and promotion of neoliberal economic and conservation strategies (Stonich, 2000, 2003, 2005). The Bay Islands are located in the Mesoamerican Barrier Reef System (MBRS), the largest continuous reef in the Western Hemisphere, which stretches over 1000 km of Caribbean coastline from Mexico, through Belize, a small portion of Guatemala and northern Honduras. The MBRS is alive with vibrant coral reefs, colourful fish and other diverse marine life (such as conch, lobsters and turtles), and is a spectacular, major tourist attraction for the region. Unfortunately, the MBRS is threatened by many human activities and increasingly by global environmental change, including climate change (Stonich, 2000).

It is beyond the scope of this chapter to fully describe the interconnections between ecotourism/tourism and marine (and terrestrial) protected areas on the Bay Islands which I have detailed elsewhere. Here it is appropriate to emphasize that the tandem growth of tourism (and ecotourism) and MPAs came about through the coordinated and collaborative efforts of many of the same institutions, interest groups and stakeholders which, out of self-interest, were interested in promoting both MPAs and the tourism industry (Stonich, 2005). These various stakeholders were composed in large part of local and national elites, bilateral and multilateral donors, international and national environmental NGOs, and later by foreign investors and speculators. One major outcome has been great inequities in terms of the distribution of risks/costs and benefits from the growth of tourism and conservation practices, despite the considerable rhetoric of so-called 'participatory approaches', considerable financial assistance from international donors, and the establishment of both local and national-level MPAs. Another outcome has been widespread resistance by local non-elite residents, including sometimes violent conflicts and confrontations. While tourism continues to expand, today the Islands are characterized by widespread environmental degradation evidenced by declines in the quality of seawater and in coral reef health; the diminished quality and quantity of potable water; and extensive deforestation and erosion (Stonich, 2000). Currently, earnings from international tourism rank third in foreign exchange earnings in Honduras (after remittances from Hondurans living abroad and export earnings from the *maquila* industry). The Bay Islands remain by far the most visited tourist destination in the country although the government is attempting to diversify the tourism sector by promoting tourism in other biologically rich and fragile areas of the country (Stonich, 2008).

A major conclusion of my work, which is central to the relationship between ecotourism and MPAs, is that it is not possible in the Bay Islands case to distinguish between traditional/mass tourism (which emphasize sun, sand and sea) and ecotourism. Consequently I have not done so in this chapter. In 1980, the first time I visited the Bay Islands, a few divers and yachters visited the Islands annually, they were not easy to get to, there was only one short paved road through a small part of the largest Bay Island (Roatan), a few small hotels and a couple of restaurants. Most travel was by small boat or dugout canoe. The first several times I visited the Islands I stayed in peoples' homes and ate with them. At the same time, the coral reefs were incredibly lovely, full of live, stunning corals and teeming with reef fish. You could also drink the water and swim in the lagoons without much fear of gastroenteritis, other diarrhoeal diseases, and respiratory or skin infections. The sand fleas were bothersome, I will say that, and it was possible to contract malaria and dengue, so 'paradise' was not perfect. However, tourism – the little that existed – was small-scale and controlled by local people. Generally it fitted within current conceptualizations and definitions of ecotourism.

Today, at least 100,000 tourists and at least 200,000 additional cruise ship passengers visit the islands and cays of the Bay Islands. Many visitors still dive, snorkel, hike and engage in other 'ecotourist' activities, but most enjoy the other nature-based tourist activities: sunbathing, swimming, boating and sipping *mojitos* on the patios of bars and restaurants while gazing at the blue Caribbean. These same pastimes are engaged in by the hundreds of cruise ship passengers who visit the Islands for several hours every day during the cruising season. At the same time, the Islands are encircled by the Bay Islands National Marine Park, a multiple-use protected area established with international donor funding. There is no sewage or drinking water system, much of the coral is dead or dying, and I would definitely advise against drinking the water without purifying it in some way. Two recent developments, both connected with the promotion of tourism, potentially endanger the Bay Islands further. Recently, the Government of Honduras declared the creation of the Bay Islands Free Trade Zone on Roatan and, in March 2007, Celebrity Cruise Lines announced plans to build and operate a US$50 million cruise terminal on Roatan. Construction of the 'Mahogany Bay – Roatan' terminal is expected to start in autumn 2007 and be completed by summer 2009. It will consist of two berths capable of accommodating super cruise vessels and up to 7000 passengers daily. Carnival Cruise Lines predicts that within 5 years of operation, the terminal will host 255 cruise ship calls and 500,000 passengers annually (Carnival Cruise Watch, 2007).

The case of the Bay Islands supports the assertion that in order to maintain and/or improve people, communities and environments through (eco)tourism development, it may be essential to conceptualize ecotourism as a type (or stage) of tourism more broadly; and more importantly, that all tourism must be *sustainable* tourism (Weaver, 2006). This belief is even more crucial in a time of climate change.

(Eco)tourism, Marine Protected Areas and Climate Change

The impacts of climate change on (eco)tourism and protected areas are so profound that it is impossible to summarize them succinctly (Eagles, 2007).

Healthy ecosystems are necessary for ecotourism, but so too are climatic factors. Climate, weather and natural resource considerations are all significant criteria in choosing vacation destinations in general (Agnew and Viner, 1999; Hall and Higham, 2005; Bigano *et al.*, 2006; Gossling and Hall, 2006a). For mass tourists (as well as ecotourists), 'favourable' climatic, weather and environmental conditions are major decisive factors (Hamilton and Lau, 2006). The tourism industry as well as tourism researchers realize this and, recently, there has been an upsurge of studies on the complex interconnections between tourism and climate change. This research generally falls into one of three categories: (i) the theoretical and scientific basis (and interrelationships) between tourism and climate change; (ii) the empirical and predicted effects of climate change on tourism flows, particular regions and tourist dependent economies (globally, regionally and nationally); and (iii) adaptation to, and mitigation of, the impacts of climate change. Two representative compendia of findings are *Tourism, Recreation, and Climate Change* (Hall and Highman, 2005) and *Tourism and Global Environmental Change: Ecological, Social, Economic, and Political Interrelationships* (Gossling and Hall, 2006b).

Table 4.1 summarizes some of the most important probabilistic predictions regarding changes in extreme weather, climate and sea-level rise events, according to the Fourth Assessment Report of the Intergovernmental Panel on Climate Change (IPCC). Confidence is very high that climate change will result in: higher temperatures, more severe and more frequent heatwaves; significant sea-level rise; increased intensity (and perhaps frequency) of extreme weather events including tropical cyclonic activity; extreme drought; and heavy precipitation events and flooding (IPCC, 2007).

Table 4.1. Changes in frequencies and intensities of extreme weather, climate and sea-level events. (Adapted from IPCC, 2007, p. 16.)

Phenomenon and direction of trend	Likelihood of future trend based on projections for the 21st century[a]
Warmer/more frequent hot days and nights over most land areas	Virtually certain
Warm spells/heat waves: frequency increases over most land areas	Very likely
Heavy precipitation events: frequency increases over most areas	Very likely
Area affected by drought increases	Likely
Intense tropical cyclone activity increases	Likely
Increased incidence of extreme high sea level (excludes tsunamis)	Likely

[a]The IPCC (2007) Summary for Policy Makers uses the following terms to indicate the assessed likelihood of an outcome or a result: virtually certain, >99% probability of occurrence; extremely likely, >95%; very likely, >90%; likely, >66%; more likely than not, >50%; very unlikely, <10%; extremely unlikely, <5%.

All of these predicted changes are likely to have significant effects on tourism in particular regions and localities. For Latin America and the Caribbean, the IPCC points to a high risk of significant biodiversity loss in many tropical areas; sea-level rise and flooding in coastal zones and islands; and drinking water shortages. The report singles out coastal zones and small islands as increasingly at risk and especially vulnerable to the consequences of climate change, sea-level rise and extreme weather-related events. Deterioration of coastal conditions through erosion of beaches is predicted to affect local resources, while sea-level rise is expected to exacerbate inundation, storm surges, erosion and other coastal hazards, thereby threatening infrastructure, settlements and facilities that support the livelihoods of coastal and island communities. In the Caribbean and many coastal areas, climate change-induced reductions in water resources are projected to become so severe by mid-century that they become insufficient to meet demand during low rainfall periods. Corals are extremely vulnerable to thermal stress and increases in sea surface temperatures are projected to result in more frequent coral bleaching events and widespread mortality. The likely impacts of climate change on the tourism industry and on tourism-dependent peoples and economies (particularly in coastal zones and islands) were singled out in the report for all of the reasons (and others) discussed above (IPCC, 2007).

Although research on how to mitigate the negative impacts of climate change on tourism in coastal zones and islands is quite limited, one common recommendation, especially for reef based, near-shore and marine tourism, is through the creation and expansion of effective MPAs (Uyarra *et al.*, 2005). This recommendation is based on the belief that healthy ecosystems are more resilient to disturbances, and thus are better able to withstand stresses caused by climate change-related events. At the same time, marine scientists and marine policy specialists have begun to emphasize the necessity of maintaining and sustaining MPAs in an era of significant climate change by concentrating on the land–sea interface (including tourism development).

Recently, the editors of *MPA News* (International News and Analysis on Marine Protected Areas) queried a number of experts about how they thought MPAs could/should remain relevant at a time when global climate change will have a significant impact on marine and coastal environments (*MPA News*, 2006). Although responses from the approximately 15 experts were somewhat diverse, the commonalities were more striking. Most urged extensive collaboration with land-based users that integrated marine planning with land-based planning in order to address pollution and conservation issues throughout watersheds. Many recommended promoting social, as well as ecological resilience, by supporting communities that depend on marine and coastal environments (including the tourism and fishery sectors) in various ways – believing that healthy communities (like healthy ecosystems) are more able to cope with, and adapt to, multiple disturbances. Although tourism was mentioned specifically only once (and ecotourism not at all) by these experts, many of their recommendations indirectly implied implementation through the tourism sector. These included such things as using MPAs to increase public knowledge and awareness of the impacts of climate change on marine and coastal ecosystems, creating community-based monitoring programmes, integrating (tourism) volunteers to observe and monitor climate-related changes of all kinds, and designing environmental education opportunities to inform the public and local communities about climate change. It is very likely that climate change will make life more unpredictable for people, communities and regions that are already dependent on tourism, but there is an opportunity (and at the same time a challenge) to create more cooperative, flexible and adaptive arrangements to deal with this unpredictability through the effective integration of (eco)tourism and (marine) protected areas.

References

Abel, T. (2003) Understanding complex human ecosystems: the case of ecotourism on Bonaire. *Conservation Ecology* 7(3); available at http://www.consecol.org/Vol7/Iss3/art10 (accessed May 2007).

Agardy, T. (1997) *Marine Protected Areas and Ocean Conservation*. R.E. Landes Academic Press, Austin, Texas.

Agardy, T. (2000) Information needs for marine protected areas: scientific and societal. *Bulletin of Marine Science* 66, 875–888.

Agardy, T. (2001). *Marine Protected Areas: A Vital Tool for Conserving Nature and Resolving Conflicts*. The Curtis and Edith Munson Distinguished Lecture Series 'Marine Protected Areas: Translating Science into Practice', Yale School of Forestry and Environmental Studies Center for Coastal and Watershed Systems. Yale University Information Technology Services Reprographics & Imaging Services Publishing Center, New Haven, Connecticut.

Agardy, T. (2005) Global marine conservation policy versus site-level implementation: the mismatch of scale and its implications. *Marine Ecology – Progress Series* 300, 242–248.

Agardy, T., Bridgewater, P., Crosby, M.P., Day, J., Dayton, P.K., Kenchington, R., Laffoley, D., McConney, P., Murray, P.A., Parks, J.E. and Peau, L. (2003) Dangerous targets? Unresolved issues and ideological clashes around marine protected areas. *Aquatic Conservation – Marine and Freshwater Ecosystems* 13, 353–367.

Agnew, D. and Viner, D. (1999) Potential impacts of climate change on international tourism. *Tourism and Hospitality Research* 3, 37–59.

Bigano, A., Hamilton, J.M., Maddison, D.J. and Tol, R.S.J. (2006) Predicting tourism flows under climate change – an editorial comment on Gossling and Hall (2006). *Climatic Change* 79, 175–180.

Brandon, K. (1996) *Ecotourism and Conservation: A Review of Key Issues*. Environment Department Papers, Biodiversity Series No. 33. World Bank, Washington, DC.

Bushell, R. and McCool, S.F. (2007) Tourism as a tool for conservation and support of protected areas: setting the agenda. In: Bushell, R. and Eagles, P. (eds) *Tourism and Protected Areas: Benefits Beyond Boundaries*. CAB International, Wallingford, UK, pp. 12–26.

Bushell, R., Staiff, R. and Eagles, P.F.J. (2007) Tourism and protected areas: benefits beyond boundaries. In: Bushell, R. and Eagles, P. (eds) *Tourism and Protected Areas: Benefits Beyond Boundaries*. CAB International, Wallingford, UK, pp. 1–11.

Cardenas-Torres, N., Enriquez-Andrade, R. and Rodriguez-Dowdell, N. (2007) Community-based management through ecotourism in Bahia de los Angeles, Mexico. *Fisheries Research* 84, 114–118.

Carnival Cruise Watch (2007) Carnival to Build $50 Million Terminal in Honduras. http://www.carnivalcruisewatch.com/2007/03/carnival_to_bui.html (accessed June 2007).

Carrier, J.G. and Macleod, D.V.L. (2005) Bursting the bubble: the sociocultural context of ecotourism. *Journal of the Royal Anthropological Institute* 11, 315–334.

Chape, S., Harrison, J., Spalding, M. and Lysenko, I. (2005) Measuring the extent and effectiveness of protected areas as an indicator for meeting global biodiversity targets. *Philosophical Transactions of the Royal Society B – Biological Sciences* 360, 443–455.

Christ, C., Hillel, O., Matus, S. and Sweeting, J. (2003) *Tourism and Biodiversity: Mapping Tourism's Global Footprint.* Conservation International and United Nations Environment Programme, Washington, DC.

Christie, P. (2005) Is integrated coastal management sustainable? *Ocean & Coastal Management* 48, 208–232.

Christie, P., Buhat, D., Garces, L.R. and White, A.T. (2003a) The challenges and rewards of community-based coastal resources management. In: Brechin, S.R., Wilshusen, P.R., Fortwangler, C.L. and West, P.C. (eds) *Contested Nature, Promoting International Biodiversity and Social Justice in the Twenty-first Century.* State University of New York, Albany, New York, pp. 231–249.

Christie, P., McCay, B.J., Miller, M.L., Lowe, C., White, A.T., Stoffle, R., Fluharty, D.L., McManus, L.T., Chuenpagdee, R., Pomeroy, C., Suman, D.O., Blount, B.G., Huppert, D., Eisma, R.L.V., Oracion, E., Lowry, K. and Pollnac, R.B. (2003b) Toward developing a complete understanding: a social science research agenda for marine protected areas. *Fisheries* 28, 22–26.

Christie, P., Lowry, K., White, A.T., Oracion, E.G., Sievanen, L., Pomeroy, R.S., Pollnac, R.B., Patlis, J.M. and Eisma, R.L.V. (2005) Key findings from a multidisciplinary examination of integrated coastal management process sustainability. *Ocean & Coastal Management* 48, 468–483.

de los Monteros, R.L.E. (2002) Evaluating ecotourism in natural protected areas of La Paz Bay, Baja California Sur, Mexico: ecotourism or nature-based tourism? *Biodiversity and Conservation* 11, 1539–1550.

Eagles, P.F.J. (2007) Global trends affecting tourism in protected areas. In: Bushell, R. and Eagles, P. (eds) *Tourism and Protected Areas: Benefits Beyond Boundaries.* CAB International, Wallingford, UK, pp. 27–43.

Farrell, T.A. and Marion, J.L. (2001) Identifying and assessing ecotourism visitor impacts at eight protected areas in Costa Rica and Belize. *Environmental Conservation* 28, 215–225.

Friedlander, A., Nowlis, J.S., Sanchez, J.A., Appeldoorn, R., Usseglio, P., McCormick, C., Bejarano, S. and Mitchell-Chui, A. (2003) Designing effective marine protected areas in Seaflower Biosphere Reserve, Colombia, based on biological and sociological information. *Conservation Biology* 17, 1769–1784.

Gossling, S. and Hall, C.M. (2006a) Uncertainties in predicting tourist flows under scenarios of climate change. *Climatic Change* 79, 163–173.

Gossling, S. and Hall, C.M. (eds) (2006b) *Tourism and Global Environmental Change: Ecological, Social, Economic, and Political Interrelationships.* Routledge, London/New York.

Hall, M. and Higham, J. (eds) (2005) *Tourism, Recreation, and Climate Change.* Channel View Publications, Clevedon, UK.

Hamilton, J.M. and Lau, M.A. (2006) The role of climate information in tourist destination decision making. In: Gossling, S. and Hall, C.M. (eds) *Tourism and Global Environmental Change: Ecological, Social, Economic, and Political Interrelationships*. Routledge, London/New York, pp. 229–249.

Honey, M. (1999). *Ecotourism and Sustainable Development: Who Owns Paradise?* Island Press, Washington, DC.

IPCC (2007) Summary for policy makers. In: Parry, M.L., Canziani, O.F., Palutikof, J.P., van der Linden, P.J. and Hanson, C.E. (eds) *Climate Change 2007: Impacts, Adaptation and Vulnerability. Contribution of Working Group II to the Fourth Assessment Report of the Intergovernmental Panel on Climate Change*. Cambridge University Press, Cambridge, UK, pp. 7–22.

IUCN-WCPA (2007) World Database on Protected Areas. International Union for the Conservation of Nature and Natural Resources, World Commission on Protected Areas; available at http://sea.unep-wcmc.org/wdbpa/ (accessed June 2007).

Jones, P.J.S. (1994) A review and analysis of the objectives of marine nature reserves. *Ocean & Coastal Management* 24, 149–178.

Jones, P.J.S. (2001) Marine protected area strategies: issues, divergences and the search for middle ground. *Reviews in Fish Biology and Fisheries* 11, 197–216.

Kelleher, G., Bleakley, C. and Wells, S. (1995) *A Global Representative System of Marine Protected Areas*. The Great Barrier Reef Marine Park Authority, The World Bank and the International Union for the Conservation of Nature and Natural Resources, Washington, DC.

Kruger, O. (2005) The role of ecotourism in conservation: panacea or Pandora's box? *Biodiversity and Conservation* 14, 579–600.

Lyons, S.C. and Wahle, C.M. (2002) *Marine Protected Areas Social Science Workshop: Notes from Breakout Groups*. National Marine Protected Areas Center Science Institute, Monterey, California.

Moreno, P.S. (2005) Ecotourism along the Meso-American Caribbean Reef: the impacts of foreign investment. *Human Ecology* 33, 217–244.

MPA News (2006) In an era of climate change: how can managers ensure that today's MPAs remain relevant over time? *MPA News* 8(6), 1–5.

MPA News (2007) Do we really need 50 ways to say 'marine protected area'? Views in MPA terminology, and efforts to categorize MPAs. *MPA News* 8(10), 1–3.

NRC (2001) *Marine Protected Areas: Tools for Sustaining Ocean Ecosystems*. National Academy Press, Washington, DC.

Sandersen, H.T. and Koester, S. (2000) Co-management of tropical coastal zones: the case of the Soufriere marine management area, St Lucia, WI. *Coastal Management* 28, 87–97.

Silva, M. and Desilvestre, I. (1986) Marine and coastal protected areas in Latin America – a preliminary assessment. *Coastal Zone Management Journal* 14, 311–347.

Stonich, S.C. (2000) *The Other Side of Paradise: Tourism, Conservation, and Development in the Bay Islands*. Cognizant Communication Corporation, New York.

Stonich, S.C. (2003) The political ecology of marine protected areas. In: Gössling, S. (ed.) *Tourism and Development in Tropical Islands: A Political Ecology Perspective*. Edward Elgar Publishing, Cheltenham, UK, pp. 121–147.

Stonich, S.C. (2005) Enhancing community-based tourism development and conservation in the Western Caribbean. In: Wallace, T. (ed.) *Tourism and Applied Anthropologists*. NAPA Bulletin No. 23. University of California Press, Berkeley, CA, pp. 77–86.

Stonich, S.C. (2008) Tourism, vulnerability, and 'natural' disasters: the case of Hurricane Mitch in Honduras. In: Gunewardena, N. and Schuller, M. (eds) *Capitalizing on Catastrophe: The Globalization of Humanitarian Assistance*. Altamira Press, Lanham, Maryland, pp. 47–68.

Trist, C. (1999) Recreating ocean space: recreational consumption and representation of the Caribbean marine environment. *Professional Geographer* 51, 376–387.

UNWTO (2007) *Tourism Highlights 2006 Edition*. United Nations World Tourism Organization, Madrid.

Uyarra, M.C., Cote, I.M., Gill, J.A., Tinch, R.R.T., Viner, D. and Watkinson, A.R. (2005) Island-specific preferences of tourists for environmental features: implications of climate change for tourism-dependent states. *Environmental Conservation* 32, 11–19.

Weaver, D.B. (1999) Magnitude of ecotourism in Costa Rica and Kenya. *Annals of Tourism Research* 26, 792–816.

Weaver, D.B. (2004) Manifestations of ecotourism in the Caribbean. In: Duval, D.T. (ed.) *Tourism in the Caribbean: Trends, Development, Prospects*. Routledge, London/New York, pp. 172–186.

Weaver, D.B. (2006) *Sustainable Tourism*. Elsevier, New York/London.

West, P. and Carrier, J.G. (2004) Ecotourism and authenticity – getting away from it all? *Current Anthropology* 45, 483–498.

West, P., Igoe J. and Brockington, D. (2006) Parks and peoples: the social impact of protected areas. *Annual Review of Anthropology* 35, 251–277.

Young, E. (1999a) Balancing conservation with development in small-scale fisheries: is ecotourism an empty promise? *Human Ecology* 27, 581–620.

Young, E. (1999b) Local people and conservation in Mexico's El Vizcaino Biosphere Reserve. *Geographical Review* 89, 364–390.

Young, E. (2001) State intervention and abuse of the commons: fisheries development in Baja California Sur, Mexico. *Annals of the Association of American Geographers* 91, 283–306.

5 Fishing for Solutions: Ecotourism and Conservation in Galapagos National Park

W.H. DURHAM

Department of Anthropology, Stanford University, Stanford, California, USA

Introduction

Ecotourism is definitely 'easier said than done'. Conceptually, the idea is most appealing: carry out responsible, educational travel to natural areas in ways that contribute to environmental conservation and enhance the livelihood of local people. Put another way, ecotourism is the business of nature tourism measured against the triple bottom line: black ink for business and the equivalent of black ink for both conservation and local well-being. With three strong motivations at the same time, no wonder it is the 'fastest growing sector of the largest industry on earth' (Taylor *et al.*, 2003, p. 977).

But the challenge of ecotourism is to deliver the goods. Instead of simply performing to the satisfaction of one set of shareholders, ecotourism requires satisfying three – including conservationists and local community members – who come with three different sets of expectations, including some which may be in conflict. Between the late 1980s and the late 1990s, there was a kind of naive optimism that ecotourism was going to bring together two big social agendas, the alleviation of poverty and the reduction of global threats to biodiversity, and stitch them together with an innovative business model. Putting these good intentions to work has proved to be a difficult task.

The challenges are perhaps nowhere better seen than in the Galapagos Islands in South America, widely viewed as one of the original 'laboratories' for ecotourism (as well as for evolution, of course). In Galapagos there are, indeed, many profitable companies running a diverse array of responsible tours, both marine (diving trips) and terrestrial (nature walks), using boats to move between visitor sites on different islands. Yes, there have been notable gains and turnarounds in Galapagos conservation, as reviewed below, including some endemic species rescued from the brink of extinction. And yes, there is greater local community benefit to tourism today than in years past. Nevertheless, I show that nature tourism in Galapagos is still far from successful in all three dimensions at the same time. Its record reveals some of the economic, institutional and structural barriers that keep ecotourism from living up to its promise, and a close look at them may well be of value in other settings. Let me begin with a brief background on Galapagos and its special properties that will serve to highlight the local historical effects of human activity.

Special Properties of Galapagos

The main features of Galapagos are widely known owing to its special place in Charles Darwin's voyage of discovery and its subsequent role in scientific and social thought. There are 13 main islands to the archipelago plus 115 small islets, all of volcanic origin, amounting to 7900 km^2 land area, which is just slightly larger than the US state of Delaware. Since annexation by Ecuador in 1832, the islands constitute their own Galapagos Province with three cantons: Isabela (with capital Puerto Villamil), San Cristobal (capital Puerto Baquerizo Moreno, also the Provincial capital) and Santa Cruz (capital Puerto Ayora, also the largest town in Galapagos). In 1959, a century after Darwin's *On the Origin of Species*, the government of Ecuador dedicated 97% of the land area to Galapagos National Park, setting aside 3% for human settlement and agriculture. In 1978 the United Nations Educational, Scientific and Cultural Organization (UNESCO) declared the islands as the very first World Heritage Site and in 1985 named it again a Biosphere Reserve. In 1986, the adjacent 70,000 km^2 of Pacific Ocean was declared a Marine Reserve by Ecuador, which was subsequently expanded to 130,000 km^2 in 1998.

Some of the less obvious features of Galapagos have combined to make the archipelago a very special place, one that offers tourists experiences unlike those anywhere else on the planet. The first of these is *isolation*: not only is the archipelago separated from mainland South America by roughly 1000 km of open ocean, but each of the 120-some islands and islets are separated from one another by surprisingly strong sea currents and winds. The result, as Darwin so aptly put it, is to make the archipelago a 'little world within itself' (Darwin, 2004 [1845], p. 336) in which each island is effectively its own little continent, separated by more than simply linear distance from its neighbours. Local isolation by currents and winds is, moreover, one of the reasons the islands were formerly called 'Enchanted' (*Islas Encantadas*); even experienced sea captains found it difficult to navigate from one island to the next and so ascribed mysterious powers to the region.

The second key property of Galapagos I summarize as *demanding ecological conditions*, owing mainly to the rugged volcanic terrain and low average rainfall of the islands at sea level. From time immemorial, would-be Galapagos colonists had first to survive the maritime journey of a thousand kilometres with all the sunlight and heat of an equatorial crossing. And then they had to survive the colonization of a craggy terrain of sand, basalt, razor-sharp lava fields and not much else. Certainly not much rain or freshwater at the lower elevations where many colonists would raft ashore: apart from El Niño years, when the archipelago is deluged in metres of rainfall, the average year brings only 300 to 400 mm rainfall total at sea level. Conditions are somewhat better at higher elevations, if a colonist made it there, but still far from tropical paradise. At 200 m, annual rainfall averages only 1000 to 1200 mm apart from El Niño years (when it can be two or three times as much).

Acting in combination over expanses of time, these first two features played a major role in shaping the assemblages of bizarre and wonderful organisms found on the different islands of the archipelago – like sea-foraging marine iguanas, giant herbivorous tortoises, oversized flightless cormorants, and daisy-like plants that grow in tall stands fifty feet high like a forest. Equally noteworthy and wonderful are the organisms not naturally found in the archipelago, including amphibians and freshwater fish (save for one lone species of cusk eel, found living in lava caves on Santa Cruz Island).

Darwin was appropriately fascinated by these odd assemblages during his visit to Galapagos in 1835. Not only did he eventually, and accurately, realize that the organisms he saw in Galapagos were the surviving descendants of species that had endured the rigors of transit and colonization, but he also recognized that they had been reshaped and adapted to this new and demanding 'little world' in the middle of the Pacific. One of his favourite examples, the sea algae-feeding marine iguana, has since become a classic in adaptation studies as has the currently endangered vegetarian finch, one of few birds in the world with literally the guts to eat just leaves.

Darwin also noted the third key ecological feature of the Galapagos: the *relative absence of competitive and/or predatory species*, especially raptors, terrestrial mammals and woody plants. Owing largely to the first two features described above, continental competitors and predators have historically not thrived in Galapagos, either because they did not survive the journey or because they could not establish a breeding population in the harsh conditions once they arrived. Interestingly, exceptions nicely test that rule: the islands *are* home to several species of flying mammals, to diminutive, durable and highly drought-tolerant 'rice rats', and to large, predatory marine mammals – the Galapagos sea lions and fur sea lions.

Because of these faunal lacunae, moreover, the same Galapagos endemics that are marvels of adaptation to local idiosyncratic conditions show a fourth special property the Galapagos shares with other oceanic islands. The archipelago's endemic species are remarkably *vulnerable to new challenges*. They simply lack the defensive, protective structures and behaviours that one is used to finding among continental biota. Worthy examples include the Galapagos petrel – a long-winged seabird that nests, of all places, in small holes in open ground on some of the higher islands; and the notorious blue-footed booby that nests and lays eggs fully exposed on flat ground, with only the marginal immunity of a circular ring of its own guano. So blatant and extreme are the vulnerabilities of Galapagos endemics that they constitute, in my view, one of the very best lines of evidence supporting modern evolutionary theory. They emphasize the point that organisms have evolved, just as Darwin surmised, to fit their local environmental circumstances.

Decline of Isolation

Against this background, the impact of recent human activity in Galapagos is readily appreciated: it plainly challenges the first three conditions that have made the archipelago so distinctive and strikingly confirms the fourth. Far from maintaining its once-splendid isolation and pristine, if harsh, natural habitats, Galapagos now suffers from globalization and all that globalization brings with it, including the rapid build-up of tourism, tourism-induced immigration, development and infrastructural elaboration, and concomitant drastic changes in habitats and biota. In many ways, the circumstances of Galapagos today are rather emblematic of globalization and the long reach of modern capitalism. The very 'poster child' of conservation efforts in Galapagos, 'Lonesome George', the last of the Pinta Island tortoises, has recently evolved into a symbol of far more global and general conservation/ development disputes (Nicholls, 2006).

Consider first the decline of isolation, nowhere better seen than in the growth of tourism in the islands (Fig. 5.1). From a humble start in the late 1960s, tourism has grown 20-fold since the 1970s to over 140,000 visitors annually – an average of over 400 new arrivals *daily*. In the service of this growth, the islands are now linked by the full panoply of contemporary means of transportation and communication, including:

- More than 35 roundtrip jet flights per week from the mainland, carrying a total of more than 2000 passengers, of whom over 70% are tourists (estimated from Fundación Natura, 2002, pp. 128–129).
- More than 70 tourism boats working year-round, with a total capacity of over 1600 passengers (Fundación Natura, 2002, p. 90).
- Over 950 motorized road vehicles including tourist buses and taxis (Cardenas, 2002).
- Frequent visits from supply ships and oil tankers, including some that result in harmful spills (Lougheed *et al.*, 2002).
- New and periodic visits from massive cruise liners, such as the *Discovery* (Rice, 2007).

Tourism has grown to the point that almost two-thirds (65.4%) of the total 'gross island product' of the archipelago comes from tourist services alone – travel agencies, boats, rentals and day tours – increasing to almost 71% when restaurants, bars and hotels are added in (Taylor *et al.*, 2003).

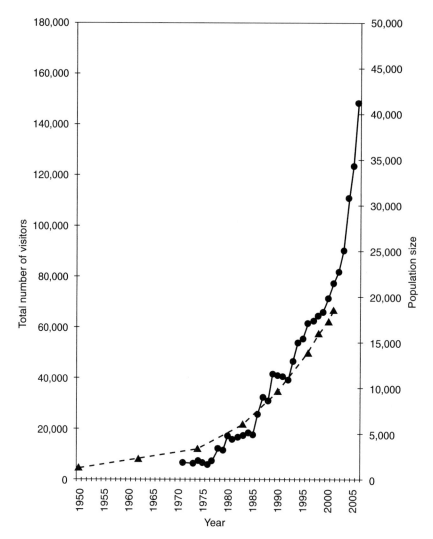

Fig. 5.1. The rapid increase in tourism and resident population in the Galapagos Islands. Shown here are the total number of visitors to the islands (circles, solid line) according to records of the Galapagos National Park, plus the resident human population of all islands (triangles, dotted line), measured at right, according to national census data.

Fortunately, the rising tide of tourism does not mean that waves of tourists spread out over the islands and go where they please; visitors are restricted to specific sites established, regulated and monitored by the National Park. Moreover, the record shows that site management works well:

> Long-term studies of impacts on key indicator species such as waved albatrosses, three species of boobies (blue-footed, red-footed and [Nazca]), and two species of frigatebirds (magnificent and great) at both visitor sites and non-visited control breeding colonies have shown no detectable impacts on reproductive success over several decades. (MacFarland, 2000)

Changing Ecological Conditions

Consider, second, the changing ecological conditions of the islands. One of the main by-products of tourism's success in Galapagos has been record levels of human population increase in the archipelago (residents, not counting tourists), closely paralleling tourism's rise, also shown in Fig. 5.1. Far from being a remote outpost of civilization, the human population has increased from census totals of 1346 in 1950 to 18,640 in 2001 – implying an extraordinarily high average rate of increase, 5.2% per annum (for comparison, 3.5% per annum is considered very high for national populations). At this writing (2007), it is likely that upwards of 25,000 people live on the four inhabited islands; some observers (e.g. Lorenz, 2007) put the figure as high as 30,000, which would imply annual increases of more than 5.2% since 2001. Sustained population growth at such high rates is inevitably a product of immigration on top of natural increase, as confirmed by several recent studies (Ecuador's nationwide annual rate of increase was roughly 2.7% by comparison). First, a study cited by MacFarland and Cifuentes (1996, p. 155) used a random sample of 214 households in the four port towns of the archipelago to find that 73% of the (presumably adult) inhabitants had immigrated to the islands since 1986. This study was conducted in 1994, before migration status became a sensitive issue in Galapagos with the 1998 Special Law (discussed below); one might therefore expect later studies to have somewhat lower percentages, which is just what one finds. An analysis of 1998 national census data by Borja (2000, p. 34) revealed that only 34.7% of Galapagos inhabitants called themselves 'native born' versus 65.3% who called themselves immigrants. Lastly, a 1998 survey of 267 households on the three most populous islands found 69.8% to have been born on the Ecuadorian mainland (Taylor *et al.*, 2003). With such high levels of immigration, the islands appear to offer a case in point of the 'tourism–income–population growth spiral' described in this last study:

> Expanding tourism can generate pressures for demographic growth by widening economic disparities between tourist destinations and outside economies, [thereby] stimulating migration to fill jobs linked directly or indirectly to tourism. (Taylor *et al.*, 2003, p. 977)

This sizeable human presence in the archipelago has helped change the ecological conditions of the islands in several ways. First, as the migration studies make clear, there are now four port towns in Galapagos (plus numerous smaller settlements), each with many of the facilities and infrastructure of urban settlements elsewhere in the world, including streets and sewers, home gardens and water-supply systems, garbage and trash dumps, and other modifications. That these changes have tempered the harsh ecological conditions on at least a couple of the islands is dramatically illustrated by the establishment of the first-ever amphibian populations in Galapagos. During the El Niño year of 1997/8, Fowler's snouted tree frog – normally a resident of wet areas of the Pacific lowlands of Ecuador and Columbia – established itself in natural and human-built freshwater supplies around towns on two of the islands, prompting a 'Wanted Dead or Alive' campaign and several efforts at control. Urban rock pigeons – as might be found in any town or city of moderate climate – are a second revealing example, becoming established in the 1970s and 1980s in and around the three largest towns of Galapagos. Because pigeons are carriers of *Trichomonas*, a deadly protozoan parasite that infects people and a wide spectrum of birds, a rock pigeon eradication campaign by the Galapagos National Park removed nearly 2000 individuals from those three sites in 2001/2. Urban water systems providing year-round pools of fresh water, together with inefficient waste treatment operations and poorly designed sewer systems, are among the habitat changes enabling these introductions and others.

Human presence in Galapagos has also given rise to habitat modification in the form of large agricultural areas on the same four islands with ports. As noted earlier, rainfall is generally scarce in Galapagos but increases with altitude, such that islands with several hundred metres of relief have an internal 'humid zone' in the volcanic uplands. Between 1832, when permanent human settlement began, and the 1990s, these zones were increasingly converted to agricultural pursuits, such as cultivating annuals (maize, manioc and sugarcane among them), grazing livestock and building up orchards of citrus and avocado – all exotic to the islands' biota. By 1974, this conversion had created 18,600 ha of agricultural lands, amounting to 2.4% of the total archipelago. By 1986 the area increased to 24,400 ha, or 3.2% of the archipelago, of which almost 50% was used for pasture. By 2000, agriculture occupied 23,400 ha, or 3.1% of the total, with again 50% being used for pasture (see Kerr *et al.*, 2004, p. 25). Galapagos-wide percentages are misleading, however, in the sense that agricultural impact varies greatly by island (being permitted only outside park boundaries on four islands) and is significant only in humid zones at that. When one measures against the land area of humid zones of inhabited islands, the figures show 93% conversion on San Cristobal Island, 74% on Santa Cruz, 15% on Floreana and 8% on Isabela (Bensted-Smith, 2002, p. 37). Ecologically, this has meant a major historical expansion of cultivars and grassland in Galapagos, complete with fields of non-native plants, fruit trees, grasses, livestock, and associated community members. More recently, Galapagos agriculture has experienced a recession as can be seen in the decline in farm area between 1986 and 2000, even though sales to tour boats are an important market for agricultural production and tourism is booming as emphasized above. Agriculture can no longer compete with earnings that can be gained elsewhere, with the result that people leave rural homesteads and move to the port towns. Consequently, abandoned farms and ranches are a common sight in agricultural zones today (Flora Lu, Palo Alto, California, personal communication, 2007).

There is one further form of environmental change that affects Galapagos severely; the only question is to what extent that change is anthropogenic. The massive climate shifts known as El Niño/Southern

Oscillation (ENSO) have a profound effect on Galapagos, bringing to the relatively dry islands as much as 2 or 3 m of rainfall, warm sea temperatures, and a major impact on flora and fauna (e.g. Jaksic, 2001). The impact is favourable for some species, such as Darwin's finches, introduced smooth-billed anis, other land birds and many invertebrates who find more food in wet years; but on other species, the impact is devastating. All of the marine foraging species, for example, from sea lions to penguins and flightless cormorants to marine iguanas, depend on food supplies that vanish in warm El Niño water. Accumulating evidence, from lake cores in Galapagos (Riedinger *et al.*, 2002) and from comparative studies across South America (reviewed in Gergis and Fowler, 2006, for example), show that El Niño events have recently increased in frequency and magnitude, in parallel with trends in greenhouse gases and climate change. But are the changes in ENSO truly a result of global warming and thus of human activity? Debate on the point continues, but separate lines of research today – one using climate models, another using the correlation of El Niño frequency and temperature change – offer new support affirming that hypothesis (see Herbert and Dixon, 2002; Tsonis *et al.*, 2003). Smooth-billed anis, introduced to the islands by a rancher who hoped they would control ticks on his cattle, offer an example of the way that human-induced climate change can facilitate the establishment of human-introduced exotics. Fowler's snouted tree frog is another example.

Introduced Species

Speaking of introductions, the combination of significant ecological change in the archipelago and its declining isolation has produced drastic change in the third special feature of Galapagos: the relative absence of competitive and/or predatory species. This change often comes as the biggest surprise to newcomers: far from being pristine, the Galapagos is now home to literally hundreds of exotic species (Watkins *et al.*, 2007; see also Table 5.1). These include:

- Thirty-six species of introduced vertebrates, including horses, donkeys, cattle, goats, dogs, pigs, cats, ducks, chickens, fish (tilapia), rats, mice and geckos.
- More than 740 species of introduced plants including some very aggressive woody plants and brambles: quinine, guava, blackberry, raspberry and lantana.
- More than 540 species of introduced invertebrates, including fire ants, cottony cushion scale, predatory wasps, bot flies (which parasitize Darwin's finches, mockingbirds and more); *Culex* and *Aedes* mosquitos (vectors for many diseases including dengue, West Nile fever and avian malaria); and disease microorganisms, such as pathogens for avian pox (a serious problem for Darwin's finches), canine distemper and trichomoniasis mentioned above.

Table 5.1. Native species, threatened and extinct, plus introductions as of 2006. (Data compiled from Bensted-Smith, 2002 for native species and from Watkins *et al.*, 2007 for introduced species.)

Species	Vascular plants		Vertebrates		Invertebrates	
	n	% of native	*n*	% of native	*n*	% of native
Native	560	100.0	112	100.0	1893	100.0
Threatened	95	17.0	54	48.2	N/A	N/A
Extinct	3	0.6	10	8.9	2–3	0.1
Introduced	748		36		543	

N/A, not applicable.

It is difficult to visit the coastal areas of Galapagos today and not see introduced organisms or their remains; in highland areas it is even worse, because the moisture there attracts and supports exotics in greater numbers.

Meanwhile, two key Galapagos institutions mentioned earlier – the Galapagos National Park and Charles Darwin Research Station (CDRS) – are active in combating these introductions, with notable successes to their credit. Surely the most impressive of these successes are the recent helicopter-assisted eradication campaigns against goats, pigs and donkeys, among the most damaging of all introductions. As of 2006, these campaigns have succeeded in eliminating donkeys, pigs and goats from Santiago Island (over 100,000 animals in all), goats from Pinta Island (over 50,000) and donkeys and goats from Isabela (over 64,000; Lavoie *et al.*, 2007).

Looking over the historical record of introductions, it is tempting to draw parallels among temporal trends in the growth of tourism and the increasing numbers of exotic species as Mauchamp (1997) and many others have done. The temptation is especially great in the case of exotic plants where the record is complete and detailed, and where it is easy to imagine seeds sticking to clothes and shoes. However, studies of biota in National Park visitation sites and of products brought into Galapagos suggest that tourists and tourism are not the main source of introductions, as confirmed by the inspection and quarantine system begun in 1998 (known as SICGAL, acronym in Spanish for Galapagos Inspection and Quarantine System). In 2001, for example, only 27% of all quarantine retentions by SICGAL (*n* = 2518) came from tourists and another 10% from tourism companies; in contrast, 64% of the retentions came from Galapagos residents, who also comprised less than a third of the passengers inspected (Zapata *et al.*, 2002). Similarly, Tye (2006) shows that what looks like a correlation of several exponential trends – the introduction of plants to Galapagos, the increase in transportation to the islands and resident population growth – falls apart under close scrutiny. The true rate of introduction for accidentals has been linear not exponential, Tye demonstrates, and the recorded rate of 'escapes from cultivation' is a function largely of botanists' changing interests over the years. Rates of introduction thus depend more on human activity than on human population growth. And their magnitude is certainly unprecedented in Galapagos history, as Tye concludes:

> One firm conclusion that can be drawn for Galapagos is that the archipelago has, since its discovery in 1535, experienced introduction of at least 550 alien plant species in 470 years, or 1.2 species per year [revised by others in 2007 to 748 species, or 1.6 per year]. This compares with a probable natural arrival rate of about one species per 10,000 years… The human-mediated rate of arrival of new plant species is thus about 13,000 times the natural rate. (Tye, 2006, p. 213)

The Vulnerability of Native Biota

The final key feature of terrestrial life in Galapagos affected by ongoing anthropogenic change is vulnerability – the vulnerability of locally evolved species, a condition which can readily be measured by endangerment or, in the worst case, by extinction. As shown in Table 5.1 using data from 2000, an impressive 17% of all native vascular plants – or a whopping 54.3% of all endemic vascular plants – are listed as 'threatened' in the archipelago, not to mention 48.2% of all Galapagos vertebrates. On top of that, three vascular plant species are known to have gone extinct since human visits began in 1535, and ten vertebrate species, including two species of the famed giant tortoises, a land iguana, and seven species of the one group of endemic mammals, the rice rats.

These serious conservation issues were already well known and well documented by the 1990s, but they were joined in 1992 by another set of urgent issues emerging from the fishing sector of Galapagos. Two sets of concerns heating up at the same time, and staying hot, raised renewed national and international alarm over the future of the archipelago. By 1995/6 the UNESCO World Heritage Committee actively considered putting Galapagos – its very first World Heritage Site 17 years earlier – on the list of World Heritage in Danger: a tragic distinction, which the government of Ecuador wanted to avoid. Following a special mission to Galapagos, the World Heritage Committee urged the President and Congress of Ecuador to prepare 'special legislation' in repair. They did as urged, and thus began in earnest the search for solutions.

Fishing in Galapagos

That fishing in Galapagos waters would surface one day as a leading issue was probably inevitable. First, there was a long-established fishing tradition in the islands going back to at least the 1920s (Merlen, 1995). With a strong family basis, this early homespun fishery focused on both local subsistence and a commercial product – dried and salted *bacalao* from an endemic sailfin grouper, a product that became a key ingredient of Easter soup on the mainland. A survey in 1981 of these fishermen and their descendents, cited in Merlen (1995, p. 100), found that '80% of the fishermen interviewed on [the island of] San Cristobal were born on the island and only 5% had no relatives within the industry'. Grounded in this local tradition is a strong feeling of entitlement today – entitlement to go on conducting local 'artisanal' fishing in Galapagos using hand lines, hand nets, and other simple technologies.

Second, in the 1960s and 1970s a vigorous second fishery had developed: a large-scale commercial fishery dedicated to lobster, especially two species of spiny lobster (still a delicacy in the islands). Originally the lobster fishery operated from large, generally foreign-owned vessels, either with their own imported divers or with buyers who would buy catches from local fishing boats and divers. By 1974, the Ecuadorian government grew concerned about overexploitation of this fishery and, in that year, passed a law prohibiting foreign vessels from entering the islands and banning all lobster exports from the country. This action prompted what Merlen (1995, p. 102) termed a 'chaotic resurgence of the lobster industry' in a new form, as many of the former lobster fishers began their own small, domestic businesses with an opportunistic bent.

Third, the Asian market for Galapagos marine products grew in the 1970s and 1980s, playing right in to any opportunism by small fishers. The first market demand of note from Asia was for shark fin, vigorously traded in Galapagos until it was found that endemic sea lions were being used for bait, and the fishery was banned in 1989. The second market demand from Asia was for sea cucumbers (*pepinos del mar* in Spanish; slug-like marine Holothurians). So great was the demand from Singapore, Taiwan and Hong Kong, for example, that it took only 4 years – 1988 to 1992 – to deplete the entire mainland coastal fishery of Ecuador. Facing declining yields in 1991, scores of *pepineros* (sea cucumber fisherman) moved to Galapagos, where they became no small part of the human population growth curve. There they continued their trade, joined by local commercial fishermen as well who could not resist as much as US$2.50 per pound for dried *pepinos*, about 20 times the return of other species (Camhi, 1995). The resulting sea cucumber harvest in Galapagos was so intense and chaotic, and its impact so far-reaching (because processing requires cooking and drying, often at illegal camps on remote islands in Galapagos National Park), that it was banned by Presidential Decree in 1992. That Decree, in turn, touched off what was to become years of protest, ranging from peaceful demonstrations to violent acts of sabotage and on to a gunfire-wounded park ranger, which came to be known as the 'Sea Cucumber War' (useful synopses are given by Pinson, 1996; Jenkins and Mulliken, 1999).

Fourth, in addition to the entrepreneurial components of the fisheries crisis in Galapagos, there were also important, unfortunate institutional aspects. Back in the 1980s, even before the sea cucumber problem, efforts were made to protect the unique marine environments of Galapagos, both because of their intrinsic biodiversity value and to ensure the protection of closely interconnected terrestrial ecosystems. By Presidential Decree in 1986, the Galapagos Marine Resources Reserve (GMRR) was created to protect sea life and habitats within the archipelago and within a 15 nautical mile buffer zone around the internal waters. Although the intention was laudable, the problems were too, as clearly identified by Heylings *et al.* (1998): (i) the category 'marine resources reserve' was unique, unrelated to the system of national parks, and had no legal basis apart from this decree, which ruled out almost any prospect of enforcement; and (ii) the decree created an unwieldy 'Interinstitutional Commission' of seven governmental entities for administration and implementation. Doomed from the start, the GMRR struggled along a few years, proposed a Management Plan in 1992, but proved 'not functional' in handling the fishing crisis. In November 1996, as the sea cucumber conflict boiled over, the executive director of INEFAN (the Ecuadorian Institute of Forestry, Natural Areas, and Wildlife) issued a decree intended to make the GMRR an official, legal, biological reserve, and giving the Galapagos National Park legitimate jurisdiction over marine as well as terrestrial areas. But even this failed on institutional grounds. As a report at the time summarized:

> The Office of [the government's own] Undersecretary of Fisheries and representatives of the fishing fleet from the mainland port of Manta rejected the declaration of the 'Galapagos Marine Resources Biological Reserve' and refused to acknowledge the Galapagos National Park's jurisdiction over it. (Fundación Natura, 1998a)

It was just at this time (December 1996), barely a month after the INEFAN decree, that the Bureau of the World Heritage Committee conducted their assessment of the recent record in Galapagos (Heslinga, 2003). The Bureau was fully aware of all the issues reviewed above, including:

- Continued exponential increase in tourism.
- Continued uncontrolled immigration, fuelling rapid population growth.
- Accelerating introduction of exotic species and diseases.
- Continuing intense local conflict over fishing.

The Bureau promptly recommended to the Committee that it add Galapagos to the Heritage in Danger List. At the following World Heritage Committee meeting, the delegate of Ecuador requested that the Committee allow the country additional time before taking that action, citing vigorous governmental efforts under way to establish a Ministry of the Environment and to draft the requested 'special legislation' addressing key Galapagos issues. The Committee decided to put Galapagos on the 'Danger List' with effect from 15 November 1997, unless Ecuador's actions proved effective.

The Galapagos Special Law of 1998

Happily, Ecuador's efforts produced novel results. In April 1997, the Galapagos National Park and the CDRS brought together a group of key players from diverse sectors involved in the crisis of the 1990s: fishing, tourism, science (from CDRS) and conservation (from Galapagos National Park). With the help of trained facilitators, an innovative (and some said 'quasi-miraculous') form of participatory decision making was begun, centred around this 'Grupo Nucleo' of key players, who took as their goal the collaborative revision of the marine reserve's now-defunct management plan, with the hopes that this might influence the 'special legislation' promised to the World Heritage Committee by the Government of Ecuador. The process was an overall success (see discussion in Heylings *et al.*, 1998; Novy, 2000) and resulted in pivotal contributions:

> The Grupo Nucleo delineated three key priorities to include in the Law: 1) the ratification of the Protected Area status of the Marine Reserve under the jurisdiction of the Galapagos National Park Service; 2) the expansion of the Marine Reserve to 40 nautical miles with exclusive rights for local, small-scale fishers; and 3) the institutionalization of participatory management. Representatives advocated institutionalizing the Grupo Nucleo to form a Participatory Management Board, the 'Junta de Manejo Participativo', for ongoing administration and management of the Reserve. (Novy, 2000, p. 87)

In addition to the success of the 'Grupo Nucleo', the presidential Commission on the Galapagos (with high-level representatives of Provincial government, INEFAN, the Galapagos National Institute (INGALA) and the Ministry of Environment) worked away on legislation for dealing with other Galapagos issues, including migration, tourism growth, tourism revenues, and other issues related to education and health care. The resulting product integrated efforts by both groups. After many months of intensive effort, lobbying and no small amount of opposition from the industrial fishing sector, a bill was approved by the National Congress and President in March 1998, called (in translation) 'The Special Law for the Conservation and Sustainable Development of Galapagos Province', or simply the 'Special Law for Galapagos'. As expected, the Law honoured all key rec-ommendations from the 'Grupo Nucleo' regarding the new and simplified Galapagos Marine Reserve (GMR). Moreover, an appropriate 'pat on the back' came through to both efforts in 2001 when the World Heritage Committee voted to include the full GMR with the terrestrial component in the Galapagos World Heritage Site.

Many features of the Special Law are important to the future of tourism, conservation and local welfare in Galapagos, above and beyond those pertaining to the GMR (see Fundación Natura, 1998b). For example, the Law clarifies institutional relations in the archipelago, recreating INGALA as the central agency for planning and policy throughout the archipelago. It expands the INGALA council to 13 members to include greater representation from diverse sectors of the islands. It also calls for the 'total control' of introduced species through sustained inspection and quarantine activities, an annual programme for the eradication of invasive species in farm areas, and stiff fines and penalties for any reported introductions or damage to protected areas. The Law further specifies a new and improved distribution system for Galapagos National Park entrance fees, not only setting the fee at a higher level (e.g. US$100 for foreign tourists aged 12 years or older) but also assuring that roughly 95% of the total will stay in Galapagos, distributed as follows.

1. Galapagos National Park, 40%.
2. Municipalities of Galapagos, 20%.
3. Provincial Council of Galapagos, 10%.
4. Marine Reserve of the Galapagos Province, 5%.
5. INEFAN, for National Protected Heritage Areas, 5%.
6. INGALA, 10%.
7. Inspection and Quarantine System for Galapagos, 5%.
8. National Navy, 5%.

According to this breakdown, roughly 50% is allocated to Galapagos conservation – a vast improvement over the previous decade, in which the allocation varied apparently arbitrarily from 12% to 32%, and went exclusively to the National Park (Fundación Natura, 1998b, p. 10). Equally noteworthy is the 40% allocated to local development (Municipalities, Provincial Council, plus INGALA) – a new allocation designed to enhance local benefits. Judging from Galapagos National Park data on foreign visitors, the aggregate year 2000 revenue from this one source was a substantial US$5.7 million, rising with the growth of tourism all the way to roughly US$9.6 million in 2006, which may be one reason it is hard to constrain the numbers of visitors.

But there are provisions in two areas of the Special Law of particular importance to ecotourism in the islands. The first has to do with immigration: as argued earlier, a growing stream of immigrants has been drawn to the islands because of the jobs and earnings related to tourism's rapid growth. The Special Law introduces residency controls designed to restrict immigration regardless of tourism growth: it limits residents to the group of people who had lived in Galapagos for 5 continuous years prior to the date of the Law (March 1998). Everyone else is thus declared a temporary resident, with renewable temporary status in Galapagos for the length of their work or service contract. Curiously, the Special Law does not explicitly address an upper limit on the number of tourist visitors to the islands, even though population and tourism growth have been so closely associated in the archipelago's history. Caps have been proposed in previous Galapagos National Park management plans, but never enforced; in the 1980s, the limit was set at 12,000 annual visitors, for example (de Groot, 1983), more than an order of magnitude below today's visitation levels.

Second, the Law deliberately provides for the 'encouragement of tourism with the involvement of the local community' (Article 48). Although it 'grandfathers' tour operation rights granted by INEFAN before the Law (which would include international and mainland tour companies, for example), it stipulates that all new tourism operations and permits will go to permanent residents only, and that only permanent residents may apply for preferential credits in support of new tourism development. It further specifies that the construction of new tourist facilities will be given authorization by INGALA only if they generate local profits, are carried out by permanent residents, and guarantee quality services with minimal environmental impact. The clear and unambiguous message of the Special Law is that tourism development in the future must have more local benefits in Galapagos. It is tantamount to admitting paltry local benefits from Galapagos tourism in the past, and it is a call for increased adherence to all three terms of the triple bottom line for genuine ecotourism in the archipelago.

The Special Law was thus watershed legislation and a dramatic statement by the Government of Ecuador of its commitment to finding a course for sustainable development in Galapagos. But much of the Law's efficacy rested on enforcement, and on the ability of INGALA to carry out the stipulated mid-course corrections. The special challenges to that responsibility included two of particular relevance here: (i) could INGALA implement and enforce residency controls effectively in the face of strong, continuing economic incentives for immigration, some of which (like preferential credit and airfare subsidies) are spelled out in the Law itself? Would it be able to regulate Galapagos population increase to more sustainable levels, like 2% per annum? (ii) Are the provisions of the Law and the enforcement of INGALA sufficient to substantially bolster local benefits coming from the tourism boom? Often cited as 'the place where ecotourism began' (Honey, 1994), will these measures put Galapagos back on track to garner the local benefits of a genuine ecotourism?

More Local Benefits from Tourism since 1998?

It is perhaps too early to provide a fully unambiguous answer to the first question about immigration. Accurate, up-to-date information about the human population of Galapagos remains difficult to obtain, and surely constitutes a research objective of high priority for the archipelago. A new census effort was undertaken by INGALA in the archipelago late in 2006, a census not based on current occupancy (an especially sensitive topic) but on normal or habitual occupancy, making it perhaps easier to downplay recent arrivals. The tally achieved, though technically not comparable to earlier censuses (so I have not included it in Fig. 5.1), was 19,184. If one ignores the comparability issue for the sake of discussion and compares that tally with the normal 2001 census count of 18,640, it would mean that INGALA and the Special Law have been almost completely effective at curtailing immigration. Judging from personal observation and the reports of others, they have not been that effective, at least not yet. As mentioned earlier, the best of informal estimates put the total population in 2005/6 as between 24,500 (INGALA, 2005; cited in Taylor *et al.*, 2006) and 30,000 (for example, Galapagos Conservation

Trust, 2005). If these latter estimates are closer to reality, they do raise questions about the efficacy of the 1998 Special Law and INGALA to bring about the regulation of island immigration. Certainly we know that the number of tourist visitors has continued to increase in an unregulated manner since 1998 (see Fig. 5.1), and thus the economic incentives to immigration remain strong and unabated. At the moment, this first question simply cannot be decided for sure. In the long run, however, it will surely be important to regulate both sides of the tourism/local population equation.

Happily, more can be said in answer to the second question about local benefits and the ecotourism trajectory of Galapagos. For this part of the analysis I draw heavily on the detailed, recent 'economy-wide' study of economic growth in the islands from Edward Taylor and colleagues (Taylor *et al.*, 2006) – a study that builds on earlier findings, mentioned above, from their survey work in 1998 (Taylor *et al.*, 2003). Noting that the Special Law has given Galapagos 'significant local autonomy' for the first time, Taylor *et al.* view Galapagos as not just a laboratory for ecotourism and evolution, but also now 'for assessing the potential effectiveness of local-based economic development and conservation' (Taylor *et al.*, 2006, p. 3). A key finding of their work is that Galapagos had, between 1998/9 and 2005, one of the fastest growing economies in the world, with tourism as its 'main motor':

> Our conservative estimates, based on changes in tourism, fishing, and government and conservation expenditures, indicate that total income in the archipelago increased 78%, to $73.2 million, over this 6-year period, for an average annual growth rate of 9.9% . . . Despite this striking increase in total income, per-capita income increased at a rate of only 1.8% annually . . . due to a highly elastic migration response. . . . The number of island inhabitants rose 60% over this period [using an INGALA estimate of approximately 24,500 residents in 2005]. If the Galapagos had had the same total income growth without migration, income per capita in 2005 would have been $4,783 instead of $2,989. . . [If one were to adjust for inflation, in real terms,] it is likely that per-capita income on the islands decreased. (Taylor *et al.*, 2006, pp. 9–10)

By their calculations, migration plus inflation (driven in part by population growth) are enough to nullify the gains of one of the world's most rapidly growing economies. They show that each foreign tourist visiting the islands in 2005 generated about US$1150 in new income for island residents. Thus, in terms of per capita income growth, the visit of every three tourists to Galapagos in 2005 effectively 'brought one new immigrant to the islands' during the same interval (Taylor *et al.*, 2006, p. 11). This is another way of saying that the immigration issue must be resolved.

But there are two further findings of the economy-wide model with important implications for ecotourism. Taylor *et al.*'s economy-wide model allows them to calculate 'multipliers' representing the effect of different categories of expenditures on Galapagos income growth. A 'multiplier' is the effect on total income in Galapagos of a given type of expenditure, taking into account the demand linkages within the archipelago's economy. A thousand dollars directly spent in the islands can be re-spent locally by the residents receiving it, for example, thus 'multiplying' its effect on total income in the islands. Thus Taylor *et al.* calculate that each US$1000 of fish sales by resident fishing households on Isabela Island increases the total income in Galapagos by US$1282. Again, this is because income in fishing households stimulates, by their local purchases in turn, growth elsewhere in the local economy. In contrast, Taylor *et al.* calculate that each US$1000 of domestic (Ecuadorian) tourist expenditure for a trip to Galapagos creates but US$429 of increase in total income in the local economy, for the simple reason that while domestic tourists often stay overnight in port towns, take some of their meals there and so on, they also spend much less of their money on the islands than the fishers do. A big chunk of their budget goes to tour packages purchased on the mainland and to domestic airfares for the flight out to the archipelago. Worse still, the study shows that each US$1000 spent by foreign tourists increases island income by only US$218. On the one hand, that is still a substantial and positive contribution: foreign tourists do add to island income. On the other hand, they add at only 50.8% of the rate for domestic tourists, and at 17.0% – less than one-fifth – of the rate for Isabela fishing households. A major challenge to Galapagos tourism is thus building the foreign (and domestic) tourist multiplier so that there is more local benefit from each visitor. Local benefit, after all, is a primary definitional goal of ecotourism. Put differently, Galapagos could receive today's benefit to income growth with a lot fewer visitors (or a much bigger benefit with the same number of visitors) if they can find ways to increase foreign visitor spending in the islands. If one were grading, as we would a university course, ecotourism's historical record in Galapagos for relative contribution to local livelihood, a multiplier of US$218 per US$1000 for current foreign tourism is not even a 'C–'.

A second finding from the Taylor *et al.* (2006) study challenges the efficacy of the Special Law to encourage tourism of benefit to the local community. This finding comes from the researcher's surveys in 1998 and again in 2005 of tourist spending patterns for their Galapagos visits (see Table 5.2). They found that foreign tourists in 1998 spent an average total of US$3677 on their visit to Galapagos, which increased to an average total of US$4180 per foreign tourist in 2005 – an increase of 12% which certainly seems a happy outcome for Ecuador and the Galapagos. However, their data show also a bigger increase in the same time interval in the average expenditure of foreign tourists on package trips purchased abroad, from an average of US$1271 in 1998 to US$2098 in 2005. This means that, in 2005, over half (50.2%) of all money spent per tourist on a trip to Galapagos is spent abroad, up from 34.6% in 1998. This is certainly neither the direction nor magnitude of change that was intended by the Special Law. Not surprisingly, average foreign tourist expenditures in the rest of Ecuador declined at the same time from 1998 to 2005 (from US$678 to US$316, a drop of 53%). There was, it should be noted, a very modest gain between 1998 and 2005 in total foreign tourist expenditures actually on the Islands: up from 6.6 cents per dollar spent on the trip, to 8.5 cents per dollar spent (a gain of 1.9 cents per dollar), due in part to an increase in philanthropic donations to the National Park (not shown in Table 5.2). But this is literally 'small change', especially compared with on-island expenditures of domestic (Ecuadorian) tourists, whose outlays in Galapagos rose from 21.6 cents per trip dollar to 35.0 cents per trip dollar (a gain of 13.4 cents per dollar). From these data and others, Taylor *et al.* (2006, p. 3) conclude as follows:

> The organization of the tourist sector in the Galapagos is evolving towards a greater emphasis on tourist packages purchased abroad and oriented toward [large boats] and recreational activities, particularly diving. In addition, returning to the islands in 2005, one immediately notes the construction of newer and more luxurious hotels and a bipolar restructuring of the [navigated tour] sector around large ships (of 100 or more berths) and yachts, with 8 to 16 berths, including luxury ships… As a result, a larger share of profits in this sector left the islands in 2005 than in [1998].

A related goal of the Special Law was to promote new tourism operations and permits among permanent residents only, and this too has not worked according to the best of available data. Following Epler and Proaño (2007), in Fig. 5.2 I have plotted the full spectrum of ship-board berths in Galapagos by the quality class of the boat and the residency of the owner, for 1998 (Fig. 5.2a) and 2005 (Fig. 5.2b). Close comparison of the data from these years shows that there has been change in the distribution all right, but it is not in the intended direction. The percentage of berths on ships with foreign owners has increased in both the 'luxury' and 'standard' classes (the 'high end' of the navigated tours). Similarly, the percentage of berths on ships with mainland owners has grown in the other two quality classes, 'economy' and 'day tour'. As a result, the percentage of berths on boats with Galapagos owners has declined across all quality classes of the spectrum – although the decrease is quite small in the case of luxury boats. In other words, data for a key variable, berths on tour boats in Galapagos, run exactly opposite to the spirit of the Special Law. The conclusion is again succinctly summarized by Taylor *et al.* (2006, p. 3): as the navigated tour sector in Galapagos 'becomes more and more capitalized, an increasing share of berths are owned by outside investors'. If indeed the Special Law has made the Galapagos into a laboratory for testing the efficacy of local-based economic development and conservation, we would have to conclude that the first experiments from that laboratory have failed to produce the desired results.

Summary and Conclusion

The Galapagos Islands retain a measure of their 'enchantment' arising from oceanic currents, volcanic landscapes and their unique biota, but no longer from their geographic isolation. The development of international

Table 5.2. Average expenditures per visitor to the Galapagos Archipelago in 1998 and 2005. (Adapted from Table 5 of Taylor *et al.*, 2006, pp. 22–23, based on exit surveys conducted at two major airports in Galapagos; *n*=514 in 1998, *n*=223 in 2005.)

	Foreign				Ecuadorian			
	1998		2005		1998		2005	
Average expenditures (US$)	$	%	$	%	$	%	$	%
Total expenditure on the islands	242.56	6.6	355.24	8.5	199.28	21.6	240.89	35.0
Total discretionary spending on cruise ships	87.41	2.4	61.47	1.5	40.97	4.4	21.17	3.1
Total of tourist packages purchased in Ecuador	220.64	6.0	229.72	5.5	381.95	41.4	251.65	36.0
Expenditure, rest of Ecuador	678.33	18.4	316.49	7.6	43.48	4.7	33.75	4.9
Direct purchase of domestic air travel	255.77	7.0	129.81	3.1	202.07	21.9	140.90	20.5
International air travel	921.04	25.1	988.66	23.7	40.69	4.4	0	0
Total of tourist packages purchased abroad	1,270.90	34.6	2,098.20	50.2	14.89	1.6	0	0
Total expenditure	3,676.70	100	4,179.60	100	923.33	100	688.36	100

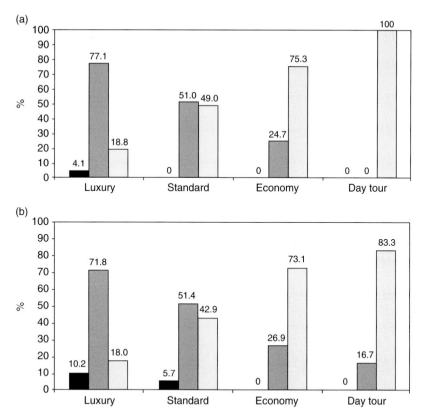

Fig. 5.2. Berths on tour boats in the Galapagos Islands in 1998 (a) and 2005 (b), by quality class and residence of owner (■, foreign owner; ■, mainland owner; ▫, owner in Galapagos). (Adapted from Epler and Proaño, 2007, p. 38, based on data from Taylor *et al.*, 2006.)

and domestic tourism in the islands has created an economic motor that propels not only one of the fastest-growing economies of the world, but also one of the fastest-growing human populations with high rates of immigration. The human population of Galapagos, in turn, has modified the archipelago's habitats, tempered its harsh ecological conditions in places, and introduced hundreds and hundreds of exotic species. Today's means of transportation offer would-be colonist species new hitchhiking possibilities on a unprecedented scale, both within the archipelago (e.g. nocturnal insects attracted by the hundreds to tour boat lights) and between the mainland and archipelago on cruise ships (four moth species new to Galapagos were caught aboard a single cruise liner in 2006; CDF, 2007). The numbers of invasive species recorded in Galapagos continue their sharp increase.

At the same time, Galapagos tourism has made many worthy contributions over the years to conservation, both directly through the supplementary monitoring of the archipelago by tourist boats and indirectly through conservation funds raised from visitor fees (see, e.g. Benitez, 2001) and donations (e.g. visitors have contributed US$3.5 million to Lindblad Expedition's Galapagos Conservation Fund). Galapagos tourism has also spawned many and diverse benefits to both the tourists themselves, in terms of education and aesthetics, and to local populations in its gateway communities, again both directly and indirectly. These benefits for people and for native species have prompted many visitors and not just a few travel writers to view Galapagos as a model for ecotourism elsewhere in the world. Ecotourism clearly has both sides in Galapagos – a fitting example of its number one paradox: success can readily undermine the very qualities that make ecotourism exciting and successful in the first place.

Meanwhile the Government of Ecuador, under international pressure, undertook an appropriate mid-course correction and, with the 1998 Special Law, attempted to regulate immigration, impede invasive species introductions, stimulate a diverse local economy and encourage more tourism benefits locally. It was a bold and timely move, and yet accumulating data today suggest that the Special Law has not yet succeeded. One reason is clearly enforcement: despite significant forward strides, migration controls need strengthening, as does the inspection and quarantine system just to keep up with tourism.

But more than that, the experience in Galapagos highlights some issues for ecotourism that, in politics, they call 'incumbency advantage' – the advantage of being there first. Number one, even with the Special Law's deliberate attempt to stimulate local benefits to Galapagos tourism, change in subsequent years went mostly in the opposite direction. Post-1998, as we have seen, there was a clear shift in the expenditures by foreign tourists away from the islands and towards pre-purchased tour packages, commonly from big companies who were early operators in the archipelago. The Special Law was not enough to stem the tide of leakage. Number two, although the Law was designed to encourage new tourism operations among Galapagos residents, through both licensing control and preferential credit, the only increases in ship berths between 1998 and 2005 went to mainland and foreign owners. The one provision in the Law for mainland and foreign owners was that tour operation rights granted by INEFAN prior to the Law would be 'respected and maintained'. Again, the advantage went to incumbents despite the Law's best intentions.

How to explain such strong incumbent's advantage in Galapagos? Incumbents have at least two structural elements in their favour in the context of this island archipelago. First, incumbents have a big marketing advantage: two-thirds or more of the visitors each year are foreign and the incumbents already have marketing channels and reputations in foreign lands. They thus start every new tourism year and season with a big advantage. Second, the layout of Galapagos National Park inadvertently favours incumbents. Because human settlements have been restricted to just a few per cent of the terrestrial area since the Park was founded, points of embarkation are necessarily distant from some of the islands and visitor sites. The incumbents again – the first to operate to those distant sites – have the advantage of the boats, technologies and experience to get there. Ironically, this advantage only grows with the accelerating increase of introduced species. Because the remote, outlier islands have the fewest introductions, they are viewed as the most pristine, desirable sites to visit, and the incumbents win again.

My conclusion is that this combination of factors – uncontrolled migration in response to burgeoning tourism revenues, plus the multiple benefits of incumbency among tourism operators in Galapagos – have conspired to reduce the social and environmental benefits of ecotourism in the islands today. They figure prominently among the forces at play that put the Galapagos 'in peril' (Boersma *et al.*, 2005) and 'at risk' (Watkins and Cruz, 2007), and sadly tend to keep it there. It will clearly take more enforcement, more creative thinking and policy formation, and possibly more legislation to pull Galapagos out of peril. One step in the right direction would be thoughtfully designed and implemented ways to trim the growth of tourism towards sustainable levels. Certainly raising the National Park entrance fee from US$100 would help, and could provide more returns to conservation and the community. As already pointed out, the migration issue must be resolved and the enforcement of residency regulations strengthened. Another step would be hybrid tourism packages that combine the advantages of boat-based tours of the islands, including the remote ones, with some days of stay-over tourism in port towns. And there is certainly merit in programmes for training and capacity-building that would allow the fishing population to convert from artisanal fishing to tourism or to engage in a mixture of the two. These and other experiments should soon be run in the laboratory, or more harm will be done.

Faced with mounting evidence that the 1998 Special Law had not succeeded, in April 2007 the President of Ecuador declared the Galapagos 'at risk' and called for specific steps to bring about change, including 'the return to the mainland of illegal residents' (Galapagos Conservancy, 2007). He also asked INGALA to consider, among other things, 'the temporary suspension of new permits for tourism and commercial flights to the islands'. Even these measures were not enough. In June 2007, the UNESCO World Heritage Committee met again and this time inscribed the Galapagos Islands on the list of World Heritage in Danger (UNESCO, 2007), as deserved.

Acknowledgements

I thank Beverly Humphrey, Laura Driscol and Kathleen Durham for their capable assistance in collecting and graphing data and literature for this chapter, Flora Lu for suggestions and unpublished data, and Amanda Stronza for feedback on the text. I thank students and alumni from my Field Seminar on 'Darwin, Evolution, and Galapagos' for always asking the hard questions.

References

Benitez, S.P. (2001) *Visitor Use Fees and Concession Systems in Protected Areas: Galapagos National Park Case Study.* Ecotourism Program, Technical Report Series No. 3. The Nature Conservancy, Arlington, Virginia.

Bensted-Smith, R. (ed.) (2002) *A Biodiversity Vision for the Galapagos Islands.* Charles Darwin Foundation, Puerto Ayora, Galapagos.

Boersma, P.D., Vargas, H. and Merlen, G. (2005) Living laboratory in peril. *Science* 308, 925.

Borja, R. (2000) La migración a Galapagos: una lecture desde los censos de 1990 y 1998. In: Fundación Natura (ed.) *Galapagos Report 1999–2000.* Fundación Natura, Quito, pp. 33–38.

Camhi, M. (1995) Industrial fisheries threaten ecological integrity of the Galapagos Islands. *Conservation Biology* 9, 715–724.

Cardenas, S. (2002) Vehicles in Galapagos: another introduced species that needs to be controlled. In: Fundación Natura (ed.) *Galapagos Report 2001–2002.* Fundación Natura, Quito, pp. 44–52.

CDF (2007) CDF studies reveal unwelcome visitors travelling with tourist boats. *Press release, 12 February.* Charles Darwin Foundation, Puerto Ayora, Galapagos.

Darwin, C. (2004) [1845] *The Voyage of the Beagle.* Reprint of the revised 1845 edition. National Geographic, Washington, DC.

de Groot, R.S. (1983) Tourism and conservation in the Galapagos Islands. *Biological Conservation* 26, 291–300.

Epler, B. and Proaño, M.E. (2007) Cuantas plazas y cuantos cupos hay en Galapagos? In: *Informe Galápagos 2006–2007.* Fundación Charles Darwin, Parque Nacional Galápagos and Instituto Nacional Galapagos, Puerto Ayora, Galapagos, pp. 36–41.

Fundación Natura (1998a) A history of the controversy over fishing and the marine reserve. In: *Galapagos Report 1997–1998.* Fundación Natura, Quito, pp. 12–13.

Fundación Natura (1998b) The Special Law for Galapagos: reforms and controversies. In: *Galapagos Report 1997–1998.* Fundación Natura, Quito, pp. 9–11.

Fundación Natura (2002) *Galapagos Report 2001–2002.* Fundación Natura, Quito.

Galapagos Conservancy (2007) Unofficial translation of the Emergency Decree signed by Ecuadorian President, Rafael Correa, on 4/10/2007. Galapagos Conservancy, Church Falls, Virginia; available at http://www.galapagos.org/news/04_2007_Decree.html (accessed July 2007).

Galapagos Conservation Trust (2005) History of Galapagos. Galapagos Conservation Trust, London; available at http://www.gct.org/history.html (accessed September 2005).

Gergis, J.L. and Fowler, M.A. (2006) How unusual was late 20th century El Nino–Southern Oscillation (ENSO)? Assessing evidence from tree-ring, coral, ice-core and documentary palaeoarchives, AD 1525–2002. *Advances in Geosciences* 6, 173–179.

Herbert, J.M. and Dixon, R.W. (2002) Is the ENSO phenomenon changing as a result of global warming? *Physical Geography* 23, 196–211.

Heslinga, J. (2003) Regulating ecotourism in Galapagos: a case study of domestic–international partnerships. *Journal of International Wildlife Law and Policy* 6, 57–77.

Heylings, P., Cruz, F., Bustamante, R., Cruz, D., Escarabay, M., Granja, A., Martinez, W., Hernández, J., Jaramillo, C., Martinez, P., Piu, M., Proaño, P., Valverde, F. and Zapata, C. (1998) Galapagos Marine Reserve. In: *Galapagos Report 1997–1998.* Fundación Natura, Quito, pp. 14–16.

Honey, M. (1994) Paying the price of ecotourism: two pioneer biological reserves face the challenges brought by a recent boom in tourism. *Americas* 46, 40–48.

Jaksic, F.M. (2001) Ecological effects of El Niño in terrestrial ecosystems of western South America. *Ecography* 24, 241–250.

Jenkins, M. and Mulliken, T.A. (1999) Evolution of exploitation in the Galapagos Islands: Ecuador's sea cucumber trade. *Traffic Bulletin* 17(3).

Kerr, S., Cardenas, S. and Hendy, J. (2004) *Migration and The Environment in the Galapagos*. Motu Working Paper 03–17. Motu Economic and Public Policy Research, Wellington; available at http://ideas.repec.org/p/wpa/wuwpot/0403001.html

Lavoie, C., Cruz, F., Carrion, G.V., Campbell, K., Donlan, C.J., Harcourt, S. and Moya, M. (2007) *The Thematic Atlas of Project Isabela*. Charles Darwin Foundation, Puerto Ayora, Galapagos.

Lorenz, S. (2007) A ground-breaking vocational school. *Galapagos News* (Galapagos Conservancy) Spring, 9.

Lougheed, L.W., Edgar, G.J. and Snell, H.L. (eds) (2002) *Biological Impacts of the Jessica Oil Spill on the Galapagos Environment: Final Report*. Charles Darwin Foundation, Puerto Ayora, Galapagos.

MacFarland, C. (2000) An analysis of nature tourism in the Galapagos Islands. In: Sitwell, N., Baert, L. and Cuppois, G. (eds) Proceedings of the Symposium on Science and Conservation in Galapagos. *Bulletin de l'Institut Royal des Sciences Naturalles de Belgique* 70, 53–63; available at http://www.darwinfoundation.org/en/library/pubs/journals/br15049801

MacFarland, C. and Cifuentes, M. (1996) Case study: Ecuador. In: Dompka, V. (ed.) *Human Population, Biodiversity and Protected Areas: Science and Policy Issues*. American Association for the Advancement of Science, Washington, DC, pp. 135–188.

Mauchamp, A. (1997) Threats from alien plant species in the Galapagos Islands. *Conservation Biology* 11, 260–263.

Merlen, G. (1995) Use and misuse of the seas around the Galapagos Archipelago. *Oryx* 29, 99–106.

Nicholls, H. (2006) *Lonesome George: The Life and Loves of a Conservation Icon*. Macmillan, New York.

Novy, J.W. (2000) *Incentive Measures for Conservation of Biodiversity and Sustainability: A Case Study of the Galapagos Islands*. World Wildlife Fund–USA, Washington, DC; available at http://www.cbd.int/doc/case-studies/inc/cs-inc-ec-galapagos-en.pdf

Pinson, J. (1996) The Pepineros: The Sea Cucumber Fishermen of Galápagos. Web Pages by Jim Pinson; available at http://jc-research.com/jim/galapagos/pepino.html (accessed June 2000).

Rice, P.C. (2007) Can the Galapagos survive cruise ship mass tourism? *General Anthropology* 14, 1010.

Riedinger, M.A., Steinitz-Kannan, M., Last, W.M. and Brenner, M. (2002) A ~6100 ^{14}C yr record of El Niño activity from the Galapagos Islands. *Journal of Paleolimnology* 27, 1–7.

Taylor, J.E., Dyer, G.A., Stewart, M., Yunez-Naude, A. and Ardila, S. (2003) The economics of ecotourism: a Galapagos islands economy-wide perspective. *Economic Development and Cultural Change* 51, 977–997.

Taylor, J.E., Hardner, J. and Stewart, M. (2006) *Ecotourism and Economic Growth in the Galapagos: An Island Economy-wide Analysis*. Agricultural and Resource Economics Working Papers 06–001. University of California, Davis, California.

Tsonis, A.A., Hunt, A.G. and Elsner, J.B. (2003) On the relation between ENSO and global climate change. *Meteorology and Atmospheric Physics* 84, 229–242.

Tye, A. (2006) Can we infer island introduction and naturalization rates from inventory data? Evidence from introduced plants in Galapagos. *Biological Invasions* 8, 201–215.

UNESCO (2007) Galapagos and Niokolo-Koba National Park inscribed on UNESCO's List of World Heritage in Danger. *Press release, Tuesday 26 June*. United Nations Educational, Scientific and Cultural Organization, Paris; available at http://www.conference.co.nz/index.cfm/31whc/News_Press_Releases/index.html (accessed August 2007).

Watkins, G. and Cruz, F. (2007) *Galapagos at Risk: A Socioeconomic Analysis of the Situation in the Archipelago.* Charles Darwin Foundation, Puerto Ayora, Galapagos.

Watkins, G., Cardenas, S. and Tapia, W. (2007) Introducción. In: *Informe Galápagos 2006–2007.* Fundación Charles Darwin, Parque Nacional Galápagos and Instituto Nacional Galapagos, Puerto Ayora, Galapagos.

Zapata, C., Cruz, D. and Causton, C. (2002) 2001: year of transition for the Galapagos quarantine and inspection system. In: Fundación Natura (ed.) *Galapagos Report 2001–2002.* Fundación Natura, Quito, pp. 103–107.

Part IV

Ecotourism in the USA

_____

6 Can Responsible Travel Exist in a Developed Country?

W.L. BRYAN

Off the Beaten Path LLC, Bozeman, Montana, USA

Introduction

While operating an outdoor, adventure-oriented travel business with strong environmental underpinnings for the last 23 years, I have been struck by the relative paucity of businesses with a viable ecotourism theme operating profitably in the 'developed' economies of North America. Pursuing this observation further, most ecotourism initiatives and activities in the Western Hemisphere have occurred in the developing world, particularly where the climate is warmer, the seasons longer and labour inexpensive. Therefore, inevitable questions arise as to why this might be the case and what might be done so that a plethora of ecotourism businesses operating in the Rocky Mountain West and other regions of North America could help influence the travel sector of these regions to become more sustainable. This chapter is an attempt to examine critically the basic underlying issues that define and shape the present situation. This is essential if one is to create strategies whereby ecotourism would be an integral part of the tourism economy not only in the Rocky Mountain West, but in other regions of the world where 'developed' economies exist and flourish.

To provide some perspective, I am a co-founder, past executive officer and now Chairman of Off the Beaten Path (www.offthebeatenpath.com), an adventure travel company and tour operator doing business in the Rocky Mountain West from Alaska to the Arizona–Mexican border, Mexico and Costa Rica in Central America and Peru, Ecuador, Chile and Argentina in South America. Our stated mission is:

> To provide travellers with exceptional travel experiences. We are committed to blending distinctive accommodations, accomplished guides, and authentic, out-of-the-ordinary experiences into each trip, providing our

> travellers with an understanding of the region and an unforgettable vacation. Integral to our service and operations is the belief that we are stewards of the regions we serve – we are devoted to protecting and promoting the vitality of our treasured geographic region and its peoples.

In short, we try to reward our guests with in-depth, analytical knowledge of the regions where we work while helping them personally design their vacations. And, in turn, we reward those quality suppliers, who we judge to be doing good work, with our customers. While lofty in our mission statement, socially accountable and environmentally friendly practices are difficult to realize at levels where we ideally wish to function and, at times, they are regrettably only marginally a part of our company's business equation. Furthermore, most tourism suppliers that we utilize in the Rockies don't abide by consumer-generated ratings, certification programmes or other independent assessments of operating standards, mainly because there aren't any. What is more, there are essentially no ecolodges or ecotour suppliers whose 'best practices' have been judged as 'good ecotourism' by a professional third party with standards that are consumer-oriented. At Off the Beaten Path, we ask why.

Why are there so few ecolodges in the Rockies (Fig. 6.1)? Why is there little or no mention of ecotourism in the myriad of marketing materials of outdoor activity-oriented suppliers in the Rockies where travellers are primarily attracted to the region's wonderful, yet very fragile, environment? Answers lie in part with the label 'ecotourism', but more fundamentally with the underlying principles of how the tourism sector operates in a capitalist, developed country. Future solutions lie first in understanding and accepting these answers and then working on developing tourism practices that truly are accountable to environments and communities where they operate. I try to address these points in this chapter.

The term 'ecotourism', while well intentioned, has been of little or no interest to the consumer and thus to the vendor who needs customers in order to have a viable and profitable business. No one likes to be called a tourist, yet alone a label with 'eco' before it. Both words have deep-rooted objections within the psyche of those of us who travel, and thus within the marketplace. We would much rather be known as a responsible and informed traveller who is very sensitive to impacts one might make on the environments and communities through which we travel. Personally, we resist the label 'ecotourist' when most of us aspire to be a responsible traveller. Most economically viable suppliers in the Rockies apparently understand this and generally don't use ecotourism, ecolodge or ecotours to market their operations, fearful that such labels could limit business instead of increasing market share. Therefore, if responsible travel is one's goal, the ecotourism concept needs a new label, one with the same meaning but one that is far more consumer-oriented. Consequently, while there may be other appropriate labels, 'responsible travel' and 'responsible traveller' are the terms used throughout the rest of this chapter.

There are other underlying tenets needing to be identified and understood as well if responsible travel (ecotourism) is to become a more

Fig. 6.1. Smith Fork Ranch lodge bar. (Photo: William Bryan.)

integral part of the tourism economy in the Rockies. Yes, except for rainfall and intense sun, climate and seasonal variables are more extreme here than in the subtropical and tropical zones of the earth. Labour costs and regulatory costs also are higher than those usually found in developing countries. Furthermore, distances between the traveller and the destination and between destinations are substantial. But, one must realize that the foundation of responsible travel is primarily built from the principles of capitalism: simply, suppliers of travel need to be profitable. One needs to understand and acknowledge this fact while developing responsible travel programmes and business entities that address and embody the principles of what has been called 'ecotourism'.

To delve further, there are four premises salient to tourism practices, either in the Rockies or elsewhere in the world, that are worth examining (Bryan, 2003).

1. Tourism is an inherently extractive industry.
2. Volume and capacity dominate and therefore define basic tourism practices.
3. Pricing and the need to make a fair profit greatly influence tourism activities and operations.
4. Developing and adhering to standards has been an age-old dilemma for the travel industry.

Tourism is an Inherently Extractive Industry

Tourism endeavours almost always take more than they give to the human and natural resources utilized in the travel experience. This is especially true in most outdoor recreational activities, such as fishing, hiking, horseback riding, mountain biking, backcountry skiing, camping and sightseeing in national parks. This is also the case in 'hunting communities' in which game is perceived as being owned by the public, but with very little acknowledgment of the rights of landowners who provide critical habitat for healthy game populations on a *pro bono publico* basis throughout the year.

Resources are also exploited in most cultural recreational experiences. Visiting a Native American tribe, a Hutterite or Amish community, spending time on a working ranch with a ranch family, or reliving romantic fantasies of rural life in small Rocky Mountain agricultural communities, all usually involve the responsible traveller receiving far more benefits and value than they return in the form of money and time to such communities (Fig. 6.2).

Fig. 6.2. Tipis at sunset. (Photo: William Bryan.)

The prevailing paradigm for most travellers is: how can I have fun as cheaply as possible while travelling and at the same time maximize value? This way of thinking primarily focuses on monetary costs, yet rarely on environmental and community costs. It comes from behaviour we all learned when we were young: any form of outdoor recreation (particularly on public lands) should be done for free or nearly for free. This attitude is very prevalent among travellers seeking outdoor recreation in the western part of the USA, where public lands and wildlife are basic parts of the experience (Fig. 6.3). To underscore this point, an article entitled 'Taxpayer-subsidized resource extraction harms species' by Losos *et al.* (1995) claims that recreation is the second greatest threat to endangered species and animals on public lands. Recreating at the expense of communities, ecosystems or species is something about which we historically have given little thought. In the context of the traveller, human and cultural resources are there to be engaged and utilized as inexpensively as possible. In many ways, it is a logical extension of traditional Judeo-Christian ideology, where natural resources are there for people to use as they see fit (Hitzhusen, 2007). This has been the dominant 'Western mindset' of our civilization. Therefore, a 'sustainability mindset' requires a new paradigm in how travel is conducted and experienced.

Volume and Capacity Dominate and Therefore Define Basic Tourism Practices

Volume is a key ingredient to a vibrant tourism economy. Volume-generated statistics are always highlighted by state travel promotion departments and bureaus and chambers of commerce as a way to gauge how well the tourism sector is doing. Traditional tourism success in the Greater

Fig. 6.3. Wolves attract tourists in Rocky Mountain West. (Photo: PhotoDisc no. 44108.)

Yellowstone has always been measured by how many people visit Yellowstone National Park during a given year (3.15 million in 2007) and the rate of growth from year to year – the more the better. Furthermore, tourism is a low-margin business, which by definition means volume has to be all-important in order to be profitable. Only recently have the thought of limits to numbers of people and the term 'resource capacity' been given much play in the tourism world. Colorado State University's Congress on Recreation and Resource Capacity in Aspen in 1999, for example, was a significant gathering of land management professionals on this issue, although academics began writing about the concept in the 1980s (e.g. Getz, 1983; O'Reilly, 1986). Today, limits on multi-day river trips on the Middle Fork of the Snake in Idaho and the Smith River in Montana, tightly regulated numbers of people in the backcountry of Yellowstone, and fishermen quotas on Montana's Beaverhead River are examples of nascent attempts to manage capacity related to public resources in the Rockies. Unfortunately, such examples are few and far between.

Ironically, in the private sector, limits on visitor volume frequently are not only accepted but often embraced as opportunities to extend profit margins. For example, when one goes 'on safari' at Animal Kingdom (Walt Disney World), for US$67, one's safari touring vehicle leaves at timed intervals that allow vacationers to never see those who are ahead or behind them, giving the impression that they are seeing animals 'on their own' and in an exclusive manner. Private lands hunting opportunities such as Papoose Creek Lodge, whose name recently changed to The Lodge at Sun Ranch (Bidwell Pearce and Ocampo-Raeder, Chapter 7, this volume) and the Flying D Ranch in Montana, where hunter numbers can be strictly controlled, get US$7500–13,500 per hunter for a trophy elk hunt. A comparable hunt on public lands costs US$2800–3500 per hunter for a 6-day hunt. Private lands' spring creek fishing in the Rockies commands a fee of up to US$200 per rod with a strict limit on how many fishermen can fish the creek daily, whereas the unregulated numbers of anglers on nearby rivers need only an out-of-state fishing license.

But, on public lands, where the private sector operates as permitted concessionaires or commercial outfitters, the permittee has a much more difficult time accepting and integrating the issues of resource capacity. For example, the permitted snowmobile outfitter operating in Yellowstone National Park has not wanted limits placed on how many sleds enter the Park on a given day even though 1200 to 1500 snowmobiles a day with two-stroke engines were common, creating more air pollution on a daily basis than automobiles create in the Park during an entire summer season (Ingersoll, 1999). This ongoing issue has resulted in a policy that now limits snowmobile numbers and requires four-stroke engines on all sleds entering the Park. But lawsuits and politics over the last several years have kept this policy in a state of flux, which has not helped the local economy (Dustin and Schneider, 2004).

There are exceptions where the private sector–public lands interaction has enhanced the concept of resource capacity. The limited number of permittees allowed to float the Colorado River through the Grand Canyon is a good example. Regardless, there is a growing controversy on our public lands concerning the issue of resource capacity. It is ironic that private enterprise rarely takes the lead in helping determine such limits, but more frequently sees them as a threat to doing business. On private property, however, operators readily embrace limits and price accordingly.

When it comes to high-quality responsible travel by tour operators, key factors are low volumes and limited capacity. Ideal sizes for small groups experiencing heritage or wildlife tourism range between 12 and 16 people. Most profitable group tour enterprises, on the other hand, must have the capability to work with 20–40 or more people at any given time. These larger sizes are essential in making trips 'affordable' to the consumer, while at the same time profitable for the supplier (see Table 6.1). Thus, an inherent problem arises. Can one have affordable yet profitable responsible travel programmes operating in and minimally impacting small communities or fragile environments? Or, is it inevitable that group travel in the 20–40 person range is the only option that can profitably exist, thereby dictating that environmental activities are usually contrived experiences where shallow, impersonal and less interactive opportunities dominate the educational efforts and cross-cultural opportunities?

The Influence of Making a Fair Profit on Tourism Activities and Operations

If one assumes that responsible travel requires interactive experiences in small groups, then one must ask who can afford such experiences and whether that sector will purchase tours where responsible travel practices are seriously attempted. Must 'responsible travel' become solely an elitist experience where only those who are willing to spend US$200 to US$500 per person daily can afford them? And, can such tours accommodate all the needs of these people, particularly the demands for high-quality accommodations and costly dietary preferences? People who want a responsible travel experience are often those who place a high value on human interactions, having expert naturalist guides, or spending a day with a rancher sharing chores, perspectives and conversation. But, are these people used to spending US$300 per person or more a day for their recreational experience? This reality seems to contradict the belief that responsible travel should be cheap and affordable. Furthermore, it conflicts with the impression many travellers have that cross-cultural exchanges and guided outdoor experiences are less costly than high tech, sophisticated equipment-oriented recreational experiences. To illustrate, a presumption is often made by consumers that a naturalist guide for a day in Yellowstone or a history guide for a day on the Lewis and Clark trail should be less costly than a fly-fishing guide, a 4×4 jeep guided day tour, a white-water rafting trip, or a guided upland bird hunting day.

In looking at an actual costing plan (Table 6.1) for a wildlife tour in the Greater Yellowstone, one can readily see why such an experience is a lot more expensive (US$368 versus US$291) per person per day than if it were a large group tour. The illustration incorporates realistic pricing guidelines and formulas for both fixed and variable costs and determining a profit. Fair wages for group travel leaders and community resource people are included. The two-van costing shows what it costs to run such a trip at a profitable level. Costing and profit projections for mini bus and standard bus tours are also shown. These typically involve only one 'content' guide with the driver built into the bus cost, compared with the two 'content' guides who also double as drivers for the two vans on the smaller tour. Both are large groups – too large by responsible travel standards for a wildlife viewing tour where the smaller the group size, the less disturbing the group is to the wildlife and the more flexibility the guide has in keeping the group at appropriate distances given the situation. All of this leads to higher safety levels for both wildlife and human observers. But with the bus-sized group, the prices are more affordable and net profits to the company are greater than those affiliated with a smaller group.

Therein lies the dilemma. Responsible travel with small group sizes, it seems, is practical only for those who can afford the higher costs involved. The figures tend to illustrate that such tourism endeavours exacerbate the problems of classism in our society. Perhaps we need then to look at responsible travel in a fundamentally different way.

Developing and Adhering to Travel Standards

The concept of industry-wide standards for the delivery of services in the tourism sector of our economy has not been a high priority among tour operators and travel suppliers. Generally, the industry-specific standards that have been created and implemented have been initiated by insurance companies and state and federal regulatory agencies. For example, a backcountry horse outfitter operating in a national forest or park comes under the guidelines developed by the US Forest Service or the National Park Service. They also operate under the guidelines of the insurance carrier from whom they get their liability insurance. Very little, if anything, comes by way of a professional association or organization of outfitters. Such associations may have voluntary best practices or competency guidelines, but very little in the way of mandatory guidelines. There are exceptions, like the river rafting industry where, because of strong competition in the marketplace, outfitter associations such as FOAM (Fishing Outfitters Association of Montana) have been very active in creating, implementing and policing their own standards. By contrast, national associations of natural history interpreters or cultural interpreters, like the National Association for Interpretation, have only voluntary standards that are not systematically adhered to or enforced.

Table 6.1. Costing plan (all costs in US$) for an illustrative tour: 'Bears and Wolves of Yellowstone – A Guided Journey, 2007, 5 nights/6 days'.

			Two vans	Mini bus	Tour bus
Number of participants			14	23	45
Fixed costs					
Guides' fees and expenses					
	Rate/day	No. of days			
Guide 1 fee	225.00	6	1,350	1,350	1,350
Guide 2 fee	125.00	6	750	N/A	N/A
Guide 1 expenses (meals, lodging, activities)			35	535	N/A
Guide 2 expenses (meals, lodging, activities)			535	N/A	N/A
Transportation					
Van 1	120.00	6	720	N/A	N/A
Van 2	120.00	6	720	N/A	N/A
Mini coach (25 passengers)			N/A	2700	N/A
Tour bus (47 passengers)			N/A	N/A	3,660
Driver room/gratuity			N/A	445	445
Miscellaneous fixed costs					
Yellowstone National Park entrance fee			160	200	300
Yellowstone Natural History Association			100	250	500
Speaker gratuity			40	40	40
Total fixed costs			4,910	5,520	6,295
Fixed cost per person			351	240	140
Variable costs (per person, net)					
Day 1: Arrive/Lake Hotel					
Lunch			10	10	10
Dinner			48	48	48
1/2 hotel room (with tax and gratuity)			104	104	104
Day 2: Lake Hotel					
Breakfast			13	13	13
Lunch			8	8	8
Dinner			48	48	48
1/2 hotel room (with tax and gratuity)			104	104	104
Day 3: Cooke City					
Breakfast			13	13	13
Lunch			8	8	8
Dinner			30	30	30
1/2 hotel room (with tax and gratuity)			40	40	40
Day 4: Cooke City					
Breakfast			10	10	10
Lunch			8	8	8
Dinner			30	30	30
Speaker			5	5	5
1/2 hotel room (with tax and gratuity)			40	40	40

Continued

Table 6.1. – *Continued.*

Number of participants	Two vans 14	Mini bus 23	Tour bus 45
Day 5: Chico			
Breakfast	10	10	10
Lunch	8	8	8
Dinner	45	45	45
1/2 hotel room (with tax and gratuity)	56	56	56
Day 6: Depart			
Breakfast	10	10	10
Miscellaneous charges per person			
Snacks, drinks, T-shirt, etc.	48	48	48
Subtotal per person	696	696	696
Fixed costs per person	351	240	140
Total cost per person (net)	1,047	936	836
Selling price (gross profit margin, %)	1,610 (35)	1,357 (31)	1,145 (27)
Total profit	7,891	9,672	13,912
1% For the Planet[a]	79	97	139
Net profit	7,812	9,575	13,773
Individual cost to go on group journey			
Trip cost	1,610	1,357	1,145
Gratuity (estimated)	100	100	100
Airfare (estimated)	500	500	500
Total	2,210	1,957	1,745
Individual cost per day	368	326	291

N/A, not applicable.

[a]1% For the Planet involves businesses donating 1% to conservation. Started by Patagonia, Inc., it is voluntary.

Therefore, except for river rafting outfitters, the idea of developing, implementing and being held accountable to 'best practice' standards in the responsible travel world in the Rockies is essentially non-existent. It is the responsibility of the supplier to follow his or her own code of ethics. To the consumer, it is 'buyer beware'.

Some professional standards do exist, at least for accommodations and related services (see Honey, Chapter 15, this volume). The star rating system in Europe is well known in the travel industry and taken very seriously by responsible travellers. In the USA, there are AAA ratings, the Mobile Guide rating system, and customer-oriented newsletters like the *Hideaway Report*, *The Angling Report* and *Passport Newsletter*. *Condé Nast Traveler* also tends to be consumer-oriented in evaluating and assessing accommodations and services. But most are arbitrary in their ratings, have sporadic reviewing procedures, and do not have clear and consistent guidelines in their assessments or categorization of services. As a result, their usefulness is not taken as seriously as the European star system and frequently not even considered in trip planning by most responsible travellers. Martha Honey has taken the leadership nationally in addressing the certification issue described in her edited book *Ecotourism and Certification* (Honey, 2002). And National Geographic Adventure, partnering with the Adventure Travel Trade Association, initiated a programme in the spring of 2007 to comprehensively evaluate the world's adventure travel outfitters. It will be interesting to see how this effort develops with both the adventure travel operator and the consumer, and whether there will be any impact on responsible adventure travel in the Rocky Mountain West.

Fortunately for the consumer, a growing number of specialty travel companies sensing the need for industry standards and certification procedures have begun collaborating to develop their own 'rules to live by', which they hope will nudge the industry to regard systematic evaluative processes more seriously. For example, the Adventure Collection, a marketing consortium comprised of ten specialty travel companies, has developed five responsible travel initiatives for each member's adherence. The ten travel companies that make up The Adventure Collection include: Off the Beaten Path, Lindblad Expeditions, Bushtracks Expeditions, Natural Habitat Adventures, Canadian Mountain Holidays, Micato Safaris, OARS, Backroads, Geographic Expeditions and the National Outdoor Leadership School (NOLS). The initiatives include internal auditing procedures related to responsible travel that each member would assess annually; environmental education syllabi for all their group trips; community accountability guidelines for communities where member companies operate and where their offices are located; and an expectation that all members have their own community/environmental projects that exemplify the principles of responsible travel. Most recently, they have begun to address the issue of striving towards carbon neutrality within each company, with Rocky Mountain operators Natural Habitat Adventures, OARS and NOLS taking the lead.

The Adventure Collection also is contemplating the development of several different responsible travel philanthropic initiatives to fund environmental and community-based programmes that further the concept of responsible travel. Lindblad Expeditions' leading role with the Charles Darwin Foundation for the Galapagos is one excellent example. While continually identifying and assessing 'big, bold moves' in the local and global accountability world, the Adventure Collection is placing a strong priority on developing responsible travel standards that are a part of member operations and result in a responsible travel leadership brand for the Adventure Collection. They are even contemplating adopting the tagline 'Shaping the Future of Travel', with sustainability being an underlying goal of their collective operations. How far they take their work and whether it will become a model for broader segments of the industry remain to be seen. But we do know that professional standards developed from within an industry or profession often have a longer shelf-life than those developed on the outside with subsequent efforts made to impose such standards on those for whom they are intended. The reasoning behind this observation is that players and entities within a professional service or business are far more aware of the nuances and operations of their business segment than those analysing from the outside. It is a fact of human nature that when there is ownership of standards, guidelines and regulations by those most affected, there is far greater acceptance and adherence than when parameters are imposed from external interests.

Responsible Travel Guidelines for Business Owners in the Rocky Mountain West

After recognizing important underlying practices of any travel business, the issue of how a travel supplier or tour operator in the Rockies can position itself as a responsible travel business remains. Businesses in the Rockies are usually sole proprietorships, corporations or partnerships. They are not community enterprises such as those often found in developing countries where there are opportunities – facilitated by non-governmental organizations – to mix socialism and capitalism (e.g. Gordillo Jordan *et al.*, Chapter 3, this volume).

What follows are some beginning thoughts on how a company in the Rockies might go about developing a responsible business model that has appropriate standards and become a leader in responsible travel.

First, defining profitability

Efficiently maximizing profits is the bottom line for most businesses. However, many suppliers of travel services in the Rockies operate their businesses for a variety of reasons of which only one may be related to profitability or 'breaking even'. These operators are commonly referred to as 'amenity-based' business owners who actually own a significant number of guest ranches, fishing lodges, outfitting businesses and other travel-related operations in the region. An amenity-based business owner is a person who owns property for its intrinsic scenic, open space or wildlife watching value in comparison to a landowner who owns property from which he or she makes a living, such as a cattle rancher, grain grower or dairy farmer. None of these ancillary businesses are the owner's primary source of income. They are owned for long-term investment, altruistic, personal or other amenity-based reasons. Profitability in these cases is defined differently from that in businesses where the business owner depends solely on the annual income from his/her travel-related business to make a living.

This issue is important for positioning any travel-related business in the Rockies, as responsible travel standards can be fundamentally affected by this particular marketplace situation. For example, the amenity-based business owner of an ecolodge in the Rockies with the goal of breaking even is in a position to more readily afford investments in alternative energy options and the construction and ongoing operation of extensive greenhouses in order to grow local, healthy foods for guests, without having to pass on all of the added costs to the consumer. In contrast, the lodge owner who depends on the business to make a living often does not have access to capital to invest in such options. Some initial questions then are: does the owner need only to 'break even' and thus determine his/her own set of variables and fixed costs to shape one's definition of 'break even'? Or, does the owner need to make a profit on an annual basis to adequately cover salary and long-term capital improvement plans? How do these business owners account for the economic appreciation factor as it relates to the land on which the business is being conducted? Methods of adherence to responsible travel standards are going to differ depending on how a Rocky Mountain travel business owner responds to these questions, as there is a very different economic playing field for amenity-based business owners versus those whose business is their primary source of livelihood.

Second, identifying basic operating issues addressed in any business plan

Table 6.2 lists the essential components of a business plan for almost any travel-related business in the Rockies. Any travel business operating in the region not only needs to account for these basic elements, but also needs to address these line items in economically self-sufficient ways (i.e. a profitable bottom line). This includes having an operation that functions smoothly and a staff with high morale and a team mentality who work well together creating both efficiency in operations and an environment that encourages repeat business. Success also involves a marketing strategy that brings an appropriate volume of customers to the company. This often is not easy given the high cost of market entry, marketplace competition, and keeping 'on top of the curve' in providing goods and services that the customer expects and demands. All standard business elements are emphasized here as they underlie any responsible travel plan for an enterprise operating in the Rockies. One must ensure first that a viable business plan is in place.

Third, the essentials of a responsible travel agenda

The realities of developing and running a business are daunting, to say nothing about how best to include in one's business the basic characteristics of a responsible travel agenda. For most operators, it is an ambitious goal to figure out how one can integrate responsible travel principles into existing operations so that additional costs/overheads do not become prohibitive to the point of pricing oneself out of the marketplace. For example, in today's competitive environment the

Table 6.2. Basic elements of a travel-related business operation.

Revenue determinants
  Size of operation
  Seasonality (annual number of days in operation)
  Pricing
  Occupancy
  Ancillary activities that generate revenues, e.g. gift shop, recipe book, selling owner-raised
    grass-fed beef, etc.

Expenses
  Start-up capital costs
  Marketing
  Initial marketing investments (e.g. market segmentation, identification of niche in
    marketplace, branding strategies, web site development)
  Annual (e.g. web site maintenance, search engine optimization, brochure, direct mail,
    public relations, loyalty strategies, etc.)

Operations
  Labour
  Training/development programmes
  Fringe benefits
  Vehicles and equipment (if appropriate)
  Insurance
  Maintenance of equipment
  Rent, utilities and taxes
  Supplies
  Food and beverages (if applicable)
  Depreciation (for capital improvements)
  Licensing/permits
  Professional assistance memberships, professional development

elements of a responsible travel agenda that should be considered in the development of an ecolodge or ranch in the Rockies include the following:

1. The facility

- Minimizing its ecological footprint on the land.
- Whether new or a renovation, decide on whether it can be LEED (Leadership in Energy and Environmental Design) certified.
- Develop strategies so as to operate in a carbon neutral manner.
- The use of local products and craftsmen in interior design and decoration.
- Selected operational elements to consider:

  ○ Appropriate use of alternative energy so that one can operate 'off the grid'.
  ○ Water conservation practices.
  ○ Tertiary waste water treatment.
  ○ Alternative fuel vehicles.

○ Recycling, composting practices in place.
○ A locally healthy foods policy and programme where:

  – There is adherence to community supported agricultural practices.
  – Ranch gardens and greenhouses are part of operations.
  – Free range and grass-fed meat products are an integral part of what is served.

2. The activities

- Ensure that education/natural history interpretation is a part of all lodge activities.
- Hiking/walking – integrate trail etiquette practices.
- Regularly schedule guided outings for guests to visit the local community, creating interactive experiences with local leaders, business people, artisans and craftsmen.
- Horseback riding – following backcountry horse etiquette; integrate trail enhancement activities into programme.
- Fishing – adhere to local standards related to keeping fish, methods of fishing, numbers and size; ensure the fishing experience integrates the environment in which it takes place.
- Hunting – implement an ethical hunting programme; be sensitive to current composition of local animal populations; follow range management and habitat enhancement practices on private lands.

3. Local community involvement

- Develop and facilitate a working relationship with community leaders so they understand the business owner's commitment to responsible travel and are willing to assist the owner when appropriate in implementation.
- Have explicit policies on the role the community plays in construction/ renovations, maintenance and ongoing operations and activities of the ranch/lodge.
- Have a staffing goal that all staff are from the region where the lodge/ ranch is located.
- Continually work towards the goal that all staff are committed to responsible travel principles and reflect that in their actions. Leadership role of the owner is essential.

Can A Responsible Travel Business Exist in the Rockies?

Can a responsible travel business exist in the Rockies? The answer is yes, but as of now there is no perfect model, only some worthwhile beginnings. Smith Fork Ranch in Crawford, Colorado (Fig. 6.4) and The Lodge at Sun Ranch in Cameron, Montana are two excellent lodge examples, as is the

Fig. 6.4. Smith Fork Ranch house at twilight. (Photo: William Bryan.)

natural history interpretation outfitter, Yellowstone Safari Company, in Bozeman, Montana. Off the Beaten Path and Natural Habitat Adventures are leading the way regarding responsible travel among tour operators in the Rockies. And there are many others that have begun to develop a responsible travel agenda. All still have significant challenges ahead if they are to assume the role of operating businesses that can be viewed as responsible travel models in the region and thus branded as such by the marketplace, the travel industry, and by those associations such as The International Ecotourism Society whose principal purpose is to promote and further the concept of responsible travel.

Despite their laudable efforts, these entities are severely hindered by the fact that there is no infrastructure in place at the national level or in the Rockies to support the ideals of responsible travel. There are no marketing associations, no branding vehicles, and no clear guidelines or standards. Furthermore, the consumer looking to travel in the Rockies is not at this time demanding a responsible travel venue, mainly because they don't know what to ask or look for. The supply side of the industry has not developed an image or brand that would play a role in driving significant market share to vendors practising responsible travel in the Rockies. But according to Yankelovich Partners (www.yankelovich.com)

in their annual *Monitors* over the past several years, the market is there. It is latent, with underlying values of wanting to learn, yearning for authenticity, choosing activities that relate directly to the land, becoming more food-literate, searching for cross-cultural experiences, and selecting custom travel or travelling in small groups are strong priorities with a growing number of travellers.

In an attempt to quantify this latent interest, in July 2005 the Adventure Collection asked the Opinion Research Corporation to do a consumer survey regarding interest in responsible travel. Seventy-four per cent of 2000 respondents who had taken an adventure travel vacation said responsible travel practices are either extremely important or very important. Only 5% said that such practices were not important. The respondents who saw responsible travel practices as an important factor in their travel decision making process were willing to pay at least 14% more for the guarantee of responsible travel practices. What was also of interest is that adventure travellers under the age of 35 years were more willing to pay more than the older respondents.

What is needed is a 'big picture' responsible travel marketing strategy like the 'Got Milk' campaign or the 'Beef...It's What's for Dinner' campaign. The American Dairy Association and the Beef Producers Council respectively created these branding campaigns for their products in the late 1990s and have continued to do so in the early years of the 21st century. However, if such marketing strategies were in place, then there needs to be a corresponding available supply of responsible travel opportunities. There also needs to be consumer-oriented travel inter-mediaries who can help the customer make responsible travel choices. In some ways, it is the age-old chicken or egg issue: what comes first, a ready supply of responsible travel operations in the Rockies or the consumer demanding services and activities adhering to responsible and sustainable practices as a part of their travel to the Mountain West?

We cannot overlook the fact that obstacles in today's marketplace are significant. Corporate tourism currently dominates the travel industry and is headed in a very different direction from responsible travel. A glaring example is that 951,431 people went on cruises in Alaska in 2006, compared with only 38,000 in 1972. To be more precise, there were 5,708,576 'bed-days' in 2006 compared with 1,715,197 in 1987 (Northwest Cruise Ship Association, www.nwcruiseship.com). Cruise companies such as Crystal, Carnival, Princess, Holland America and Royal Caribbean are creating contrived expedition experiences in Alaska so as to fill their large cruise ships in the summer, knowing that they are at capacity in the winter in the Caribbean and other subtropical and tropical regions around the world. South-eastern Alaska in the summer has largely become a corporate theme park for industrial tourism, not unlike what is occurring in Las Vegas, Orlando, Branson and Anaheim. High volume, corporate profits and shareholders' dividends are dominating what used to be a highly individualistic 'mom and pop' travel industry with some semblance of authenticity and legitimate cross-cultural interactions.

Consolidation efforts emerged around the millennium as a new corporate strategy of the present-day specialty travel world. Roll-ups of adventure travel companies took place at an alarming rate in areas of the tourism sector where US$20–50 million companies were once considered large. Many large and small sole proprietor companies merged into US$300–500 million corporate entities with the names of Grand Expeditions and Far & Wide and tried to dominate the up-market specialty travel landscape. Owner–managers and family businesses gave way to Chief Executive Officers, Chief Operating Officers, Initial Public Offerings and trading on the NASDAQ. Fortunately, these initial roll-up strategies did not work. Nevertheless, large corporate acquisitions and consolidation strategies continue to take place in the adventure travel world. Intrawest's acquisition of Abercrombie & Kent and Canadian Mountain Holidays is a prime example that corporate consolidation is still viewed as a viable big business strategy.

While these developments are occurring in the Rockies and other regions in the country, little critical thought is being given to where tourism as an industry is headed or should be headed. Tourism is still viewed in the region overall as a desired growth industry where expansion is supported in a generally unfettered way. Academic programmes at Rocky Mountains universities are not focusing on critical issues regarding responsible travel and the environmental, social and economic impacts of outdoor recreation and tourism. Rather, university tourism programmes are more apt to be found in MBA (Master of Business Administration) programmes, hotel management schools, colleges of technology or in business research institutes rather than in entities that critically assess ways tourism can be more accountable and less extractive to both community and environment.

In recent years recreation programmes have emerged in the region's public universities that are beginning to address sustainable tourism issues. The College of Forestry and Conservation at the University of Montana, the College of Natural Resources at the University of Idaho, the College of Health at the University of Utah, the College of Natural Resources at Utah State and the Environmental Studies Program at the University of Colorado all have a relatively minor emphasis in the area of sustainable tourism. The one exception is the College of Natural Resources at Colorado State University where sustainable tourism appears to have more of an emphasis. They also are developing a regional reputation in addressing issues of recreational carrying capacity on public lands and the extractive nature of tourism as it relates to travel in the Rocky Mountain West.

With the possible exception of modest interests in sustainable travel at the Center of the American West at the University of Colorado and the Center for the Rocky Mountain West at the University of Montana, there are no institutes or think-tanks on sustainable travel and responsible travel policies in the Rocky Mountain West. No one is looking in a constructive and critical way at the direction in which the tourism sector of the economy should go, that is less extractive and more sustainable.

This is somewhat appalling in that travel is a multi-billion dollar industry in all Rocky Mountain states accompanied by a very healthy rate of growth. But it is important to remind ourselves that it is an industry still dominated by the four premises described at some length earlier in this chapter. Therefore, public policy institute funding coming from the travel sector is more logically going to go towards promoting growth in travel and not towards sustainability and responsible travel policies and practices. A serious and substantive regional debate has yet to occur over the type and quantity of travellers the Rockies can sustain.

Also, we lack professional associations or non-profit organizations that provide support to responsible travel enterprises in the areas of appropriateness, accountability, sustainability and standards. The basic extractive nature of tourism and how it might be mitigated is not being addressed in any systematic manner in the Rockies today. Nor are there programmes in institutions of higher learning that are critically examining issues of justice and equity as they relate to tourism practices. Further-more, there is only a beginning sense of the need to research and examine carefully the substantial and far-reaching issues of resource capacity as they relate to public and private lands.

If industrial tourism continues at a metastasized rate of growth, and travel is not seriously questioned regarding its extractive nature in the Rocky Mountain West, the concept of responsible travel can easily fade into the catacombs of a large corporate and capitalistic culture of travel where the bottom line rules all. That is why real-life experiments in the Rockies and in the USA need to be given the opportunity and support to thrive and succeed. We need:

- To accept the fact that responsible travel can be a viable business practice and can operate in a sustainable manner.
- To support existing and build new responsible travel models and experiments at both the local and regional levels.
- Networks and organizations that can interact and build upon each other's experiences so that issues of volume, pricing and standards are adequately developed and that markets for such entities are more clearly defined, as are the strategies to reach such markets.
- More non-profit institutions like The Center on Ecotourism and Sustainable Development (CESD) at the national and international levels furthering the concept of sustainable travel.
- To develop public policy research and development institutes and programmes at the Rocky Mountain region's universities and in the region's non-profit independent institutional arena, directed at realizing the vision of the travel sector of the economy being sustainable and dominated by best practices in responsible travel.
- Industry-generated standards and certification programmes that involve both the supplier and the consumer.
- Significant national branding strategies that help educate and persuade consumers to actively pursue responsible travel experiences.

It is not simply that it *can* be done, it *has* to be done. The people, communities and environments targeted by the tourism business in the Rocky Mountain West have to demand that the vision of sustainability supported by responsible travel principles and actions must be how tourism is constructed, grown and practised. If this vision is not realized, tourism will continue to be extractive in nature with most tourism revenues flowing out of the region to corporate headquarters elsewhere, with the best of the West from an environment, community and cultural perspective being eroded to only a shadow of its former self. Let us be mindful and encouraged that there is movement and progress on sustainable travel issues among more and more small, regional travel businesses. These developments need to be nurtured and helped to grow to be pivotal industry forces within the tourism industry. But so much of the journey is still ahead, with the cultural and natural integrity of the Rocky Mountains, and the rest of the world, hanging in the balance.

Web Site Addresses Relevant to the Chapter

Off the Beaten Path	offthebeatenpath.com
Yellowstone National Park	http://www.nps.gov/yell/siteindex.htm
Papoose Creek Lodge	papoosecreek.com
Flying D Ranch	montanahuntingcompany.com
1% for the Planet	onepercentfortheplanet.org
Fishing Outfitters Association of Montana	foam-montana.org
National Association for Interpretation	interpnet.com
Hideaway Report	www.andrewharpertravel.com/show.dll/hideaway
The Angling Report	anglingreport.com
Passport	passportnewsletter.com
Adventure Collection	adventurecollection.com
Adventure Travel Trade Association	adventuretravel.biz
Charles Darwin Foundation	darwinfoundation.org
LEED	usgbc.org
Smith Fork Ranch	smithforkranch.com
Yellowstone Safaris	yellowstonesafari.com
Natural Habitat Adventures	nathab.com
The International Ecotourism Society	ecotourism.org
Intrawest	intrawest.com
Center of the American West	centerwest.org
Center for the Rocky Mountain West	crmw.org
College of Health/University of Utah	http://www.health.utah.edu
College of Forestry and Conservation/ University of Montana	http://www.forestry.umt.edu
College of Natural Resources/ University of Idaho	http://www.cnrhome.uidaho.edu/default.aspx? pid=44951
College of Natural Resources/ Utah State University	http://www.cnr.usu.edu

References

Bryan W.L. (2003) Appropriate cultural tourism – can it exist? Searching for an answer: three Arizona case studies. In: Rothman, H. (ed.) *The Culture of Tourism, The Tourism of Culture. Selling the Past to the Present in the American Southwest.* Published in cooperation with the Clements Center for Southwest Studies at Southern Methodist University. University of New Mexico Press, Albuquerque, New Mexico, pp. 140–163.

Dustin, D. and Schneider, I.E. (2004) The science of politics/the politics of science: examining the snowmobile controversy in Yellowstone National Park. *Environmental Management* 34, 761–767.

Getz, D. (1983) Capacity to absorb tourism: concepts and implications for strategic planning. *Annals of Tourism Research* 10, 239–263.

Hitzhusen, G.E. (2007) Judeo-Christian theology and the environment: moving beyond scepticism to new sources for environmental education in the USA. *Environmental Education Research* 13, 55–74.

Honey, M. (2002) *Ecotourism and Certification: Setting Standards in Practice.* Island Press, Washington, DC.

Ingersoll, G.P. (1999) *Effects of Snowmobile Use on Snowpack Chemistry in Yellowstone National Park, 1998.* Water-Resources Investigations Report 99–4148. US Geological Survey, Denver, Colorado.

Losos, E., Hayes, J., Phillips, A., Wilcove, D. and Alkire, C. (1995) Taxpayer-subsidized resource extraction harms species. *BioScience* 45, 446–455.

O'Reilly, A.M. (1986) Tourism carrying capacity. *Tourism Management* 7, 254–258.

7 A Montana Lodge and the Case for a Broadly Defined Ecotourism

A. Bidwell Pearce[1] and C. Ocampo-Raeder[2]

[1]PO Box 66, Garrett Park, Maryland, USA; [2]Department of Anthropology, University of Maine, Orono, Maine, USA

Introduction

William Bryan's thoughtful chapter in this volume addresses the significant structural challenges in the marketplace to the development of legitimate ecotourism or 'responsible travel' options in the USA and other developed settings. In addition to the issues Bryan raises, we believe that there are also challenges to ecotourism in the USA that stem from preconceived notions within the travel industry and ecotourism community. We observe that ecotourism efforts in the USA have often been categorically dismissed by analysts for reasons of geographic or socio-political setting, rather than on the basis of careful analysis of the social and environmental impacts of these operations.

Ecotourism operations around the world struggle to reconcile their ambitious mission with the concrete realities of their setting. It is no small task to balance the goals of nature conservation, community benefits and profitability that successful ecotourism requires (Fennell, 2002; Garrod, 2003). Many ecotourism ventures have discovered that despite best intentions, their operations do not result in the economic incentives for conservation that they envisioned (Bookbinder *et al.*, 1998). In fact, earnings from ecotourism may actually be used in ways that are antithetical to conservation (Wunder, 2000). Another concern is that ecotourism income may not be channelled to the people who actually use or impact natural resources locally, making the link between economic benefits and conservation ineffectual (Stonich, 2000).

Aside from these well-intentioned 'pitfalls', there are also a great many operations that exploit the ecotourism label for commercial gain without the least intention of providing substantial environmental or community benefits (Honey and Stewart, 2002). As noted by others in this volume, such 'greenwashers' typically label any travel experience in a natural setting as ecotourism. The existence of these 'shams' seriously jeopardizes the ecotourism community's ability to educate travellers about responsible travel, as opposed to mere nature consumption.

Clearly then, between the pitfalls and the shams, the ecotourism industry is beset by challenges on all sides. As a result, there are few examples of ecotourism ventures that have achieved substantial long-term community benefits, concrete progress in nature conservation and economic profitability. Yet, the ecotourism community has rightly resisted despair. Instead, new organizations and initiatives are emerging in the hope of developing certification programmes, effective marketing and business structures that work for conservation (Buckley, 2002; Honey, 2002). As this activity progresses, organizations like The International Ecotourism Society (TIES) have regarded past ecotourism pitfalls as experiments in the common goal of developing successful ecotourism models. They have embraced those involved in well-intentioned failures as allies in this mission, while attempting to limit the ability of exploitative shams to profit from their efforts.

But even within this pragmatic 'works in progress' approach, eco-tourism efforts in the USA still seem to us to be marginalized. First, we note that there exist numerous ventures in the USA that share the same good intentions as ecotourism operations abroad and that achieve some degree of success in meeting ecotourism ideals. In addition, research indicates that there is high demand for ecotourism experiences in the USA (Wight, 1996; Stein *et al.*, 2003). How peculiar it is, then, that most of the ecotourism literature continues to focus almost exclusively on cases from abroad? Second, compared with other areas of the world, the USA lags far behind in the effort to develop ecotourism guidelines appropriate to its social and environmental contexts. Some progress is being made, such as the 2005 and 2007 TIES conferences in Maine and Wisconsin, which included workshops on guidelines for US ecotourism. But the USA pales in comparison to Europe or Central America, for example, where there are already active, rigorous programmes for ecotourism certification. Finally, we feel there is a tendency to dismiss ecotourism efforts in the USA as free-riders in the 'sham' category, rather than as allies in an evolving industry. Some reactions to presentations of an ecotourism lodge in Montana illustrate the problem; below we use the case study of Papoose Creek Lodge, an ecotourism operation in Montana, to explore why stronger relationships have not developed between the ecotourism community and travel operators in the USA.

A Montana Case Study

Papoose Creek Lodge (PCL), whose name has changed since the time of writing this chapter to The Lodge at Sun Ranch, is located in the Madison Valley (35 min from the entrance of Yellowstone National Park) in Madison County, Montana (Fig. 7.1). The infrastructure for PCL is found

Fig. 7.1. Main cabin at Papoose Creek Lodge. (Photo: Constanza Ocampo-Raeder.)

within a 20 ha aspen and spruce grove along Papoose Creek. The immediate lodge property encompasses and maintains three different ecotones: (i) riparian; (ii) sage grass; and (iii) the mentioned aspen grove (Fig. 7.2). The adjacent land, called the Sun Ranch, is much larger (approximately 10,000 ha) and is where the bulk of the lodge activities take place. The ranch property also has a variety of different ecotones including grasslands, forest, willows and riparian areas (Fig. 7.3). In addition, the ranch has three creeks that feed the Madison River: Wolf, Squaw and Moose Creek. The water rights for all creeks including Papoose Creek have been donated to Trout Unlimited for fishery and water quality conservation projects.

Cynthia Lang, one of the co-owners of PCL, spoke at the Stanford workshop in the International Year of Ecotourism about the lodge's environmental education programme for guests, their efforts to minimize the environmental impacts of lodge operations, and their involvement in various conservation projects. She spoke of cabins constructed with reclaimed timber (Fig. 7.4), efforts to help restore native trout species, and a guest speaker series featuring local environmental experts. The conference participants, including academics, travel professionals and representatives of ecotourism non-profit organizations, seemed intrigued and impressed with these aspects of the lodge. However, several raised

Fig. 7.2. Ecotones represented in Papoose Creek Lodge property. (Photo: Constanza Ocampo-Raeder.)

Fig. 7.3. View of the Sun Ranch property. (Photo: Constanza Ocampo-Raeder.)

Fig. 7.4. Guest cabin constructed with reclaimed timber. (Photo: Constanza Ocampo-Raeder.)

objections to using the ecotourism label for PCL based on a lack of evidence for community benefits from lodge operations. One participant challenged the underlying ecotourism mission of a lodge in Montana owned by people who live in California and have other business interests. These objections, then, seemed to question whether ecotourism could exist in a guise other than the 'sustainable development project' with which it is commonly associated abroad.

One year after the Stanford workshop, the authors had the opportunity to do some consulting work with PCL. The owners of the lodge had undergone a sort of rapid self-assessment of where they stood relative to their ecotourism mission statement: 'to operate our guest lodge in a purposeful way that strives to preserve and enhance the natural, cultural and economic resources of our surrounding area'. They were dissatisfied with the lodge's progress in this regard and asked us to coordinate a programme that would advance the lodge's environmental mission. In the course of this work, we encountered a second set of objections to using the ecotourism label for Papoose Creek. Tour operators and travel agents with whom the lodge did business objected that because Papoose Creek was not in an 'exotic' locale and the accommodations were not rustic, it didn't 'look' like ecotourism. These travel professionals knew that guest ranches were marketable and didn't see any reason to confuse the issue by calling Papoose Creek an ecotourism lodge. They were accustomed to marketing ecotourism packages in rainforest settings and guest ranch packages in Rocky Mountain settings.

Many of the observations about PCL, both from within and outside the ecotourism community, are valid. The lodge is in the Madison Valley of south-west Montana, where the vast majority of the population is white and speaks English. The lodge is also very luxurious (Fig. 7.5). With an outdoor hot tub, a gourmet chef and expensive furnishings, the lodge has more creature comforts than most people have in their own homes. The owners of the lodge do not rely on the income it generates, but have undertaken this project because of their love of the Madison Valley and interest in piloting business models with conservation benefits. The lodge is not co-owned by the local community, nor does it provide a large source of employment or income for the local population.

Given the differences between PCL and more normative ecotourism lodges, is there any reason to call it ecotourism? Should the owners just keep their environmentalism to themselves and run a standard guest ranch? Or should they come up with another label for the lodge that highlights its environmental mission? Based upon our work with the lodge, we believe that Papoose Creek should continue to promote itself as ecotourism. We observed several ways in which the lodge is currently contributing to the welfare of the local community and we believe that other community links will soon develop. Additionally, we suggest that the promotion of Papoose Creek as an ecotourism lodge will be good for the ecotourism industry as a whole. We argue, therefore, that organizations like TIES ought to provide room within their certification guidelines and promotional efforts for tourism operations like PCL.

Fig. 7.5. Interior view of main cabin at Papoose Creek Lodge. (Photo: Constanza Ocampo-Raeder.)

First, PCL does have the potential to contribute economically to the local community, if only on a small scale. During the 2003 season, more than a third of the lodge's full-time staff comprised people from the immediate local area, and about two-thirds were from the Rocky Mountain region. Papoose Creek also makes a conscious effort to purchase locally produced, sustainable products. They display and promote the work of local artists and artisans in the lodge. So while the lodge is not a huge influence at the scale of the local population, it is making helpful and sustainable connections with specific individuals and businesses in the local community.

Their efforts to hire and purchase locally are often frustrated by the remoteness of the Madison Valley and its low population density. As is the case with many ecotourism lodges, the local economy often cannot supply the lodge's specific needs. However, even if the lodge hired and purchased exclusively at the local level, Papoose Creek would still not represent a large source of employment or income for locals. That being the case, it is unlikely that the existence of PCL in the Madison Valley will funda-mentally transform the way that the local community at large values or manages natural resources. This limitation has nothing to do with the fact that the lodge is privately owned. Papoose Creek is simply too small an operation relative to the local economy to have that kind of impact, as is likely to be true of any ecotourism operation in the USA. It seems unwarranted to disqualify a lodge as ecotourism based upon such issues of scale, as long as its influences, however limited, are positive in terms of environmental sustainability. As many authors have noted, ecotourism cannot be a panacea for environmental problems, even at a local level (Kiss 2004; Kruger 2005). Instead, it is one of a variety of strategies, some market-based and others not, that can work in concert to promote environmental responsibility.

Second, despite the limited potential for Papoose Creek to directly influence the local economy, other components of the lodge's operations contribute to community welfare and sustainability. In particular, the environmental education programme at PCL benefits the local community in several ways. For example, lodge guests – who are typically US citizens and voters, as well as people of considerable economic and political influence – are exposed to all of the stakeholders in Western environmental issues in a non-confrontational setting. The lodge provides a voice for local people who often feel under-represented and misunderstood in national political debates about such issues as public lands management and endangered species protection. One family rancher expressed to us that simply by exposing guests to the perspectives and values of local ranchers, Papoose Creek was contributing to their struggle to maintain their lifestyle in the Madison Valley. Many of the guests whom we met at Papoose Creek commented that their stay at the lodge gave them a better understanding of the complexity of environmental issues in the USA. Some guests came to the realization that issues of local participation and just distribution of costs and benefits were as relevant to natural resource management in the

Madison Valley as they were in developing countries. PCL, then, fosters dialogue about environmental conservation in the USA that does not typically occur in a public venue.

The lodge's environmental education programme with guests can also help to shape their future behaviour in the local Madison Valley landscape or the Rocky Mountain region. The tourism and real estate industries in the Rockies are very closely related. Stories abound of people who initially visited the Madison Valley on a fly-fishing vacation and then decided to buy a summer retreat or retirement home in the area. Guests at Papoose Creek are educated about the environmental costs of unplanned development, as well as alternative strategies for land-use planning. Lodge guests who decide to buy property locally may be more likely than other recreational buyers to use conservation easements, support clustered development or buy a home site within a protected family ranch. This would certainly be a concrete benefit for a community that is struggling to balance the imperatives of a growing recreational real estate industry with the widely shared desire for preservation of open space.

While these community benefits associated with Papoose Creek's environmental education programme may not be as profound as those stemming from direct economic links, they still represent positive advances. The lodge will undoubtedly develop more direct links with community livelihood in the future. However, it is also important to recognize that the small scale of the Papoose Creek operation relative to the local economy also means that this ecotourism 'experiment' poses fewer dangers than more ambitious projects in developing nations. In the Madison Valley there is no danger that participation in Papoose Creek will dramatically alter the local economy, as can happen when subsistence producers begin to engage in the market through ecotourism (e.g. Belsky 1999; Rodríguez, Chapter 10, this volume). Therefore, we feel that Papoose Creek has unquestionably maintained a 'positive balance' in terms of community benefits.

Aside from the potential community benefits and environmental education, a third rationale for labelling Papoose Creek an ecotourism lodge is the potential benefit to the ecotourism industry as a whole. Including operations like Papoose Creek under a general rubric like 'ecotourism' is an opportunity to educate travel agents and travellers that 'ecotourism' is not a style, comprising a rainforest setting and mosquito nets, but a set of principles and practices related to social and environmental responsibility. The USA has always had a large market for 'nature-based travel'. Yet little effort has been made to help consumers make distinctions between general nature travel in the USA and environmentally responsible travel. Withholding an ecotourism label from operations like Papoose Creek, based on its inability to create economic links on a scale like those of a sustainable development project, would be giving up a chance to create such distinctions in the US travel market.

Likewise, lodges like Papoose Creek could also be instrumental in the process of expanding the market of 'true' ecotourists, as they attract and educate 'incipient' ecotourists. Very few of the guests at Papoose Creek during the 2003 season came to the lodge specifically for its ecotourism label. Some did not even realize that the lodge had an environmental mission. Once at the lodge, however, the vast majority of lodge guests took an active interest in the environmental education programme, asked questions about the environmental mission, and reported that these aspects of the lodge were an unexpected 'bonus' for their vacation. These guests may be more likely to seek out ecotourism packages, as opposed to simply nature-based travel, in the future. In fact, it became common practice for the guests to solicit a list of 'suggested ecotourism destinations' from the authors during their time at Papoose Creek. We expect that if Papoose Creek did not use the ecotourism label, guests would be less likely to translate their positive experiences at the lodge into broader participation in ecotourism. Of course, substantiating these hypotheses will require future testing with surveys of lodge guests.

Clearly PCL could continue to serve its particular environmental mission statement without using an ecotourism label. They could call it a 'green lodge' or a 'conservation lodge', or could forego any label at all. However, we believe that using the ecotourism label is the best way for them to influence the future travel choices of their guests. Ecotourism is ultimately a market-based approach to conservation and community development, and hence marketing strategies must be considered not just for individual businesses and projects, but for the ecotourism community as a whole. And, of course, a primary rule of marketing is to 'keep it simple'.

While in academic discussions we may want to subcategorize lodges along a variety of lines, we feel it is important to promote a spectrum of responsible travel under a large umbrella name like 'ecotourism' that travellers can easily understand. As William Bryan points out in Chapter 6, this volume, this term may not be how travellers prefer to identify themselves. However, it already has a significant presence in the marketplace and may be worth holding on to for that reason. Our main point is that by consistently promoting environmentally and socially responsible travel options with a single label, we can 'create' responsible travellers in one locale and export them around the world. Lodges like Papoose Creek could be instrumental in the process of expanding the market for ecotourism because they attract 'incipient' ecotourists.

This is not to say that TIES or other groups should loosen standards or turn a blind eye to ecotourism shams. In fact, we feel that certification should be a main priority of the ecotourism community. And certification programmes should continue to stress social impacts and community benefits. However, certification should leave room for a variety of tourism strategies that promote conservation, while also being socially responsible. Certification should recognize that community benefits can come in many forms other than direct household income for locals, and that some travel settings present greater opportunities for influence on the local economy than others. Of course, however, all ecotourism ought to follow the most important tenet of the Hippocratic oath: 'first, do no harm'. Clearly if a project has significant negative consequences for the local community or for the environment it should not be considered ecotourism.

In our view, ecotourism consists of three equally important aspects: (i) low environmental impacts paired with conservation benefits; (ii) environmental education for guests; and (iii) sustainable links with the local economy. Not all of these aspects are equally represented in all ecotourism projects, nor can they all be developed at once. Some ecotourism projects may be stronger in terms of promoting sustainable local benefits; others may have more of an influence through environmental education. The important thing, as noted above, is to maintain a positive balance in each aspect, no matter how slight. If certification focuses upon developing processes through which ecotourism ventures can be tailored to specific socio-economic and environmental settings without sacrificing its mission, then a whole spectrum of creative approaches will not only fit comfortably within its domain, but will also serve to inform, promote and inspire each other.

References

Belsky, J.M. (1999) Misrepresenting communities: the politics of community-based rural ecotourism in Gales Point Manatee, Belize. *Rural Sociology* 64, 641–666.

Bookbinder, M.P., Dinerstein, E., Rijal, A., Cauley, H. and Rajouria, A. (1998) Ecotourism's support of biodiversity conservation. *Conservation Biology* 12, 1399–1404.

Buckley, R. (2002) Tourism ecocertification in the International Year of Ecotourism. *Journal of Ecotourism* 1, 197–203.

Fennell, D. (2002) Ecotourism: where we've been; where we're going. *Journal of Ecotourism* 1, 1–6.

Garrod, B. (2003) Local participation in the planning and management of ecotourism: a revised model approach. *Journal of Ecotourism* 2, 33–53.

Honey, M. (1999) *Ecotourism and Sustainable Development: Who Owns Paradise?* Island Press, Washington, DC.

Honey, M. (ed.) (2002) *Ecotourism and Certification: Setting Standards in Practice.* Island Press, Washington, DC.

Honey, M. and Stewart, E. (2002) The evolution of 'green' standards for tourism. In: Honey, M. (ed.) *Ecotourism and Certification: Setting Standards in Practice.* Island Press, Washington, DC, pp. 33–72.

Kiss, A. (2004) Is community-based ecotourism a good use of biodiversity conservation funds? *Trends in Ecology and Evolution* 19, 231–237.

Kruger, O. (2005) The role of ecotourism in conservation: panacea or Pandora's box? *Biodiversity and Conservation* 14, 579–600.

Stein, T., Clark, J. and Rickards, J. (2003) Assessing nature's role in ecotourism development in Florida: perspectives of tourism professionals and government decision makers. *Journal of Ecotourism* 2, 155–172.

Stonich, S. (2000) *The Other Side of Paradise: Tourism, Conservation, and Sustainable Development in the Bay Islands.* Cognizant Communication Corporation, New York.

Stronza, A. (2000) 'Because it is ours': community-based ecotourism in the Peruvian Amazon. PhD dissertation, University of Florida, Gainesville, Florida.

Stronza, A. (2001) Anthropology of tourism: forging new ground for ecotourism and other alternatives. *Annual Review of Anthropology* 30, 261–283.

Wight, P. (1996) North American ecotourists: market profile and trip characteristics. *Journal of Travel Research* 34, 2–10.

Wunder, S. (2000) Ecotourism and economic incentives: an empirical approach. *Ecological Economics* 32, 465–479.

Part V

Educating Tourists

8 Environmental Interpretation versus Environmental Education as an Ecotourism Conservation Strategy

J. KOHL

Private Consultant, Tres Ríos, Costa Rica

Introduction

The rapid loss of biological diversity continues despite the hundreds of conservation projects being carried out today. Cultural diversity is also diminishing, owing to globalization and encroachment. Languages are one indicator of cultural integrity, and 90% of the 6000 living languages and dialects are on the decline (Waas, 1998). The urgency for protection increases every day.

Ecotourism has been proposed as a major strategy to protect biodiversity. According to Brandon (1996), key benefits from ecotourism can be clustered into five groups:

1. A source of financing for biodiversity conservation, especially in legally protected areas.
2. Economic justification for protected areas.
3. Economic alternatives for local people to reduce over-exploitation on protected areas and wildlands and wildlife resources.
4. Constituency-building, which promotes biodiversity conservation.
5. An impetus for private biodiversity conservation efforts.

One tool that allows ecotourism to achieve the first cluster is environmental interpretation. Interpretation is often confused with environmental education, but the two are distinct fields – each, for example, having its own professional association and research journal. In the present chapter I argue that this distinction matters for conservation. More specifically, I show that environmental interpretation, rather than environmental education, is the more appropriate strategy for connecting ecotourism with conservation in protected areas. Also, I show that in a public-use planning context, education can be explicitly tied to conservation.

Interpretation as a field has been developing throughout the 20th century, taking on a formal form with the publication of Freeman Tilden's seminal work, *Interpreting Our Heritage* (1957). Interpretation is literally the translation from one language to another. In the field of environmental interpretation it refers to translating the natural, cultural and even historical legacy or heritage of places and objects to a form people can easily understand. An interpreter helps ecotourists see underlying significance and develop an appreciation for the story behind what is being seen. Although some proponents of interpretation focus solely on the benefits for learning, interpretation can also help bolster conservation beyond simply educating visitors (Kimmel, 1999).

In protected areas, interpreters can help visitors gain a deeper appreciation for the park's significance, particularly in relation to larger ecological and social problems. Because education is generally considered an essential component of ecotourism, interpretation is the principal tool by which visitors are 'educated'. This is a voluntary relationship between visitor and interpreter. An example, on which I elaborate below, is Lindblad Expeditions, which hosts ecotourists on interpretive, multi-day tours aboard cruise vessels. Each day interpreters take visitors to different on-shore sites. Interpretation can be carried out through signs, brochures and other non-personal media, such as slide shows in the case of Lindblad.

Although in developed countries such as the USA, Australia and Spain there are established communities of professional interpreters, in the developing tropics, the skill set is still in infancy. Park administrators often talk about offering interpretive services and indeed many park administrations own Ham's (1992) classic interpretive reference book, *Environmental Interpretation*. Most parks offer information signs. Galapagos National Park even has an interpretive plan, although it has not been implemented (T. Villegas, personal communication, 2001). In Costa Rica, the Latin American country most famous for its national parks, the University of Costa Rica suspended its interpretation minor programme in 2002 due to a lack of available faculty (M. Mayorga, personal communication, 2004). The programme was reopened in 2007 with the arrival of a young professor.

Environmental Interpretation Has a Long Way To Go in the Developing Tropics

Again, despite the many conservation projects, threats and challenges to biological and cultural diversity conservation continue to mount. One can conclude that the problem is getting bigger despite the success of projects, or that the projects are generally failing, or both. Certainly the rates of natural resource exploitation and human population growth are increasing. To compound these global problems, many conservation projects, including interpretation when used as a conservation tool, do fail for a variety of methodological reasons.

Because ecotourism is one strategy of general international development, I cite some examples of failure from this field. Ferguson (1994) argued that development projects in general are not designed to manage political challenges and thus they ignore them, focusing exclusively on technical solutions. Projects then fail when the problem proves to be more political than technical in nature. There is evidence that some large development agents such as the World Bank and the US Agency for International Development (USAID) worry more about positive reporting than good project design. When Clements (1999) evaluated randomly selected projects and compared his results with those reported he found in all cases that project results were exaggerated. Project success can be greatly limited by an inability of project implementers to learn and apply rigorous scientific standards. Pullin and Knight (2001) have challenged the conservation field to move from project design and implementation based on intuition and personal experience to projects based on evidence. This move would mirror the transition the public health field has been through since the late 1980s. The same need for greater effectiveness precipitated USAID's establishing the now defunct Biodiversity Support Program, whose tagline was 'Doing Conservation Better'. A couple of the Program's staff went on to create a new organization, Foundations of Success, whose slogan is 'Improving the Practice of Conservation'.

Projects involving ecotourism and interpretation suffer these problems as much as any other field. Interpretation, however, has the added linguistic, cultural and educational barriers, impeding its implementation in developing countries (Kohl *et al.*, 2001). Perhaps the biggest problem with the successful use of interpretation for conservation in developing countries has been the very conception of interpretation. It is very often confused with environmental education, even among academics (Knapp *et al.*, 1997). I regularly hear park professionals in Central America interchanging the terms. Sometimes both are used in reference to behaviour change, sometimes to make people aware, sometimes so that tourists will go back and carry out behaviour in their own countries, sometimes just for visitor enjoyment. Because these distinctions matter for making ecotourism an effective tool for conservation, I define them here.

Typically, interpretation takes place during the leisure time of visitors who voluntarily participate in programmes usually only for a couple of hours, though some last up to a few days, such as Lindblad Expeditions' interpretive cruises. Because interpretation is largely recreational and short in duration, it normally should not have aspirations of behaviour change. As Knapp (1997, p. 10) wrote:

> People need time to attain the sensitivity, knowledge, and attitudes
> necessary for a positive environmental ethic. Time is certainly one
> characteristic that an interpretive experience lacks.

The National Association for Interpretation (2007) defines its practice without any reference to education: interpretation is a mission-based communication process that forges emotional and intellectual connections between the interests of the audience and the meanings inherent in the resource (Fig. 8.1). Environmental education, on the other hand, tends to be knowledge-based, curricular and sequential over time, with the express goal of developing an environmentally conscious and active citizenry. Consider the definition of environmental education by the North American Association for Environmental Education (1983):

> Environmental education is a process which promotes the analysis and understanding of environmental issues and questions as the basis for effective education, problem solving, policy making, and management. The purpose of environmental education is to foster the education of skilled individuals able to understand environmental problems and possessing the expertise to devise effective solutions to them. In the broader context, environmental education's purpose is to assist in the development of a citizenry conscious of the scope and complexity of current and emerging environmental problems and supportive of solutions and policies which are ecologically sound.

At the heart of both approaches and all other environmental communication methodologies (such as social marketing, fiction writing, documentaries, etc.) are the same basic human cognitive and affective mechanisms. Considering these points, nevertheless, one should employ interpretation, rather than environmental education, with ecotourists

Fig. 8.1. Visitor centre outside Bolivia's Madidi National Park. (Photo: Jon Kohl.)

visiting protected areas. Parks should avoid the delusion of long-term behaviour change by short interpretive encounters, or at least until new behaviour models are developed that can explain how small, voluntary interpretive experiences can lead to lasting behaviour change.

Long-term behaviour change should not be confused with visitors taking certain actions as a result of their interpretive experience. Knapp *et al.* (1997) developed a framework of goals for programme development in environmental interpretation, with behaviour change at the top of the list. The authors admit that they derived these goals without considering the time, audiences and media that interpreters normally have at their call. This confusion and concurrent misunderstanding about behaviour change has led to a host of assumptions unsupported by established learning theory. These assumptions can kill development and ecotourism projects using education even before they start. Some common assumptions include the following:

1. Lasting attitudes and even behaviour can be changed in short interpretive encounters. Trail signs that say, for example, 'do not throw trash' are rarely, if ever, effective.
2. Attitude change leads directly to behaviour change. McKenzie-Mohr and Smith (1999) have reviewed a variety of studies that debunk this assumption. Nature guides often hope that if visitors can be shown how marvellous nature is, then they will more likely protect it in the future.
3. It is harder to get adults to change their behaviour, so programmes should focus on children, even if children are not the appropriate target audience for a particular problem. It is better to start with children, they say, who will grow up and behave better some day. This is the overriding principle at many zoos.
4. Information is interpretation and is sufficient to provoke appreciation. By extension, people can remember the information if they are interested. An ecotourism student-guide working at a zoo in Panama told the author, 'If you can't remember, you are not interested'.

Misunderstanding combined with poor skills at conceptualizing and writing objectives compound problems. In an article aptly titled 'If you don't care where you get to, then it doesn't matter which way you go!', Nay *et al.* (1976) explain that if an objective is not operational, then it is not possible to achieve specific objectives. Thus an objective must be measurable and plausible, and those in charge of the programme must have the motivation, ability and authority to manage. Also the popular SMART goal criteria (using the term 'goal' and 'objective' interchangeably in this case) call for goals to be specific, measurable, attainable, relevant and time-bound. In any case, few effective project objectives make it to the field.

In summary, environmental interpretation, rather than environmental education, is the appropriate communication intervention for ecotourists, especially if the objective is to make ecotourism an effective tool for conserving cultural and biological diversity in protected areas.

Clarifying the Conservation Role of Interpretation in Ecotourism

With preliminary concepts of ecotourism and interpretation in place, we can clarify the conservation role that interpretation might play in ecotourism. To do this, I use a public-use management perspective. The question is how might a park administrator use heritage interpretation with visitors to promote conservation of protected resources? The term 'public use' refers to all non-extractive uses other than for sport or science by protected area visitors whether they are ecotourists, local people, school groups, investigators, reporters, politicians or others. 'Public use' does not include timber cutting, commercial or subsistence fishing, mineral extraction, or other extractive commercial uses (World Heritage Centre and Rare, 2007). It does encompass all of tourism as well as visitation by people who are not tourists. According to the World Tourism Organization, a tourist is anyone who visits a site away from their home, stays at least one night, and consumes tourist services.

To study how interpretation affects conservation, we must first examine how public-use programming achieves resource conservation. For this, I present a concept model (Fig. 8.2). A concept model diagrams the relationships between a set of factors that are believed to influence a certain end or target condition. Any concept model is a simplification of real life, trying to balance sufficient detail with efficient legibility. The art of concept modelling is to show just enough to develop an effective project, and not more. The following four main building blocks of a project concept model come from Margoluis and Salafsky (1998):

1. *Target condition*: in other systems it is the output or dependent variable that a project intends to influence. It might be biodiversity in a certain park, public health in a certain community, or dependence on foreign oil.
2. *Factor*: in other systems the factor is called the predictor or independent variable. These are the specific events, situations, conditions, policies, attitudes, beliefs or behaviours that project designers think influence the target condition. In terms of biodiversity, some factors are considered direct threats to biodiversity and others indirect threats. The difference is that direct threats are those that actually cause damage to target condition and the indirect threats drive the direct threats. Both kinds are factors.
3. *Activities*: these are the actions proposed to modify particular factors in order to influence the target conditions.
4. *Relationships*: also known as hypotheses or assumptions, relationships describe the cause-and-effect connection between one factor and another. Arrows represent them.

Aside from site-specific concept models such as the one shown in Fig. 8.2, Rare has also adapted the methodology for general intervention strategies. Rare (known as RARE Center, an abbreviation for RARE Center for Tropical Conservation, at the time of the intervention) is a US-based conservation organization that works globally to equip people in the

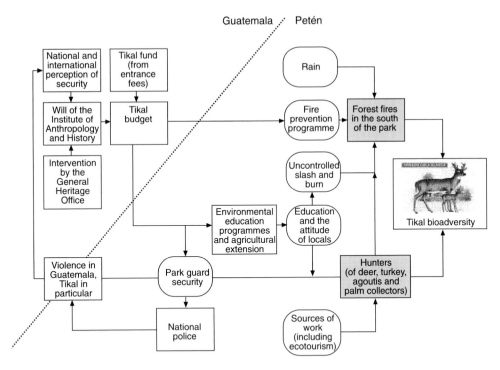

Fig. 8.2. This site-based concept model was developed by Rare for Tikal National Park in Guatemala, using the strict modelling procedure from Margoluis and Salafsky (1998). The target condition is the park biodiversity. The two direct threats are fires and hunters–harvesters (shaded). A series of indirect threats influence the direct threats (in ovals), such as fire prevention programmes, education of populations, park security, sources of work, slash and burn, and rainfall. Other factors influence the indirect factors such as the national police, park budget, etc. Notice how factors have actually been divided up geographically in Guatemala City (on the left) and the Petén Province where Tikal is found, on the right.

world's most threatened natural areas with the tools and motivation they need to care for their natural resources. Using the same mechanics and terminology but instead of describing a site, Rare's concept model describes generalized causal chains (cause-and-effect relationship between several factors) a strategy intends to follow across its portfolio of sites. Of course, a general model for the strategy cannot be applied uniformly to all sites. Not all factors will apply to any given site.

The cause-and-effect chains, by which interpretation can help protect resources, are chosen using several criteria. First, ideally a chain of assumptions should have some evidence that supports it. The more evidence and established theory that already exists, the more certain a project designer can feel about building that relationship into the model. Second, a project designer should consider impact. It is possible to include a factor that has a definite but small effect, but its clutter effect might outweigh any positive contribution to the model.

A project designer – whether park manager or ecotour operator – could also include factors beyond the control of the project. For example, international terrorism affects visitation which affects revenues and ultimately conservation. But the project is not designed to confront international terrorism, hurricanes or protests by labour unions. All of these threats could easily be linked in a model. Adding them does not usually help to design the project, so they should probably be omitted.

Rare used the strategy-specific modelling to describe how its public-use planning programme could affect conservation in a generalized protected area (see Fig. 8.3). This model provides the causal chains that link the public-use planning intervention with actual mitigation of biodiversity threats.

Description of the Factors

- *Public-use planning*: this is the Rare intervention that helps a park develop a strategic public-use plan.
- *Park public-use management capacity*: this capacity refers to the education, organization and discipline of an organization to implement and update a public-use plan.
- *Public-use products*: parks offer a wide variety of products to the public. They include private-sector tour packages, activities and services, and formal study programmes for college students, such as those tied to birdwatching, interpretive programmes for children, or even packages for researchers to carry out their projects in the park.
- *Control capacity*: a park can use a set of techniques to control visitors such as hard-line regulations, soft-line education and interpretation, incentives, and manipulation of the physical environment to control

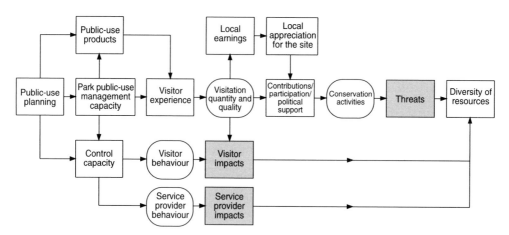

Fig. 8.3. Public-use planning programme.

behaviour and movement (clean walls, barriers, lines of sight, waterways, etc.). 'Control capacity' is a sub-set of the more general 'public-use management capacity'.

- *Visitor experience*: the novelty, enjoyment and educational value of the visitor experience depend in large measure on the kinds of products offered, their quality and the park's management of their context. As most visitors to a park are part of a non-captive audience (meaning they can get up and leave any time they desire; the opposite are students obliged to be there by their teacher), the park like any business needs to pay utmost attention to the quality of the visitor experience, so that visitors remain happy, participate in conservation and speak highly of the park to other people.
- *Visitor behaviour*: the control measures regulate visitor behaviours, especially those that relate to impacts on protected resources.
- *Service provider behaviour*: the control measures regulate service provider behaviour (restaurants, transportation, street vendors, outside guides, etc.), especially that which relates to impacts on protected resources.
- *Visitation quantity and quality*: the number of visitors is the quantity. The quality refers to two dimensions of a visitor: how much they spend and how much impact they inflict on resources. Typically older, more educated visitors can pay more and are more conscious not to damage resources; thus, in industry lingo, they are 'higher quality' and desired by parks. When word gets around that the park is offering higher-quality experience opportunities, this normally attracts more people including higher-quality visitors.
- *Visitor impacts*: if the park can control visitor behaviour in public-use zones, then visitor impacts should be minimized in those same zones.
- *Service provider impacts*: if the park can control service provider behaviour in public-use zones, then service provider impacts should be minimized in those same zones.
- *Local earnings*: with greater visitation, more visitors spend money in the area and more money finds its way to local businesses. This assumption carries the additional premise that local participation constitutes a part of the public-use mix in the protected area. Without local participation, this branch does not apply.
- *Local appreciation for the site*: if local businesses earn money from visitation, then their appreciation of the site should increase, since people value that which is important to them. The reverse is also true.
- *Support generation mechanisms*: simply having more visitors and more local people who appreciate the park does not mean that conservation benefits are sure to follow. The park must make active efforts to develop channels by which motivated stakeholders can contribute. Parks must know how to solicit donations, set up activities for volunteers, and organize the efforts of like-minded supporters.
- *Support (donations and actions)*: both visitors and locals can contribute donations or carry out actions for park conservation. The more locals

appreciate it and the greater the visitor experience (as well as the more visitors in general), the greater the support. Because visitors throughout the world already make contributions, the key assumption is that they can be primed with a very positive experience leading to greater donations. Also the Theory of Planned Behaviour (Ajzen, 1991) shows that when people believe they have the knowledge, ability, confidence and opportunity to carry out the action ('perceived behavioural control'), they are more likely to have the intention to act. Additionally the kinds of messages the park uses can influence a person's making a contribution (McKenzie-Mohr and Smith, 1999). Parks can provide that knowledge through a well-targeted solicitation.

- *Conservation activities*: such activities serve as the recipients of the resources generated through contributions, participation and political support.
- *Threats*: conservation activities mitigate threats, if well chosen, designed and evaluated.
- *Diversity of resources*: diversity can include all biological, cultural, archaeological or historical resources in a protected area.

In the case of the public-use model, there are principally three cause-and-effect chains: (i) visitor experience; (ii) control capacity; and (iii) working through local stakeholders. The heart of the concept model focuses on the visitor experience. As Ham *et al.* (1993) argued:

> Because... tourists like to receive information about the places they visit, interpretation must be seen as part of the service they pay for, and which they expect. Simply put, interpretation constitutes the intellectual part of the experience tourists seek. Interesting information presented in an entertaining way adds to the quality of the experience, which creates satisfied customers and gives the tourism entrepreneur [including the park interpretation staff] an important competitive edge.

Simply, the better the public-use planning, the better the interpretation (and other services implicit in the 'Park public-use management capacity') that will result and the better the visitor experience opportunities are in the protected area. If the park offers better products (also by helping the private sector develop better products as seen in the factor 'Public-use products'), then it is assumed that more visitors will come and if the park so desires more visitors of higher quality. The model also assumes that visitors who have better experiences will feel a greater connection to the site and its resources. People with greater emotional involvement are more likely to want to support the park to protect the resources they have just come to appreciate. As such, if the park makes the appropriate solicitation, visitors are more likely to make contributions of one form or another. With greater contributions, the park can support to a greater extent its conservation activities. It is clear that within every assumption are many smaller assumptions. Project designers need to be able to identify those assumptions and identify – and perhaps eliminate – those that are less likely to prove correct.

Another way interpretation can protect resources is through moderating both visitor and service provider impacts. The chain says that with good planning, the park will have better capacity to control visitor and service provider behaviour. If their behaviour is controlled, resources are protected from visitor and service provider impacts. Interpretation contributes to control by explaining to visitors and service providers the importance of their behaviour to conservation (positive incentive) or how their non-compliance will demand sanctions (negative incentive). Park managers can use interpretation to control behaviour through signage, through guides and guards, and with presentations designed for service providers.

The last chain uses interpretation through local communities. This chain is really a sub-set of the visitor experience chain. It says that as the quality and quantity of visitation goes up, earnings of local service providers increases, also increasing their appreciation for the site. This appreciation can result in increased contributions by locals to the conservation activities of the park.

Ham and Krumpe (1995) argued for another chain, that of using interpretation directly with local communities who do not recreationally visit public-use facilities in an attempt to effect behaviours more conducive to park protection. Because communities which never visit park public-use facilities are not technically visitors, that chain is not included in this model. A park might have another model on community development and extension that would include this strategy.

Strategies for Using Interpretation to Conserve Resources

This modelling approach, which was not specifically designed to highlight interpretation, clarified the central role interpretation can play in linking public use – and importantly, ecotourism – to conservation. This model shied away from promoting the conservation benefits that result from economic benefits to local communities, even though it is commonly assumed that if local communities benefit economically, they will support conservation (e.g. Bookbinder *et al.*, 1998). Modellers at Rare tried to model these chains but found there were so many assumptions and so little direct evidence that it made more sense for the programme to focus on visitor experiences. Indirectly there are many theories of economic multiplier effects, standard of living effects, income distribution effects, attitudes of locals towards conservation based on economic benefits from tourism, and other theories that make the economic effects of visitor behaviour very difficult to predict, despite popular opinion. This analysis of popular assumptions is precisely why concept models are valuable to project designers.

Similarly, this model emphasizes that general education models, such as the need to educate ecotourists, alone do not contribute to conservation. The education must be tied directly to benefits for the park offering the education. It does the local park little good if, for example, its ecotourists go back to their country and build bird nest boxes.

Once these chains are clarified, then project designers use them to design interventions. They ask themselves what they need to do for the desired changes in the target condition to come about. They can judge the wisdom of their intervention against the standard in the concept model instead of choosing designs for arbitrary, personal or political reasons. For example, Rare has considered the following ideas in its interventions:

1. The park needs a strategic planning process to identify the products and ways of generating the best visitor experiences.
2. The park needs training in how to translate its conservation needs (i.e. support for a new policy, more shovels, US$5000 for a new guard post, volunteers to plant trees) into resources that can be solicited from different kinds of visitors.
3. Guides need to be trained to identify which kinds of visitors are most likely to contribute which kinds of contributions and then solicit them in a tactful manner.
4. To ensure that funds coming into the park are actually used for conservation and not just for administrative costs, the designer might insist that the park identify a percentage of net income towards a particular project or set of projects (i.e. 5% of net income goes to the nest box building project).
5. Because contributions of all types will be coming in (monetary, political support, donated services, manual labour), there needs to be a more sophisticated registry of donations to ensure that they end up going to the desired destination.
6. The park needs to open up a separate account to ensure that conservation funds do not get mixed back into general operation.
7. The park needs to demonstrate that it has effective conservation projects in place in order to receive resources and then convert them into conservation. Little good it does to spend great effort in designing the public-use programme to generate resources and then waste them on ineffective projects.

Conclusion

To use interpretation effectively requires that the practitioner (park manager or tour operator) understands something about learning and behaviour theory. Unfortunately, especially in many protected areas around the world, this kind of understanding is hard to come by and interpretation is still hardly practised, especially by host national park staffs. The typical challenges of implementing conservation projects combined with the misunderstanding of interpretation and environmental education make it hard to deliver interpretation products.

None the less, according to the concept model analysis, when the power of interpretation is used to improve the visitor experience, delivering effective messages, setting up a system of solicitation and tracking contributions, and finally having an available conservation project to take advantage of the resources, interpretation can be used directly to effect conservation. Lindblad Expeditions offers the best example of this model in action. It is a cruise ship-based natural interpretation experience where tourists spend several days on the 80-passenger boats steaming down the Pacific coast of Ecuador, including the Galapagos, for example. The on-board naturalists give regular interpretive programmes and guide trips in small boats to natural attractions along the coast. Throughout the cruise, the naturalists carry out a carefully crafted package of messages, at the end of which a solicitation is made. The tour operator collects and donates about US$4000 weekly to conservation activities in Galapagos National Park. Since its inception, the Galapagos Conservation Fund has raised more than US$4 million (as of October 2007) that have been used in a variety of local projects such as the eradication of feral pigs from the island of Santiago and the support of National Park Marine Reserve patrol boats (Lindblad Expeditions, 2007).

According to the model, nature guides, donation boxes and post-trip solicitations to garner contributions for conservation could use that same approach locally. Says Tom O'Brien, conservation coordinator at Lindblad:

> We have developed a coordinated interpretive strategy for our naturalists that defines how specific conservation messages are introduced over the course of the visitor experience. That coordinated communication of specific messages is critical, and that is what I would apply to any visitor experience, no matter how long or short.

References

Ajzen, I. (1991) The theory of planned behaviour. *Organizational Behavior and Human Decision Processes* 50, 170–211.

Bookbinder, M., Dinerstein, E., Rijal, A., Cauley, H. and Rajouria, A. (1998) Ecotourism's support of biodiversity conservation. *BioScience* 12, 1399–1401.

Brandon, K. (1996) *Ecotourism and Conservation: A Review of Key Issues*. Environmental Department Paper #33. World Bank, Washington, DC.

Clements, P. (1999) Information standards in development agency management. *World Development* 27, 1359–1381.

Ferguson, J. (1994) *The Anti-Politics Machine: 'Development', Depoliticization, and Bureaucratic Power in Lesotho*. University of Minnesota, St Paul, Minnesota.

Ham, S. (1992) *Environmental Interpretation: A Practical Guide for People with Big Ideas for Small Budgets*. North American Press, Golden, Colorado.

Ham, S. and Krumpe, E. (1995) How site-based interpretation can be used to change behaviours and contribute to biodiversity and ecosystem conservation in Central America. Discussion paper submitted to the Academy for Educational Development GreenCOM Project, Technical Advisory Group Meeting, 19 October.

Ham, S., Sutherland, D. and Meganck, R.A. (1993) Applying environmental interpretation in protected areas of developing countries: problems in exporting the US model. *Environmental Conservation* 20, 232–242.

Kimmel, J. (1999) Ecotourism as environmental learning. *Journal of Environmental Education* 30, 40–44.

Knapp, D. (1997) The relationship between environmental interpretation and environmental education. *Legacy*, May/June.

Knapp, D., Volk, T. and Hungerford, H. (1997) The identification of empirically derived goals for program development in environmental interpretation. *Journal of Environmental Education* 28, 24–34.

Kohl, J., Brown, C. and Humke, M. (2001) Hurdles to teaching guides to interpret biodiversity conservation. *Legacy*, July/August.

Lindblad Expeditions (2007) Lindblad Expeditions: Our Philosophy. http://www. expeditions.com/Our_Philosophy85.asp (accessed March 2008).

McKenzie-Mohr, D. and Smith, W. (1999) *Fostering Sustainable Behavior: An Introduction to Community-Based Social Marketing.* New Society Publishers and the Academy for Educational Development, British Columbia, Canada and Washington, DC.

Margoluis, R. and Salafsky, N. (1998) *Measures of Success.* Island Press, Washington, DC.

National Association for Interpretation (2007) National Association for Interpretation homepage. www.interpnet.com (accessed March 2007).

Nay, J.N., Scanlon, J.W., Schmidt, R.E. and Wholey, J.S. (1976) If you don't care where you get to, then it doesn't matter which way you go! In: Abt, C.C. (ed) *The Evaluation of Social Programs.* Sage, Beverly Hills, California, pp. 97–125.

North American Association for Environmental Education (1983) *Defining Environmental Education: The NAAEE Perspective.* NAAEE, Troy, Ohio.

Pullin, A. and Knight, T. (2001) Effectiveness in conservation practice: pointers from medicine and public health. *Conservation Biology* 15, 50–54.

Tilden, F. (1957) *Interpreting Our Heritage*, 3rd edn. University of North Carolina Press, Chapel Hill, North Carolina.

Waas, M. (1998) Taking note of language extinction. *Applied Linguistics Forum* 18, 1, 4–5; available at http://www.colorado.edu/iec/alis/articles/langext.htm (accessed May 2007).

World Heritage Centre and Rare (2007) *Park Planning for Life, Programme Manual for the Public Use Planning Program.* United Nations Educational, Scientific and Cultural Organization, Paris.

9   Educating Ecotourists: Lessons from the Field

J. DUBIN

Global Explorers, Fort Collins, Colorado, USA

Introduction

Although a single definition of ecotourism remains elusive, the majority of definitions include a few primary elements. It is generally agreed that ecotourism involves responsible travel to natural areas, a positive contribution to conservation and a positive contribution to local communities. In addition, one of the basic tenets of ecotourism is to engender in the tourist a greater understanding of the importance of conservation and increase the tourist's ecological literacy (Goodwin, 1996). Essentially, ecotourism is an opportunity to educate people of various ages about conservation (Hall, 1992; Kimmel, 1999).

A few defining characteristics of ecotourism indicate that ecotourists may be a particularly appropriate audience for conservation lessons. For example, ecotourists are a self-selected group of tourists who indicate, by the very nature of their chosen destination and activities, their interest in the natural world and potential receptivity to lessons about conservation. Ecotourists are also generally removed from their regular routine throughout the experience, which may allow them to gain new perspectives on familiar conservation messages or spark a new interest in conservation. In addition, research shows that lessons learned through direct experience have a greater chance of influencing behaviour than do lessons learned through books or other means (Cornell, 1979; Miles, 1991). For example, reading about tropical deforestation and experiencing deforestation as an ecotourist are likely to result in very different levels of understanding.

Although educating the ecotourist is one of the goals of ecotourism and ecotourists should theoretically be receptive to these lessons, the question remains: what do ecotourists really learn? Do they, in fact, learn lessons about conservation, and are they inspired by their experiences to take action or change their attitudes in meaningful ways? It is difficult to measure exactly what ecotourists learn because an ecotourism experience is complex and multi-layered. Its lessons may not be apparent, even to the ecotourist, until well after its completion. It is also hard to generalize about ecotourism across the industry because a standard definition of what constitutes a 'true' ecotourism experience does not yet exist. With this in mind, I conducted a case study to determine how a specific ecotourism experience educationally impacted a select group of eco-tourists. The insights from this research may potentially be used to help tailor the educational experiences of ecotourists in other places.

Objectives

The objectives of the present study were twofold. The first was to determine the educational effectiveness of a specific ecotourism experience. For the purposes of the study, lesson types are classified in four distinct categories: (i) enhancement of ecological knowledge; (ii) cultural lessons; (iii) personal growth; and (iv) conservation/advocacy. I chose these lesson categories as they reflect the educational goals of the ecotourism experience I used for the case study.

The second objective was to identify demographic and descriptive factors that influence the educational impact of a specific ecotourism experience on ecotourists. A review of environmental education research suggests that characteristics of the learner (e.g. age, gender) and the experience itself (e.g. preparation) may influence the learning outcome of an experience (Gutierrez de White and Jacobson, 1994; Rickinson, 2001). I hypothesized that various characteristics of ecotourists and the ecotourism experience would be similarly correlated with the learning outcome. Based on my own observations, I hypothesized that the amount and perceived efficacy of educational preparation prior to the experience would be positively correlated with the learning outcome, and would be one of the most influential factors.

Case Study

I gathered data from a population of ecotourists in Peru's upper Amazon Basin who were participating in one of a series of week-long environ-mental and cultural education workshops created and facilitated by a US-based non-profit organization, Children's Environmental Trust Foundation, International (CET). CET workshops are the culmination of a year of extracurricular academic study and preparation by groups of US middle and high school students (aged 12 to 18 years) and their adult chaperones. At their homes throughout the year prior to the actual immersion workshop, participants study tropical rainforest ecology, the culture of the local villagers they visit while in Peru, the concept of biodiversity, and the complex issues of deforestation and conservation.

CET workshops include intensive natural science educational experiences that immerse participants in the field. These activities are led by instructors and include ornithological, amphibian and entomological censuses, ecological transects, fishing expeditions and canopy ecology studies. In addition, workshops include several activities that aim to give participants a better understanding of the lives of people living in this remote area.

Finally, upon completion of the 1-week ecotourism experience, workshop participants are committed to one year of environmental or social advocacy either in their local community or on a broader scale. Advocacy projects of former participants include raising funds to build a new roof for a rural school in Peru, planting dune grass on the shores of Lake Michigan to mitigate beach erosion, creating a rainforest conservation colouring book for local kindergarten students and beginning a recycling programme in the local junior high school, among many others.

I obtained information from participants through the use of a survey instrument. Participants were surveyed at the close of the week-long workshop. A total of 326 people participated in the six 1-week workshops. Two hundred and sixty-seven people completed the survey. The response rate was 82%. Middle school students accounted for 54% of the sample, high school students 14%, and college students and adult chaperones 31%. The respondents comprised 58% females and 42% males. The most well-represented age categories among participants were 12 to 17 years and 36 to 45 years, accounting for 63% and 14%, respectively.

This was a biased sample of ecotourists, as respondents were all participants in a specific educational workshop, and approximately two-thirds were young people. As a part of the workshop, all respondents received the same type of preparatory information about tropical ecology and local cultures both before arriving at the workshop site and, more significantly, once they were on-site, at the workshops.

Survey Questions by Area

The survey was designed to measure the impact or meaning of the experience in four primary areas. The survey questions were divided into the four topic categories listed below.

1. Environment/enhanced ecological literacy:

- Better understanding of the tropical rainforest environment.
- Better understanding of the importance of global ecosystems.
- Meaningfulness of the experience educationally.

2. Culture:

- Meaningfulness of the experience for expanding cultural awareness.
- Development of a new appreciation for other cultures.

3. Personal growth:

- Meaningfulness of the experience for personal growth.
- Greater self-awareness.

4. Environmental advocacy and conservation:

- Meaningfulness of the experience for inspiring advocacy.
- Interest in learning about home environment.
- Willingness to make positive changes in one's own life as a result of the experience.
- Willingness to make positive changes in one's home community as a result of the experience.
- Intention to become involved in local organizations, clubs or environmental groups to become a better advocate of environmental issues locally and/or globally as a result of the experience.

In addition, the survey instrument included nine questions designed to gather demographic and characteristic data about each respondent.

Results

Answers to a few of the initial survey questions give us an idea about participants' motivations for travel and the amount and value of the preparatory work participants engaged in prior to travel. Survey respondents indicated that they participated in the workshop for a variety of reasons. Thirty-four per cent reported that visiting the tropical rainforest was their primary reason. Sixteen per cent reported that their primary reason was to learn about another culture. Studying tropical ecology was the primary reason for an additional 10% of respondents.

Just less than 70% of the survey respondents found the study and research they did prior to the workshop helpful (47%) or very helpful (22%). Twenty-two per cent of the respondents reported that it was somewhat helpful, while only 6% reported that it was not too or not at all helpful.

Survey respondents reported that they spent a varying amount of hours each month preparing for the workshop. The largest response category was 3–4 h per month (33%). Another 24% reported 1–2 h and 18% reported 5–6 h. An additional 11% reported more than 8 h.

The remaining questions relate to the four primary lesson areas described above.

Environment

The data show that the experience was effective at increasing participants' ecological literacy (Table 9.1). Ninety-three per cent of survey respondents

Table 9.1. Summary of responses to survey questions about environmental knowledge.

	Not at all meaningful (%)	Not very meaningful (%)	Somewhat meaningful (%)	Meaningful (%)	Very meaningful (%)	No response (%)
Educationally meaningful	0	1	9	45	45	0
	Strongly disagree (%)	Disagree (%)	Neutral (%)	Agree (%)	Strongly agree (%)	No response (%)
Better understanding of tropical rainforest	0	0	4	36	57	2
Better understanding of importance of global ecosystems	0	2	18	42	37	1

reported that they agreed (36%) or strongly agreed (57%) that the week-long experience was meaningful in increasing their understanding of the tropical rainforest. In addition, 42% agreed that they have a better understanding of the importance of all global ecosystems as a result of participating in the workshop. An additional 37% strongly agreed with this statement. Only 20% either disagreed or were neutral in their response. Finally, 45% of respondents indicated that the experience was very meaningful to them educationally, with an additional 45% reporting that it was meaningful.

Culture

According to the data, the experience had an even greater impact on participants' cultural literacy (Table 9.2). Seventy-two per cent of respondents reported that the experience was very meaningful in expanding their cultural awareness. An additional 24% responded that it was meaningful in this way. A resounding 75% of respondents reported that they strongly agreed that as a result of participating in the ecotourism experience, they have a new appreciation for other cultures. An additional 19% agreed. These both represent the highest responses for the 'very meaningful' and 'strongly agree' categories of this survey.

Personal growth

The survey responses indicate that the workshop experience was meaningful to participants' personal growth (Table 9.3). Just over half (52%) of the respondents reported that the workshop was very meaningful and nearly a third reported that it was meaningful. Only 3% reported that it was not very meaningful. When asked if they discovered new things about themselves as a result of participating in the workshop,

Table 9.2. Summary of responses to survey questions about culture.

	Not at all meaningful (%)	Not very meaningful (%)	Somewhat meaningful (%)	Meaningful (%)	Very meaningful (%)	No response (%)
Culturally meaningful	0	1	3	24	72	0
	Strongly disagree (%)	Disagree (%)	Neutral (%)	Agree (%)	Strongly agree (%)	No response (%)
New appreciation for other cultures	0	1	4	19	75	1

Table 9.3. Summary of responses to survey questions about personal growth.

	Not at all meaningful (%)	Not very meaningful (%)	Somewhat meaningful (%)	Meaningful (%)	Very meaningful (%)	No response (%)
Meaningful for personal growth	0	3	13	31	52	0
	Strongly disagree (%)	Disagree (%)	Neutral (%)	Agree (%)	Strongly agree	No response (%)
Discovery of new things about myself	4	6	18	29	40	2

40% of the respondents strongly agreed while about a third (29%) agreed. Four per cent strongly disagreed with this statement, which is the largest 'strongly disagree' response of this survey.

Conservation and advocacy

When asked how meaningful the workshop was for inspiring respondents' involvement in environmental advocacy, only 33% reported that it was very meaningful while 45% reported that it was meaningful. Eighteen per cent reported that it was somewhat meaningful and 4% reported lower responses.

Only 19% of the respondents strongly agreed that the workshop helped inspire them to learn more about their home environment while 43% agreed. Twenty-five per cent reported that they were ambivalent – they were midway between agreeing and disagreeing with the statement. Seven per cent disagreed and 4% strongly disagreed.

Nearly all respondents either agreed (29%) or strongly agreed (62%) that they will try to make positive changes in their lives as a result of participating in the workshop. The remaining 6% of respondents reported ambivalence – they neither agreed nor disagreed with the statement.

A significant majority of respondents reported that they agreed (46%) or strongly agreed (39%) that they will try to make positive changes in their communities at home as a result of their participation in the workshop.

The remaining 14% were either ambivalent or disagreed. Only about a quarter of respondents (22%) strongly agreed that they would get involved in environmental groups upon their return home as a result of participating in the workshop. About a third (35%) reported that they agreed with the statement while about 40% were either ambivalent or they disagreed (Table 9.4).

Correlation of Ecotourist and Ecotourism Experience Characteristics with Meaningful Learning

I ran a series of multiple regression analyses using the survey questions highlighted above. I used the same independent variables for each regression model. These included: specific group the respondent travelled with; reason respondent reported for travelling; amount of time spent on workshop preparation; how helpful the respondent found the educational preparation prior to the workshop; respondents' satisfaction with his/her own Spanish language preparation; gender; age; and level of education completed. In addition, I added data from respondents who attended a similar CET workshop in Costa Rica and who completed the same survey. I wanted to see if there was a correlation between any of the variables and the specific workshop each respondent attended.

I chose a series of four 'meaningfulness' questions for the dependent variables. Each question asked respondents to rate the workshop on a scale from 1 to 5 to indicate the meaningfulness of the experience in each of the primary learning areas described above.

The results are summarized in Table 9.5.

Table 9.4. Summary of responses to survey questions about environmental advocacy/conservation.

	Not at all meaningful (%)	Not very meaningful (%)	Somewhat meaningful (%)	Meaningful (%)	Very meaningful (%)	No response (%)
Meaningful for inspiring advocacy	1	3	18	45	33	1
	Strongly disagree (%)	Disagree (%)	Neutral (%)	Agree (%)	Strongly agree (%)	No response (%)
Learn about home environment	4	7	25	43	19	1
Positive changes in my own life	0	0	6	29	62	2
Positive changes in community	1	1	12	46	39	1
Get involved in local environmental organizations	3	10	27	35	22	2

Table 9.5. Results of multiple regression analyses.

Variable	Education	Cultural awareness	Personal growth	Advocacy
Workshop (1=Costa Rica)	−0.1356	−0.4948*	−0.1023	0.12311
Project	−0.0229	−0.0183	−0.0011	0.00314
Reason for travel	4.41×10^{-5}	0.00562	0.03497	0.03720
Time	0.04253	0.03225	−0.0381	0.04964
Ed prep helpful	0.20234*	0.14025*	0.26998*	0.22064*
Spanish	0.02344	0.04525	0.21772*	0.04751
Age	−0.0319	−0.0573	−0.0144	0.02582
Gender (1=male)	−0.0163	−0.1949*	−0.2156*	−0.2641*
Education	0.0033	0.04209	−0.0260	−0.0502
R^2	0.0797	0.11487	0.0879	0.0879
F	3.6601	4.9842	3.9577	3.9601
P	0.0001	1.08×10^{-6}	4.37×10^{-5}	4.33×10^{-5}

*$P<0.05$.

A multiple regression analysis of the independent variables described above versus the responses to the question about the educational value of the workshop, indicated that this response was positively correlated with how helpful the respondents found the preparatory study prior to the workshop. Although the regression results indicate that this model does not explain much of the variance of this variable (adjusted $R^2=0.0797$), the overall model is significant ($F=3.6601$; $P=0.0001$).

According to a multiple regression analysis of the same independent variables versus the cultural variable, female participants on the Peru workshop (rather than the Costa Rica workshop) who also reported that they found the research and study prior to the workshop helpful were more likely to report that the workshop was meaningful in expanding their cultural awareness. Once again, the amount of variance in this factor explained by this model is not very high (adjusted $R^2=0.11487$), but the overall model is significant ($F=4.9842$; $P<0.0001$).

The third regression model indicated that females who reported that the prior study and research was helpful and that they were satisfied with their amount of Spanish preparation were positively correlated with reported meaningfulness of the workshop for respondents' personal growth. The amount of variance explained by this model is low (adjusted $R^2=0.0879$) and the overall model is significant ($F=3.9577$; $P<0.0001$).

Finally, the fourth regression analysis on the question of advocacy also indicated that females who reported that the prior study and research was helpful were positively correlated with reported meaningfulness of the workshop in terms of inspiring respondents' involvement with environmental advocacy. Again, the amount of variance described by this model is low (adjusted $R^2=0.0879$) although the model is significant ($F=3.9601$; $P<0.0001$).

Power of Cultural Experiences

Overall, the results show that the ecotourists I surveyed were positively impacted in each of the four target learning areas. However, the survey results indicate that the cultural lessons of the experience are apparently the most meaningful. The results show that nearly 100% of the survey respondents found the experience meaningful or very meaningful in expanding their cultural awareness. Participants responded even more strongly to a question about their appreciation of another culture. Three-quarters of the respondents strongly agreed that they had gained this appreciation as a result of the ecotourism experience. This represents the highest response to any question of the survey. This high response to the cultural element of the workshop is not unexpected. Although natural science activities are a large focus of the ecotourism experience, participants also have numerous opportunities for cultural interaction. I have personally observed that ecotourists of all ages and backgrounds become emotionally moved by their visits to local communities and by the human connections they form with local school children, artisans, local guides and lodge employees.

It is interesting to note that the responsible exposure to and interaction with local community members had the strongest immediate impact on the ecotourists I surveyed, even though for most respondents this was not their primary motivation to participate in the workshop. When asked the primary reason they chose to participate in the workshop, the largest percentage of respondents (34%) indicated that they were simply interested in visiting the tropical rainforest. The more specific category, 'I wanted to learn about another culture', was not nearly as well represented (16%). This indicates that the majority of ecotourists surveyed may not have been anticipating the impact of the cultural interaction they experienced. Therefore, the impact may be even more significant because it was unexpected.

It follows that if conservation education is a goal of ecotourism, a culturally oriented conservation message would perhaps be most motivational to this audience. In fact, I have found that the most attractive advocacy projects for participants in this particular set of workshops tend to involve helping people in some capacity to support conservation directly or indirectly. Examples include supporting school children in rural communities, particularly with educational supplies and initiatives, supporting street kids in urban areas, or supporting micro enterprise initiatives among rural community members. This may be a result of personal human ties formed during the experience and because the results of these projects are generally visible and measurable.

Advocacy and Conservation

Although, according to the data, the advocacy and conservation lessons and inspiration appear to have had the lowest immediate impact of the four lesson areas, the responses are still significant. Respondents indicated through their responses to a series of questions that the majority anticipated they would make changes in their lives at home as a result of their participation in the workshop. The most significant positive response in this series of questions involved the most ambiguous of all of the questions. Nearly all respondents either agreed or strongly agreed that they would make positive changes in their lives as a result of participating in the workshop. Fewer respondents reported they agreed or strongly agreed that they would make positive changes in their communities at home as a result of their participation. When asked if they would become involved with environmental groups upon their return home, an even lower percentage agreed or strongly agreed. This last question was the most specific of the three and possibly the hardest for participants to commit to.

It is logical that the lowest percentage of respondents felt they could commit to taking a specific step such as joining an environmental organization, while the greatest percentage of respondents felt they could commit to making general positive changes in their lives. This could include any number of things from working to achieve better grades, to recycling at home, to becoming active in an environmental group, to watching less television, to treating a sibling more respectfully. This question was deliberately left open. It is much easier for respondents to say they will do something 'in the moment' at the workshop itself than to actually take those steps to do what they intended.

If nothing else, it is valuable to note that nearly all respondents reported that the experience inspired them to make positive changes in some way in the future. This lends strong support to the idea that an ecotourism experience can inspire action particularly to support conservation. The challenge is to channel that inspiration. In my recent work with Global Explorers, a non-profit organization dedicated to youth international immersion, we have seen that successful channelling of that inspiration relies on three things: (i) a positive experience with service both before and during the trip; (ii) taking time on the trip to discuss in detail specific ways that participants could follow-up when returning home; and (iii) reminding participants upon their return of the commitments they made abroad.

One important issue to keep in mind is that these data reflect responses at the close of an ecotourism experience before the experience had been fully processed. It would be valuable to measure responses to the same questions well after the experience was completed, to determine how it influenced respondents and what action they actually took.

Value of Preparation

Unfortunately, the regression analysis did not yield strong results; however, it is instructive to note that the one significant variable that is consistent in each model is the perceived helpfulness of the workshop preparation. The models show that this variable is positively correlated with the meaningfulness of the workshop in all four lesson areas. This indicates that ecotourists could potentially gain more from an ecotourism experience if they received some form of preparatory information about the natural history and cultures of the areas they will be visiting. Providing reading lists, a booklet with information specifically prepared for ecotourists visiting a particular area, short preparatory lectures on-site or even educational activities sent to ecotourists prior to the experience may help enhance the educational value of the experience. In addition, I have observed that ecotourists may gain more from the experience if they are educated about ecotourism in general and what it means to be a responsible ecotourist.

Conclusion

While the present case study was conducted with a small segment of the ecotourist population, the lessons may potentially be applied to a more general population of ecotourists. The data indicate that the cultural element of the ecotourism experience has the greatest impact on ecotourists, presumably for the emotional response elicited by responsible cross-cultural interactions. The data also suggest that the ecotourism experience is successful at inspiring advocacy among participants, potentially for conservation-oriented issues. However, a follow-up study would be necessary to distinguish between intention and action. Finally, the results of this study indicate that helping ecotourists prepare educationally for the experience serves to enhance their learning in all areas. This can be achieved in a number of ways, including providing a reading list, informational booklets and introductory talks on-site prior to activities.

It is a primary goal of ecotourism to educate ecotourists, in part to inspire them to support conservation. In the words of Baba Dioum, a Senegalese conservationist:

> In the end, we will conserve only what we love. We will love only what we understand. We will understand only what we are taught.

People committed to the business of ecotourism have an unparalleled opportunity and a responsibility to help ecotourists 'understand' in order to fully achieve the goals of ecotourism.

References

Cornell, J. (1979) *Sharing Nature with Children.* Dawn Publications, Nevada City, California.

Goodwin, H. (1996) In pursuit of ecotourism. *Biodiversity and Conservation* 5, 277–291.

Gutierrez de White, T. and Jacobson, S.K. (1994) Evaluating conservation programs at a South America zoo. *Journal of Environmental Education* 25, 18–22.

Hall, C. (1992) Ecotourism/the global classroom. Conference Report. *Journal of Travel & Tourism Marketing* 1, 79–82.

Kimmel, J. (1999) Ecotourism as environmental learning. *Journal of Environmental Education* 30, 40–44.

Miles, J. (1991) Viewpoint: teaching in wilderness. *Journal of Environmental Education* 22, 5–9.

Rickinson, M. (2001) Learners and learning in environmental education: a critical review of the evidence. *Environmental Education Research* 7, 207–321.

Part VI

Outcomes for Communities

_____

10 Tourism, Indigenous Peoples and Conservation in the Ecuadorian Amazon

A. RODRÍGUEZ

Green Consulting, Quito, Ecuador

Introduction

According to the United Nations Food and Agriculture Organization (FAO, 2007), 93,900 km² of forest were cleared per annum during the past 10 years, with annual rates of forest loss positive for all continents with tropical forests. Africa and Latin America and the Caribbean are currently the regions with the highest losses. Africa, which accounts for about 16% of the total global forest area, lost over 9% of its forests between 1990 and 2005. Latin America and the Caribbean, with over 47% of the world's forests, saw an increase in the annual net loss between 2000 and 2005 from 0.46% to 0.51% (FAO, 2007). Specific locations in Latin America showed annual deforestation rates much higher than the continental rates, such as the Western Amazon (Colombia, Ecuador and Peru) at 0.65% each year between 1986 and 1999. Within South America, Ecuador had the highest deforestation rate between 1990 and 2000, averaging 1.2% per annum (FAO, 2001). The FAO estimated overall deforestation in Ecuador to be 2380 km²/year from 1980 to 1990 and 1370 km²/year from 1990 to 2000, especially in the north-eastern Amazonian region.

In the Amazon, the causes of deforestation are linked to activities such as timber exploitation, agriculture and cattle farming; and indirectly linked to oil exploitation, which has allowed for the establishment of settlements along opened access routes (Mena *et al.*, 2006), while tourism in the Amazon increased rapidly in the decade of the 1980s (Drumm, 1991). At the start, tourism was seen as a low-impact economic activity, which could possibly replace other activities associated with deforestation. Twenty years later, opinions are divided on the impact tourism has had on the Amazon (Kiss, 2004).

Given the relative lack of markets among Amazon communities to commercialize agricultural products, such as cocoa, groundnuts or annatto, economic opportunities are limited. What, then, are the alternatives? Development agencies, non-profit organizations and indigenous villages point to tourism as one of the most viable options. If tourism is part of the solution, what is the real impact of tourism on deforestation and poverty?

Tourism in the Amazon seems to have a future, and interest in the demand for nature products continues to be high. For example, tourists report that one of the main reasons to travel to Ecuador is to see nature and wildlife, local cultures and to engage in photography and low-risk adventure tourism, all of which coincide with the offer of community-based tourism in the Amazon (Delgado *et al.*, 2007). In a study carried out by Green Consulting for the CAIMAN ('Conservation in Managed Indigenous Areas') project (Rodríguez and Epler Wood, 2003), 12 leading North American nature tourism companies were interviewed. All had experience working with lodges in the Amazon. Three community-based ecotourism companies were especially popular: Kapawi in Ecuador, Posada Amazonas in Peru and Chalalán in Bolivia. Of the 12 companies interviewed, 75% had used one or more of these three accommodations; according to the operators, clients gave positive feedback in the majority of cases.

Limitations of Community-based Ecotourism in the Amazon

Enterprises in the Amazon managed by indigenous communities have not always been successful (Wray, 1995). A fundamental challenge appears to be related to the differences between market economies and traditional economies based on the so-called 'gift economy'. Like the market economy, a gift economy is based on the exchange of goods. However, the essence of the gift economy is to maintain the flow of goods between giver and receiver in a cycle of reciprocation (Gauss, 1990). By generating a perpetual exchange in this way, the gift economy unifies members of a community (Wray, 1995). That is, through reciprocity, a gift economy can help reconcile fundamental tensions between individual desires and needs of the society as a whole. In a gift economy, quality of life is measured neither in terms of money nor the accumulation of tangible goods. Instead, other indicators, such as access to education, time with the family, health, and access to natural resources, determine good quality of life.

Some of the core differences between these economies are set out in Table 10.1.

The Huao Lodge

The Huao Lodge is a tourism operation based in Huaorani indigenous territory in the Ecuadorian Amazon. The lodge offers comfortable facilities at accessible prices with the opportunity to carry out cultural and nature tourism with the involvement of local communities. The lodge's development took several years owing to the need to establish

Table 10.1. Comparison between the gift economy and the market economy.

Gift economy	Market economy
Non-monetary	Monetary
Favours social organization	Favours individualism
Focused on well-being of community	Focused on well-being of individual
Tends to strengthen social cohesion	Tends to weaken social cohesion
Unlimited access to resources	Limited access to resources
Patrimony is a common resource	Patrimony is exploited for personal benefit
Promotes dispersed settlements	Promotes nuclear settlements
Accumulation of wealth is penalized	Accumulation of wealth is rewarded

conditions for ecotourism, organize the communities involved, establish legal procedures, train personnel and promote the destination itself. All research and procedures involved in the implementation of the lodge were carried out in conjunction with the Huaorani communities and Tropic Journeys in Nature, a private enterprise, and mainly funded by Proyecto CAIMAN (a USAID initiative).

Despite the fact that the average monthly income of a Huaorani family was just US$31.35 in 2004, 100% of Huaorani families agreed that their lifestyle was of high quality – in Ecuador the minimum wage in the private sector was US$170 for the year in question (Rodríguez, 2004). Nevertheless, monetary income alone cannot be considered an indicator of poverty or restricted quality of life. Factors such as self-subsistence, small populations in large territories, access to housing and non-traditional education, and a gift economy make it inappropriate to define the Huaorani communities as impoverished. Tourism, the sale of handicrafts and temporal work are the main sources of monetary income for the Huaorani. These activities are occasional and are not perceived by the Huaorani as critical to achieve a good quality of life (Rodríguez, 2004). For the Huaorani, the five top factors determining quality of life are (in order of importance): (i) education for children; (ii) time spent with family; (iii) health; (iv) living in a well-preserved forest; and (v) food.

Amazon communities are becoming increasingly integrated within the market economy as they strive to fulfil new needs, including school materials for children, western clothing and air transport and medicines in case of an emergency. However, such connections with the market economy can be very disruptive within communities, creating conflicts, changes in settlements and the dissolution of community activities, like reciprocal work exchanges. Paradoxically, development projects in the Amazon that attempt to improve quality of life by integrating communities with the market economy affect the very foundations of the communities by promoting a type of economy that does not adapt to local conditions. This apparently irreconcilable clash of economies reduces the possibility of success in ecotourism projects in the Amazon.

If the duality between a market economy and gift economy is a factor affecting ecotourism's success among indigenous communities in the

Amazon, another factor of equal importance is the difference between the principles governing a community and those that govern a business.

In a community there are a series of norms in place to avoid the verticality of society. For example, the so-called *priostes* (those chosen to pay for a big party, celebration or other important event) are generally those who have accumulated too much economic power within a community. The party constitutes a mechanism to preclude the accumulation of wealth. In many cases, the *priostes* can end up bankrupt. The same occurs with individuals who have acquired too much success and therefore stand out in the community. There are mechanisms in place, formal or informal, to penalize those who are most successful. These two examples show just some of the many differences between the community and the business world. In the business world, those who accumulate wealth are classified as successful; and consequently those who are successful are rewarded. Tendencies of community and business are compared in Table 10.2.

The Kapawi Ecolodge

The Achuar Indians live in the south-eastern region of Ecuador. Their territory encompasses 787,000 ha of well-preserved tropical rainforest, and they have a population of approximately 6000 inhabitants in 64 communities. In 1995, the Achuar built the Kapawi Ecolodge in collaboration with the tourism company CANODROS, S.A. as part of a conservation and development strategy in the area. Kapawi has a capacity for 38 guests and has won much international acclaim and several international prizes (Stronza, 2003).

In spite of its success, the differences between the so-called 'community world' and the business world have caused conflicts within the Achuar communities and between the communities and the private enterprise. For example, the lodge's employees who are too successful or have accumulated

Table 10.2. Comparison between community and business tendencies.

Community-based enterprise	Privately owned business
Many community members want employment, high rotation	Few employees, multi-tasked, low rotation
Immediate distribution of profits	Profits at end of fiscal year
Non-hierarchical structure (community members do not accept a boss)	Hierarchical structure
Paid activities (dances, musical shows) translated into variable costs	Reduction in variable costs
Sale of products (handicrafts, food) at high prices in benefit of the community	Purchasing of products (handicrafts, food) at low prices in order to increase profit margins
Successful people sanctioned	Successful people rewarded
Lodge belongs to everyone and everyone has equal rights	Lodge belongs to the company and everyone must abide by the rules
Competitiveness looked upon unfavourably	Competitiveness looked upon favourably

too much money are 'punished' and forced to return to their communities. This has caused problems as far as training personnel is concerned, given that as soon as the Achuar workers begin to acquire skills (especially those who need to learn English), they resign and return to their communities. On the other hand, the lack of interest on behalf of the Achuar to assume more complex and demanding posts, partly due to the frustration of being forced to return to their communities, along with the Achuar employees' rejection of having to answer to an Achuar 'boss', has resulted in an inability to assume full management of the Kapawi lodge.

The difference in principles between the community and the private enterprise can be so conflicting that, on occasions, the community prefers to destroy the enterprise, despite the fact it belongs to them, rather than go against the fundamental foundations of the community. For example, in 2005, San Miguel de Bala, a community lodge on the borders of the Madidi National Park in Bolivia, experienced financial problems. One of the problems was due to the inclusion of dance shows among its activities wherein the earnings of the several members of the community who participated surpassed the lodge's income. However, in a business planning workshop, the community stated that it would prefer to see the business go bankrupt before taking opportunities away from community members (Rodríguez, 2005a). In other cases, such as La Chonta in Amboró National Park in Bolivia, community members distributed earnings immediately in order to benefit members of the community instead of distributing profits at the end of the fiscal year. This left the lodge without a cash flow, and no money to reinvest (Rodríguez, 2005b).

These differences have resulted in misunderstandings, tensions and conflicts between private enterprises (or external organizations, including non-governmental organizations (NGOs)) and indigenous communities, in some cases leading to the dissolution of contracts or partnerships. The partnership for the Napo Wildlife Center in Yasuni National Park with the Kichwa Añangu Indians ended in 2007, and Kapawi ended prematurely in 2008.

Other limitations of community-based ecotourism in the Amazon include the following:

1. An overdose of enthusiasm, with the belief that tourism is the answer to all of the community's problems.
2. Lack of knowledge about how the tourism system functions and the phases of development, a problem that ends in a badly planned product. This is critical, given that NGOs and donors have focused on the physical construction of lodges without analysing the necessities of demand, training in services, accounting systems or marketing.
3. Incapacity to market a product due to a lack of knowledge of the tourism market, which can be extremely complex.
4. High transportation costs.
5. Difficulty in competing – in economic terms for the community – with short-term non-sustainable activities (oil, logging, etc.).

Tourism, Community Welfare and Incentives for Conservation

Despite the social and economic challenges described above, ecotourism nevertheless represents a relatively sustainable and profitable activity for Amazon communities. So far, ecotourism has helped a number of indigenous groups in Ecuador to defend their resources. Several ecotourism cases have shown that maintaining intact flora, fauna and cultural traditions affords people greater chances in the long run to generate income and sustain themselves. As Randy Borman (Chapter 2, this volume) has noted, 'At Zabalo [a Cofan community], the primary incentive to curtail macaw hunting came from the demonstrable fact that a macaw viewed by a tourist was worth more money than a macaw in the pot for the table' (see also Borman, 2001). In Kapawi as well, the Achuar have made use of their hunting skills to become world-class ornithologists and their income has increased. In the Napo Wildlife Center, the Quichua Añangu community decided to cease involvement in large-scale extractive industries, like oil, and take a risk on the conservation of the forest. They live directly off earnings generated by tourism activities. The environment has benefited, and the profits obtained by the lodge are invested in health and education for the community (Napo Wildlife Center, 2007).

Four Huaorani communities residing on the riverbanks of the Shiripuno, owners of the Huao Lodge, have blocked the entry of oil and timber companies, a measure other Huaorani communities have been unable to achieve. They depend on hunting for their subsistence and have been involved in monitoring to such an extent that they are able to identify species most hunted, species with declining populations and those of greatest importance for tourism (Rodríguez, 2004). The Huaorani recognize that certain species must be conserved and that some have greater value as tourism attractions than as game. The motives for conserving certain species (responses from 14 families) are as follows (in order of importance): (i) due to their importance as a tourist attraction ($n=8$); (ii) for future generations ($n=3$); (iii) to prevent extinction ($n=2$); and (iv) to avoid entering into conflict with tourism ($n=1$).

In hunting practices, there is a direct relationship between tourism and the conservation of native species. For instance, the Amazon tapir is not frequently hunted; neither does it appear – to the Huaorani – to be a species whose population is declining. Nevertheless, the Huaorani consider it a species that should be conserved because it is a preferred attraction for tourists, as is the White-throated toucan. On the other hand, deer and the Grey-winged trumpeter, both species that are frequently hunted, are not given such high importance by the Huaorani for conservation. These species are not considered attractions as they are nocturnal and rarely seen by tourists.

From 1996 to 2005, tourism operations generated US$1,225,724 in direct or indirect contributions to the local communities and the NAE, the Achuar Nationality of Ecuador (CANODROS, 2007). These earnings have served as an important incentive to block the entry of oil companies in Achuar territory. So far the Achuar have been categorical in rejecting the use of their territory for the purposes of high-impact extraction activities. Also with an eye to conservation, the Kapawi Ecolodge is equipped with systems that help to minimize environmental impact (e.g. solar energy, sewage treatment systems and low-emission engines). A strict social code has been established also to minimize negative impacts of host–guest interactions. These include prohibitions on photography in the communities, giving money or gifts to children, or making visits without prior consent of the Achuar.

Chalalán Ecolodge in the Bolivian Amazon has improved local incomes significantly by providing rotational employment opportunities for some 60 people (Stronza, 2006), while providing an alternative to cattle ranching and timber. It has also helped to stem the migration of young people to distant cities. The scheme has strengthened community organization and encouraged villagers to protect an area which is outstanding for its scenic beauty and wildlife (Chalalán Ecolodge, 2007).

Conclusions

The experiences of several indigenous communities in the Ecuadorian Amazon have shown that economic development options are limited. Outside extractive activities or extensive agroindustries, like soybeans, cattle ranching and palm oil, ecotourism is one of the more promising alternatives. Although earnings from ecotourism may seem to outsiders as minimal, many indigenous families identify them as substantial. For instance, a Huaorani family receiving an additional US$30/month from tourism can increase monthly income by 100%.

Concern over introducing the market economy to indigenous communities in spite of the damaging effects it may produce has been characterized by a female Huaorani citizen: 'The truth is that we don't need money; we are content with our lives; we only worry about our children's health and education'. Another woman commented: 'Here children die because there are no medicines, no nurses and because we don't have money should an emergency arise'. Such economic changes may also be important incentives for conservation, as tourism becomes a kind of compensation for environmental services maintained by Amazon communities.

To be effective and supportive of conservation, community-based ecotourism must also be profitable to a substantial sector of the local population. Achieving profitability requires effective marketing that will attract clients and impeccable service that will maintain the accounts. Support from the private sector, NGOs and government is fundamental to the success of community-based initiatives in the Amazon. Finally, despite overenthusiastic declarations, community-based ecotourism cannot be the answer to conservation per se. As the Cofan have acknowledged: 'Unless we can guarantee the long-term stability of the environment on a macro level, there is little use in trying to create a conservation ethic at our community level' (Borman, 2001).

References

Borman, R. (2001) Survival in a Hostile World: Culture Change and Missionary Influence among the Cofan People of Ecuador, 1954–1994. http://www.cofan.org/survival.htm (accessed September 2007).

CANODROS (2007) *Plan de transferencia Kapawi*. CANODROS S.A./Achuar Nationality of Ecuador/Fundación Pachamama, Quito.

Chalalán Ecolodge (2007) Chalalán Ecolodge homepage. http://www.chalalan.com (accessed September 2007).

Delgado, E., Rodríguez, A. and Izurieta, J. (2007) *Punta del Faro, Estudio de Factibilidad para la Operación Turística*. Programa de Manejo de Recursos Costeros (PMRC), Quito.

Drumm, A. (1991) *An Integrated Impact Assessment of Nature Tourism in Ecuador's Amazon Region*. School of Environmental Sciences, University of Greenwich, Quito.

FAO (2001) Global forest resource assessment. Food and Agriculture Organization of the United Nations, Rome; available at http://www.fao.org/forestry/site/28679/en/ (accessed March 2008).

FAO (2007) FAO Deforestation Facts and Figures. Food and Agriculture Organization of the United Nations, Rome; available at http://www.fao.org/forestry/site/28679/en/ (accessed March 2008).

Gauss, M. (1990) *The Gift, Forms and Functions of Exchange in Archaic Societies*. W.W. Norton, New York.

Kiss, A. (2004) Is community-based ecotourism a good use of biodiversity conservation funds? *Trends in Ecology and Evolution* 19, 231–237.

Mena, C., Bilsborrow, R. and McClain, M (2006) Socioeconomic drivers of deforestation in the northern Ecuadorian Amazon. *Environmental Management* 37, 802–815.

Napo Wildlife Center (2007) Napo Wildlife Center homepage. http://www.napowildlifecenter.com (accessed September 2007).

Rodríguez, A. (2004) *Establecimiento de Condiciones para una Operación Ecoturística de Base Comunitaria en la Comunidad Huaorani de Quehueri-ono, Proyecto CAIMAN*. Unidad de Implementación del Programa de Desarrollo de la Amazonía Norte (CONFENIAE-BID-UDENOR), Quito.

Rodríguez, A. (2005a) *Plan de Negocios y Mercadeo para el Albergue San Miguel de Bala*. Conservación Internacional and PNUD, Quito, La Paz.

Rodríguez, A. (2005b) *Planificación Empresarial para el Ecoturismo Comunitario en la Región del Parque Nacional Amboró: Resultados y Recomendaciones*.The Nature Conservancy, Quito.

Rodríguez, A. and Epler Wood, M. (2003) *Identificación de Oportunidades para el Desarrollo de Productos Ecoturísticos en Territorios Awá y Huaorani. Proyecto CAIMAN*. Chemonics Internacional/US Agency for International Development, Quito.

Stronza, A. (2003) *The Kapawi Indigenous–Corporate Partnership for Ecotourism in Ecuador*. Case Number SI-42. Stanford Graduate School of Business, Stanford, California.

Stronza, A. (2005) *Trueque Amazónico: Lessons in Community-based Ecotourism*. Critical Ecosystem Partnership Fund, Washington, DC.

Stronza, A. (2006) *See the Amazon through Our Eyes: History of the Chalalán Ecolodge*. Conservation International, Washington, DC.

Wray, N. (1995) Economía indígena e integración al mercado: el caso de los Quichua del Alto Napo, Ecuador. In: Smith, R.C. and Wray, N. (eds) *Amazonía: Economía Indígena y Mercado Los Desafíos del Desarrollo*. COICA, Lima and OXFAM América, Quito.

11 Ecotourism Equations: Do Economic Benefits Equal Conservation?

F. DE VASCONCELLOS PÊGAS AND A. STRONZA

Department of Recreation, Park and Tourism Sciences, Texas A&M University, College Station, Texas, USA

Introduction

Advocates of ecotourism often invoke a 'win–win–win' message of ecotourism's potential for people, profits and the planet. Since the late 1980s, global environmental organizations and multilateral development agencies have invested heavily in ecotourism with the hope that it can meet people's needs while also protecting the environment. Sometimes the goals have been mutually reinforcing and, in places, ecotourism has succeeded at building social and economic foundations for conservation (Alexander, 2000). In other places, ecotourism has failed to deliver benefits either for people and or the environment (Belsky, 1999). In yet other cases, ecotourism has benefited people, but caused direct damage to species and ecosystems (Isaacs, 2000). Success and failure in ecotourism have varied over time as well. Short-term economic gains in some places have led to degradation of resources over time (Barrett *et al.*, 2001). An overriding challenge for conservationists is to find the conditions under which ecotourism works for people and environment, both now and into the future.

At the core of many ecotourism projects is a social and economic paradigm that functions, at least in the aspirations of project managers, as something like an equation (Malek-Zadeh, 1996). The equation posits that ecotourism (E), when multiplied by economic benefits (B) and divided equitably among local residents (R), equals conservation (C): E (B/R)=C. Calculating this 'equation' in real life often entails calculating 'E' as numbers of tourists, rooms occupied, vacation days or expenditures, and measuring 'B' as total revenues, number of jobs created or volume of local commerce generated. The 'C' for conservation seldom gets measured in the same way by researchers across sites, although often it is summarized as a 'conservation ethic', expressed in reported attitudes or values, or as a set of behaviours, such as the limiting of harvest rates or the establishment of a reserve or protected area (Agrawal and Redford, 2006).

An extension of the paradigm that economic benefits from ecotourism lead to conservation is the idea that more ecotourism can lead to more economic benefits for locals and thus more conservation; or, conversely, that the cessation of ecotourism will lead to the decline of benefits and thus the demise of resources that could have otherwise been conserved. The mechanism linking ecotourism with conservation in this paradigm is the creation of economic incentives from employment and income. Essentially, this is the idea of market-based conservation (Barrett and Arcese, 1995; Salafsky et al., 2001).

An alternative view of ecotourism and conservation pays explicit attention to social and political variables. As some scholars have found, empowerment and the devolution of control over management and ownership of ecotourism operations can be critical for forging real linkages between ecotourism and conservation (see Durham, Chapter 5, this volume). Here an 'equation' to capture this view might be: $E\ (B/R)+P=C$, where 'P' is local participation in decision making. In this case, the mechanism linking ecotourism with conservation is still economic incentive (as in the first equation), but it is also increased by local capacity among local residents. This is the idea of conservation through empowerment and strengthened local institutions (Pretty and Ward, 2001). In this scenario, local residents who gain skills and experience managing ecotourism also gain the capacity to manage other communal resources collectively – both for the benefit of conservation and for their own livelihoods.

The ecotourism literature is rife with illustrations of the first paradigm, but relatively scant of the second. For example, in the Brazilian Amazon, Wallace and Pierce (1996) found that ecotourism improved local economies minimally via revenues and the generation of some employment, although 80% of the labour force came from outside communities and most positions were low-paid and short-term. Residents were not involved in ownership or management of the ecotourism operation. Mbaiwa (2004) found that tourism in community-based natural resource management projects of Botswana generated income and employment for traditional peoples in the Okavango Delta, but also enhanced people's sense of pride and self-worth, and led to various community development initiatives. In that case, people engaged actively in managing ecotourism, a process that has strengthened their local institutions and collective ability to manage resources.

In this chapter, we compare outcomes of the two 'equations' (or conservation paradigms) with a descriptive analysis of selected case studies in ecotourism. The chapter begins by reviewing a (non-exhaustive) set of case studies that illustrate the first equation. Again, that equation predicts conservation as an outcome primarily of economic benefits from ecotourism. Second, we turn to the alternative paradigm, which posits that conservation results when economic benefits from ecotourism are combined with the institution-building benefits of community participation. We then provide a brief case study of ecotourism and sea turtle protection in Praia do Forte,

Brazil. In that case, local residents have received economic benefits – employment and income – from ecotourism, but have not participated in management. This is an example of the first equation. We argue with this case that economic benefits are important for short-term conservation goals of ecotourism, but that greater involvement of the community in conservation efforts may help sustain conservation success over time.

In some ways, what we argue is not new. In fact, an early definition of ecotourism, by Tensie Whelan (1991) is as follows:

> Ecotourism, done well, can be a sustainable and relatively simple alternative. It promises employment and income to local communities... while allowing the continued existence of the natural resource base... It can empower local communities, giving them a sense of pride in their natural resources and control over their communities' development. (Cited in Campbell, 2002, p. 302.)

Though empowerment and community participation in ecotourism appear in definitions and principles of ecotourism, scholars seldom measure these social facets empirically or in direct relation to conservation. What they do measure more often are economic benefits. The social changes tend to appear as just that, somehow less connected with conservation decisions and behaviours. Yet social facets of ecotourism – particularly the degree to which and how local residents participate in ecotourism – alter many aspects of community life in host destinations that ultimately affect conservation. The changes in people's abilities and inclinations to work together are especially relevant to their potential for collective action for resource management. Thus, we argue for the need to evaluate connections not just between economics and conservation, but also between social empowerment and conservation.

The First Equation: Economic Incentives as Tools for Conservation

The expectation that ecotourism can protect biodiversity, improve local welfare and generate sustainable development is prevalent among conservationists (Kruger, 2005; Agrawal and Redford, 2006). Proponents tout economic benefits from ecotourism as especially important to achieving these interlocking goals. Income and employment opportunities, in particular, often appear in case studies as indicators of successful ecotourism projects (Bookbinder *et al.*, 1998; Gössling, 1999; Wunder, 1999). Such factors act as potential incentives for local residents to shift out of other activities that are relatively detrimental to local natural resources, such as large-scale agriculture, logging and hunting (Langholz, 1999). In Papua New Guinea, for example, the environmental non-governmental organization (NGO) Conservation International has promoted birdwatching ecotourism to create financial incentives for residents of the community of Maimafu to cease hunting of some bird species (West, 2006). In Ecuador, income and employment from ecotourism activities in the Cuyabeno Wildlife Reserve were also important incentives for the community to support conservation efforts (Wunder, 1999). In Costa Rica, ecotourism became a primary source of income to many families near Tortuguero National Park where visitors pay to see sea turtles nesting on the beaches. Troëng and Drews (2004) found that ecotourism with sea turtles generated important economic alternatives for local residents, especially during the off-peak, regular tourism season. The authors also concluded that economic benefits from such activities were bringing critical incentives for protecting sea turtles.

Yet, there are limitations to this first equation between ecotourism and conservation. Some ecotourism projects have not generated economic benefits, or at least not enough, to build incentives for conservation among host communities (Jacobson and Robles, 1992). Many ecotourism enterprises create relatively few jobs relative to the number of local residents (Fiallo and Jacobson, 1995; Lindberg et al., 1996). In Mexico, employment opportunities from the Monarch Butterfly Reserve fell short of achieving the expected economic outcomes, and logging activities continued unabated in the region (Barkin, 2003). Lindberg and colleagues (1996) reported similar results in Belize, where tourism activities failed to generate financial support for protected area management. Belsky (1999) found that sporadic ecotourism in Gales Point Manatee, Belize, actually decreased local livelihood security and triggered a 'violent backlash against conservation' (p. 662).

Even when provided, economic benefits may not be sufficient to discourage local people from engaging in activities that are detrimental to local resources. In Mexico, for example, Young (1999) found that economic revenues from grey whale watching in Laguna San Ignacio and Bahia Magdalena did not reduce extractive pressures on inshore fisheries. External events can also jeopardize the fate of natural resources that local residents may be trying to manage through ecotourism. In Mexico, national policies affecting agriculture and land tenure led to the degradation of forests and habitats the locals were trying to protect in the Monarch Butterfly Reserve (Barkin, 2003).

The ecotourism equation that pays attention primarily to economic change may overlook the ways in which ecotourism can profoundly alter social dynamics within host communities (Zografos and Oglethorpe, 2004). In Papua New Guinea, West (2006) found that tourism brought more work for women in the village of Maimafu. The women became responsible not only for family chores, but also for producing handicraft items to sell to tourists. Similarly, Gentry (2006) showed that Belizean women involved in the tourism industry experienced especially high levels of stress and illness, problems associated with double workday responsibilities. In Drake Bay, Costa Rica, Stem et al. (2003) found ecotourism associated with communal and familial disintegration, and increased use of alcohol and drugs. Weinberg et al. (2002) reported similar problems stemming from ecotourism in communities near Monteverde, Costa Rica.

These kinds of social problems combined with competing demands for local resources – ecotourism versus fishing – have led to conflicts among local residents in Baja, Mexico (Young, 1999). Similarly, in Ostional, a wildlife refuge in Costa Rica, local residents compete with the ecotourism industry for the use of sea turtles (Campbell, 2007). As in so many examples of wildlife conservation, the protection of the turtles may come at the direct expense of local access of resources. Because local economic benefits from sea turtle egg harvesting are superior to those generated by sea turtle ecotourism, the limitations on harvesting will most likely generate resentment rather than increase local support for conservation (Campbell, 2007).

The examples cited show mixed conservation outcomes. In some cases, economic benefits were sufficient in gaining at least a modicum of local support for conservation. These are examples of ecotourism as an effective market-based tool for conservation (Salafsky and Wollenberg, 2000; Spiteri and Nepal, 2006). In other cases, economic benefits from ecotourism fell short for conservation. In the worst cases, ecotourism generated conflicts and other social problems that ultimately diminished rather than increased chances for collective action for conservation and community development.

The Second Equation: Participation and Economic Benefits

Participatory models of ecotourism emphasize local involvement in the planning, management and ownership of ecotourism enterprises. Conservationists began talking about ecotourism as a tool for conservation in the late 1980s, often as an epitome of sustainable development and 'integrated conservation and development projects' (Brandon and Wells, 1992). The discourse about participatory ecotourism mirrors that of participatory conservation (e.g. Western and Wright, 1994; Brechin *et al.*, 2002). Both aim to reverse top-down approaches to resource management and externally driven strategies for development. Both include empowerment and social justice as goals over and above resource protection and both intend to build local capacity to manage – and benefit from – conservation projects (Scheyvens, 1999).

What both sets of scholars have shown conclusively is that social relations of power – among the state, environmental NGOs, tour operators and communities – influence the outcomes of conservation programmes. Stonich (2000), for example, found that at least some devolution of control from private tour operators and the government to local residents was critical for building local support for conservation in the Bay Islands, Honduras. Borman (1999) also noted the importance of local control over ecotourism for protecting Cofan indigenous territories and achieving community economic development goals. The catalysing effect of local participation may be that it can help build social capital as local residents work collectively to manage ecotourism (Pretty and Ward, 2001). As they manage ecotourism, they strengthen their own local institutions and enhance their chances to translate economic benefits from ecotourism into broader goals. Therefore, although economic benefits from ecotourism may lead to significant changes in local economies (which will either support or undermine conservation), participation in ecotourism ownership and management may lead to new learning and institutional support for conservation in the longer term.

A number of ecotourism projects in the tropics illustrate the second equation for ecotourism. They are programmes in which local residents participate in ecotourism management and decision making – thus shifting the locus of power and building capacity and strengthening local institutions within host destinations. In the Native Community of Infierno in Tambopata, south-eastern Peru, the ecotourism lodge, Posada Amazonas, is co-owned by local families in partnership with the tour company, Rainforest Expeditions. Since 1996, the partners have shared management of the lodge and split profits (see Gordillo Jordan *et al.*, Chapter 3, this volume).

Stronza has been conducting research in Infierno since 1996 on the interactions between ecotourism, economic benefits, community participation and conservation. Results so far have shown that the effects of economic benefits from ecotourism are ambiguous for conservation. Though employment has led to a general decline in farming and hunting, new ecotourism income (which represents an average increase of 15% per household) has enabled greater market consumption and expansion of production (Stronza, 2007). People report continued hunting in the community's 3000 ha reserve, for example, despite communal decisions to prohibit all use of the area except for ecotourism. The consensus among many community members is that tourism profits are not sufficient to sustain conservation, especially in the absence of trust that others will also cooperate to protect resources. As one man explained, 'I would like to take care of the forest. But what if I am making sacrifices and no one else is? My neighbours have cleared most of their forest to raise cattle'.

Participation in ownership and management of Posada Amazonas, however, has been associated with stronger communal organization and trust, and greater network of support beyond the community. These changes, in turn, have enabled people to work together to initiate a number of their own conservation and development efforts. For example, in 2006, the community council saved US$12,000 from tourism profits to gain legal title to a 1700 ha 'ecotourism concession' from the Peruvian government. They also formed multi-family cooperatives to make handicrafts, manage Brazil nut harvests, and build a new river port. These efforts have required organization, leadership and cooperation with outside entities – all skills improved through the experience of co-managing Posada Amazonas.

These findings suggest that ecotourism as not merely an economic 'tool' for conservation so much as a cause of new understandings, skills and social relationships. Decisions to conserve natural resources in ecotourism settings occur not solely in the light of cost–benefit calculations of prices and time. They also occur as the result of new feelings of capacity, the strength of local institutions and ties with outside actors, and overall social and economic stability.

Other studies have revealed similar results. In Ecuador, Wunder (2000) reported a reduction of hunting among some communities near the Cuyabeno Wildlife Reserve. The communities that had communal rules in place for hunting were those involved in ecotourism management; those that did not have rules were involved in ecotourism only as employees or income earners (Wunder, 2000). Participation in ecotourism management seemed to be associated with greater support for conservation and awareness of impacts on resources. In Mexico, Foucat (2002) described an example of ecotourism managed through a local cooperative, the Cooperativa de Servicios Ecoturisticos la Ventanilla. Members of the cooperative have decision-making power regarding cooperative activities, and all residents involved in ecotourism are members of the cooperative. Ecotourism is the main source of revenue for local residents. In addition to economic benefits, ecotourism has also been associated with greater wildlife conservation and environmental awareness.

Sea Turtle Protection in the Fishing Village of Praia do Forte, Brazil

The Brazilian Sea Turtle Conservation Programme (TAMAR) represents one of the few conservation programmes in the world that has successfully protected endangered species at both local and national levels while also addressing local needs (Spotila, 2004). For some, this achievement makes TAMAR a model for sea turtle conservation worldwide (Mast, 1999). Created in 1980, TAMAR is a federal government programme supported by the Brazilian Institute for the Environment. TAMAR's mission is to protect five species of sea turtles in Brazil through sustainable development. In 1988, leaders of TAMAR established the Fundação Pró-TAMAR to support, raise funds and co-administer the project with the Brazilian government (Marcovaldi and Marcovaldi, 1999).

Today, TAMAR has 22 research stations and monitors 1100 km of beaches in nine Brazilian states. The organization employs approximately 1200 people, 85% of whom are from the coastal communities where TAMAR works. The national headquarters of both TAMAR and Fundação Pró-TAMAR are located in the fishing village of Praia do Forte. The TAMAR Research Station in Praia do Forte was established in 1982. The Visitor Center (Fig. 11.1), built a few years later, started small with a few tanks showing marine wildlife. The village is approximately 80 km north of Salvador, Bahia's state capital, and is home to about 2000 residents (Mata de São João, 2004). The Visitor Center is the busiest and the most profitable of TAMAR's visitor centres. Most of the revenue from the Visitor Center comes from the TAMAR store, which sells many items made by local cooperatives. More broadly, the Visitor Center is one of the most popular tourism destinations in all of Brazil. During the 2005/6 nesting season, approximately 600,000 people visited the Center (TAMAR, 2006).

In September 2007, 110 people worked at TAMAR's Praia do Forte Visitor Center, mostly locals from the village and adjacent communities.

Fig. 11.1. The Projeto TAMAR (Brazilian Sea Turtle Conservation Programme) Visitor Center in Praia do Forte, Brazil. (Photo: Fernanda de Vasconcellos Pêgas.)

Associated with the Visitor Center is the 'Turtle by Night' ecotourism programme, which is offered during the sea turtle nesting season from December to February. During the programme, tourists have the chance to release hatchlings and observe nesting sea turtles. The Visitor Center also provides environmental education via media, interpretation and guided visits, led by biologists and trained personnel. Revenues from 'Turtle by Night', the environmental education programmes and Visitor Center return to the community in the form of wages paid to residents employed by TAMAR (Projeto TAMAR, 2007).

De Vasconcellos Pêgas has been conducting an ethnographic study in Praia do Forte since 2006, focusing on the social, cultural and economic impacts of TAMAR's sea turtle protection and ecotourism programmes, and local perceptions and values of sea turtles. In 35 semi-structured interviews with local residents, she found that economic benefits from TAMAR were perceived as important for the community. Respondents noted that the provision of employment in the Visitor Center, the fact that TAMAR is a pull factor for tourism and the education opportunities offered to school children are benefits for Praia do Forte. People said things like, 'TAMAR is everything for the village' and 'I want my child to work for TAMAR because he can learn and get skills to get a better job opportunity in the future'. De Vasconcellos Pêgas also found a certain amount of trust and social obligations between the village and the TAMAR programme. More than one resident noted, 'TAMAR is like a father figure for the community'. TAMAR directors also emphasized a general sentiment that the well-being of the village is as important as the well-being of TAMAR.

Part of the bond between TAMAR and the community is based on the history of the village. As stated by many in the community, both the Research Station and the Visitor Center grew side by side with the community. At the time of TAMAR's initiation, the village was home to about 500 residents and there was, of course, no Visitor Center or Research Station. Another reason for the bond between the project and the village is the exchange of information – traditional knowledge from the fishermen and technical support from TAMAR. Many have noted that TAMAR has always provided support to the fishermen, assistance otherwise not available.

Such perceptions of TAMAR may be linked to a history of economic dependency. Until 1970, the community of Praia do Forte was located within a coconut plantation. Residents relied on wages from plantation labour and fishing for survival. Employment, education and infrastructure were provided by the owners of the plantation. Despite hardships, residents stated that whatever was needed was provided. Government assistance was limited and often absent. For many, the arrival of TAMAR in 1982 helped change this situation; although, essentially, 'the provider' shifted from the plantation to the conservation programme. The assistance from TAMAR makes it a 'father figure' in a way that reflects the history of the plantation. Though problematic from a perspective of colonialism and dependency, the relationship between TAMAR and the community is working on some levels. It is also a success from the perspective of sea turtle conservation (Fig. 11.2).

When TAMAR started in 1980, local residents harvested sea turtle nests and nesting females regularly. By 2007, TAMAR had minimized harvest rates and introduced livelihood alternatives to many villagers. Today, unless pressured by natural threats such as high tides and predators, about 70% of sea turtle nests remain intact (Projeto TAMAR, 2007). One indicator of success is the release of more than eight million

Fig. 11.2. Sea turtle nesting site in Praia do Forte, Brazil. (Photo: Fernanda de Vasconcellos Pêgas.)

sea turtle hatchlings nationwide over the past 27 years. In Praia do Forte, local residents also show support for protecting sea turtles. In interviews with de Vasconcellos Pêgas in 2006, many agreed with the need for sea turtle conservation and the enforcement of laws against harvesting. As one resident said, 'I think the laws are good because they help protect the turtles... those who break [them] should be penalized'.

In some ways, the TAMAR programme in Praia do Forte represents the first 'ecotourism equation' outlined in our chapter. Through the Visitor Center and Research Station, TAMAR offers employment opportunities, environmental education programmes and technical support to fishermen. All of these have become incentives for local residents to support TAMAR and, by extension, TAMAR's efforts to protect sea turtles. As one resident explained, 'People come here to see the turtles... so we need the turtles and TAMAR here to have an income'. Leaders of TAMAR describe the community as a strong and essential component in its successes to date in protecting sea turtles. However, TAMAR does not include local residents of Praia do Forte in its management decisions or strategic planning for conservation and tourism. In fact, in some ways, the TAMAR project has been the opposite of empowering, as its relationship with the village perpetuates years of economic dependence on plantation agriculture.

Yet, most residents in Praia do Forte have not described this lack of participation as a problem, at least not yet. Instead, many report general feelings of support for TAMAR and for sea turtle conservation. Furthermore, conservation efforts have been relatively successful. The challenge for TAMAR and the village of Praia do Forte may lie in the future. Will economic benefits from TAMAR continue to be sufficient for sustaining local support for sea turtle protection? A couple of factors indicate that the answer is yes: a majority of families in Praia do Forte report significant economic benefits from ecotourism and TAMAR, and many families have shifted away from agriculture and fishing to sea turtle tourism. Most state that fishing is not economically beneficial to them anymore and that they would rather have their children working in other activities, such as with TAMAR.

However, there are potential challenges on the horizon. Of special concern is the fact that most youth in the village of Praia do Forte do not remember having any direct connection with sea turtles, fish or other marine resources. Their traditional and cultural ties with the resources on which their parents and grandparents depended directly have been severed. Now they see sea turtles as essentially cash cows, and thus they support conservation. If TAMAR leaves, however, or if the ecotourism economy crashes, the chances for ongoing conservation are less promising. New generations would lack the cultural knowledge and skills for subsistence, as well as the capacity to seek other development alternatives. As the ecotourism and conservation programmes have not been participatory, they have not helped build local capacity for self-determination in new directions.

Had TAMAR engaged local residents more fully in management and decision making, perhaps the future for sustainable development and sea turtle conservation efforts would be more promising. Perhaps the youth would have gained other skills that would have enabled them to take direction of their own development for future years, either with TAMAR or with the growing tourism industry. The complex array of social, political and economic variables make predicting the outcomes of alternative scenarios mere guesswork. However, results from the case studies of the 'second equation' in ecotourism do provide partial evidence that participation leads to possibilities that are empowering for local residents and not just 'enriching' in an economic sense.

Conclusion

Proponents of ecotourism often describe it as a tool for conservation and development. In many cases, ecotourism earns that label and effectively provides local residents of host destinations with alternative sources of income, employment opportunities, better infrastructure and even empowerment. In some cases, such benefits become incentives for conservation of the wildlife and other resources (or attractions) tourists pay to see. In other cases, ecotourism does more than provide incentives and instead catalyses collective action for broader community-based efforts in conservation and development. For example, ecotourism can lead to locally devised rules for resource management and/or self-initiated programmes for development, as in the case of Posada Amazonas and the community of Infierno. Ecotourism is not, however, free of challenges and limitations. The sample of case studies in this chapter suggests that long-term support for conservation is difficult to gain, even when economic incentives are in place. As many in this volume have noted, ecotourism is not a panacea for interlocking environmental, social and economic problems.

Our message then is that ecotourism may be more likely to succeed for long-term and locally sustained goals of conservation and development when local residents are engaged as decision makers and co-managers. Community participation in ecotourism can be especially critical for strengthening local institutions for collective action. We have also noted, however, that local participation is not necessarily required for ecotourism to create the right incentives for conservation. In the case of sea turtle protection in Brazil, the TAMAR Project in Praia do Forte has exhibited signs of success in conservation over the past 25 years, even though villagers have not participated in TAMAR as managers and decision makers. Employment opportunities and income provided by TAMAR, along with environmental education programmes and technical support to fishermen, have been sufficient to build local support for sea turtle conservation. The TAMAR example shows that, at least in the short term, the first ecotourism equation may be true: economic incentives from ecotourism do (or can) equal conservation. In the longer term, the approach of engaging and empowering local residents may prevent problems shared by many ecotourism operations, including conflicts over resource use and negative social and cultural impacts.

References

Agrawal, A. and Redford, K. (2006) *Poverty, Development, and Biodiversity Conservation: Shooting in the Dark?* Working Paper No. 26. Wildlife Conservation Society, New York.

Alexander, S. (2000) Resident attitudes towards conservation and black howler monkeys in Belize: the Community Baboon Sanctuary. *Environmental Conservation* 27, 341–350.

Barkin, D. (2003) Alleviating poverty through ecotourism: promises and reality in the Monarch Butterfly Reserve of Mexico. *Environment, Development and Sustainability* 5, 371–382.

Barrett, C. and Arcese, P. (1995) Are integrated conservation–development projects (ICDPs) sustainable? On the conservation of large mammals in sub-Saharan Africa. *World Development* 23, 1073–1084.

Barrett, C., Brandon, K., Gibson, C. and Gjertsen, H. (2001) Conserving tropical biodiversity amid weak institutions. *BioScience* 51, 497–502.

Belsky, J. (1999) Misrepresenting communities: the politics of community-based rural ecotourism in Gales Point Manatee, Belize. *Rural* Sociology 64, 641–666.

Bookbinder, M.P., Dinerstein, E., Rijal, A., Cauley, H. and Rajouria, A. (1998) Ecotourism's support of biodiversity conservation. *Conservation Biology* 12, 1399–1404.

Borman, R. (1999) Cofan: story of the forest people and the outsiders. *Cultural Survival Quarterly* 23, 48–50.

Brandon, K. and Wells, M. (1992) Planning for people and parks: design dilemmas. *World Development* 20, 557–570.

Brechin, S., Wilshusen, P., Fortwangler, C. and West, P. (2002) Beyond the square wheel: toward a more comprehensive understanding of biodiversity conservation as social and political process. *Society and Natural Resources* 15, 41–64.

Campbell, L. (2002) Conservation narratives and the 'received wisdom' of ecotourism: case studies from Costa Rica. *Journal of Sustainable Development* 5, 300–326.

Campbell, L. (2007) Local conservation practice and global discourse: a political ecology of sea turtle conservation. *Annals of the Association of American Geographers* 97, 313–334.

Fiallo, E. and Jacobson, S. (1995) Local communities and protected areas: attitudes of rural residents towards conservation and Machalilla National Park, Ecuador. *Environmental Conservation* 22, 241–249.

Foucat, V. (2002) Community-based ecotourism management moving towards sustainability, in Ventanilla, Oaxaca, Mexico. *Ocean & Coastal Management* 45, 511–529.

Gentry, K. (2006) Belizean women and tourism work: opportunity or impediment? *Annals of Tourism Research* 34, 477–496.

Gössling, S. (1999) Ecotourism: a means to safeguard biodiversity and ecosystem functions? *Ecological Economics* 29, 303–320.

Isaacs, J. (2000) The limited potential of ecotourism to contribute to wildlife conservation. *Wildlife Society Bulletin* 28, 61–69.

Jacobson, S. and Robles, R. (1992) Ecotourism, sustainable development, and conservation education: development of a tour guide training program in Tortuguero, Coast Rica. *Environmental Management* 16, 701–713.

Kruger, O. (2005) The role of ecotourism in conservation: panacea or Pandora's box? *Biodiversity and Conservation* 14, 579–600.

Langholz, J. (1999) Exploring the effects of alternative income opportunities on rainforest use: insights from Guatemala's Maya Biosphere Reserve. *Society and Natural Resources* 12, 139–150.

Lindberg, K., Enriquez, J. and Sproule, K. (1996) Ecotourism questioned: case studies from Belize. *Annals of Tourism Research* 23, 543–562.

Malek-Zadeh, E. (1996) *The Ecotourism Equation: Measuring the Impacts.* Bulletin No. 99. Yale School of Forestry, New Haven, Connecticut.

Marcovaldi, M. and Marcovaldi, G. (1999) Marine turtles of Brazil: the history and structure of Projeto TAMAR–IBAMA. *Biological Conservation* 91, 35–41.

Mast, R. (1999) Guest Editorial: Common sense conservation. *Marine Turtle Newsletter* 83, 3–7.

Mata de São João (2004) *Adequação do plano director urbano de Mata de São João ao estatuto da cidade.* Prefeitura Municipal de Mata de São João, Brazil.

Mbaiwa, J. (2004) The sociocultural impacts of tourism development in the Okavango Delta, Botswana. *Journal of Tourism and Cultural Change* 2, 163–184.

Pretty, J. and Ward, H. (2001) Social capital and the environment. *World Development* 29, 209–227.

Projeto TAMAR (2007) O que o TAMAR faz. http://www.tamar.org.br/t_func.asp (accessed September 2007).

Salafsky, N. and Wollenberg, E. (2000) Linking livelihoods and conservation: a conceptual framework and scale for assessing the integration of human needs and biodiversity. *World Development* 28, 1421–1438.

Salafsky, N., Cauley, H., Balachander, G., Cordes, B., Parks, J., Margoluis, C., Bhatt, S., Encarnacion, C., Russell, D. and Margoluis, R. (2001) A systematic test of an enterprise strategy for community-based biodiversity conservation. *Conservation Biology* 15, 1585–1595.

Scheyvens, R. (1999) Ecotourism and the empowerment of local communities. *Tourism Management* 20, 245–249.

Spiteri, A. and Nepal, S. (2006) Incentive-based conservation programs in developing countries: a review of some key issues and suggestions for improvements. *Environmental Management* 37, 1–14.

Spotila, J. (2004) *Sea Turtles: A Complete Guide to Their Biology, Behavior, and Conservation.* Johns Hopkins University Press, Baltimore, Maryland.

Stem, C., Lassoie, J., Lee, D. and Deshler, D. (2003) How 'eco' is ecotourism? A comparative case study of ecotourism in Costa Rica. *Journal of Sustainable Tourism* 11, 322–347.

Stonich, S. (2000) *The Other Side of Paradise: Tourism, Conservation and Development in the Bay Islands.* Cognizant Communication Corporation, New York.

Stronza, A. (2007) The economic promise of ecotourism for conservation. *Journal of Ecotourism* 6, 170–190.

TAMAR (2006) *Relatório Técnico Anual Bahia – Junho de 2005 a Maio de 2006.* Projeto TAMAR– Brazilian Institute for the Environment, Praia do Forte, Brazil.

Troëng, S. and Drews C. (2004) *Money Talks: Economic Aspects of Marine Turtle Use and Conservation.* WWF International, Gland, Switzerland.

Wallace, G. and Pierce, S. (1996) An evaluation of ecotourism in Amazonas, Brazil. *Annals of Tourism Research* 23, 843–873.

Weinberg, A., Bellows, S. and Ekster, D. (2002) Sustaining ecotourism: insights and implications from two successful case studies. *Society and Natural Resources* 15, 371–380.

West, P. (2006) *Conservation is Our Government Now: the Politics of Ecology in Papua New Guinea.* Duke University Press, Durham, North Carolina.

Western, D. and Wright, R.M. (1994) The background to community-based conservation. In: Western, D. and Wright, R.M. (eds) *Natural Connections: Perspectives in Community Conservation.* Island Press, Washington, DC, pp. 1–12.

Wunder, E. (1999) *Promoting Forest Conservation Through Ecotourism Income? A Case Study from the Ecuadorian Amazon Region.* Center for International Forestry Research, Bogor, Indonesia.

Wunder, S. (2000) Ecotourism and economic incentives – an empirical approach. *Ecological Economics* 32, 465–479.

Young, E. (1999) Balancing conservation with development in small-scale fisheries: is ecotourism an empty promise? *Human Ecology* 27, 581–620.

Zografos, C. and Oglethorpe, D. (2004) Multi-criteria analysis in ecotourism: using goal programming to explore sustainable solutions. *Current Issues in Tourism* 7, 20–43.

Part VII

National Perspectives

12 Protected Areas and Tourism in Cuba

T. Borges Hernándes[1], L. Coya de la Fuente[1] and K. Lee Wald[2]

[1]Ministry of Science, Technology and Environment – CITMA, Havana, Cuba; [2]San Jose, California, USA

Introduction

Understanding ecology and ecotourism in Cuba's social, political and economic context is not as easy as it might be with other countries. North Americans, especially, are burdened by many misconceptions about this island nation resulting from decades of misinformation. Much of this reflects the hostility towards the Cuban Revolution by the US government and by corporations and individuals who once owned property and wielded significant influence on the island. In addition, this hostility often reflects the corporate media's own perceptions as to how the world should be run – and for whom.

A number of groups and organizations (academic, research, friendship, people-to-people exchanges, or just simply tourism- and ecotourism-focused) that send people to Cuba say they want to encourage people to go there with an open mind; to investigate, to learn, to enjoy Cuba's natural beauty and diversity, and to extend a helping hand. This is especially true for those who would like to be partners with their Cuban colleagues in helping protect the natural ecosystems that exist there.

Their objective is for people to go to Cuba to do more than just enjoy the pretty scenery – whether the Spanish and French colonial architecture of its cities, the white sand beaches and warm crystalline water, the tropical mountain rainforests, or the offshore cays. That means seeing Cuba as it really is, with all the advantages and all the problems that come from being an independent, sovereign and socialist developing nation, but at the same time facing enormous obstacles placed by its colonial history and the ongoing economic, political and military opposition of its neighbour to the north.

When Cuba first began looking at ecotourism – or what they called the 'ecologizing of tourism', which meant extending ecological concepts to all aspects of tourism – they were if anything overly optimistic. In many parts of the world, ecologists are fighting against governments and developers to preserve the environment. In Cuba, it is the government itself which is setting careful limits on development so as not to endanger what it considers to be its most valuable natural resource. The Cuban government wants to preserve the best this Caribbean island has to offer while allowing its citizens to enjoy what the modern world has to offer. Not an easy combination to achieve.

The obstacles

Perhaps the first and foremost obstacle is the *USA's economic blockade* that impacts every aspect of life in Cuba. This means that Cuban conservationists often cannot get the materials they need to maintain a clean environment. This is especially true when they are trying to repair or replace equipment originally made and purchased in the USA more than half a century ago. For instance, antiquated sewer systems and the deterioration of water treatment plants have greatly increased the pollution of major cities' waterways and harbours. Filter systems that should clean the smoke and other elements discharged from factories, cement plants and sugar mills before being released into the air have been idled for lack of spare parts.

The second obstacle, *economic necessity*, is closely linked to the US economic blockade and the demise of the Soviet Union, which was Cuba's main trading partner; but would exist in any case simply because Cuba is a developing Third World country. The population has many basic needs which the government is hard-put to fulfil. And while having a planned, socialist economy mitigates the power of various commercial enterprises to impose their own, usually selfish, agendas over social needs such as a clean environment, it does not eliminate this problem completely.

The resulting *scarcity–need–scarcity cycle* is the third obstacle. Being a poor, underdeveloped, blockaded country means that Cuba has a greater need to conserve, recycle and reuse. The economic crisis that followed the fall of the Soviet Union heightened this awareness. But at the same time, ironically, it sometimes made this more difficult to carry out. For instance, Cuban neighbourhood committees – known as CDRs – have been collecting reusable and recyclable materials since the 1960s: bottles and other glass, cartons, newspapers, even toothpaste tubes that were lined with a material that could be recycled. But as a result of the energy crisis in the 1990s, just when Cuba needed more than ever to conserve in this way, there was a sharp drop in transportation available for picking up recyclables. Many CDRs and stores stopped collecting such materials because they were not being picked up, they had no place to store them and there was no way to get them to the recycling centres in bulk. It became an individual responsibility, and most individuals only have bus, bicycle or feet to get to those places.

As if all of this wasn't bad enough, Cuba faces a fourth obstacle: *nature and climactic conditions.* As an island in the Caribbean, Cuba suffers from everything from devastating hurricanes and tropical storms to flooding and prolonged droughts. And the ferocious salt air that eats away at everything, from plants to concrete, makes life even harder. While plant life grows with tremendous exuberance, so do all the pests that destroy it.

The advantages

None of this means we should be discouraged, however, because Cuba also has a tremendous amount going for it. The advantages include:

- Centuries-long history of high regard for the natural environment in the face of degradation of the forests and the environment in general.
- Determination of current leaders in most fields – and up to the highest levels – to protect the natural environment.
- Major legislation starting with the Cuban Constitution mandating environmental protection and placing this above other economic or social interests.
- The absence of large, vested private commercial interests with significant influence in decision making when it comes to environmental legislation and practice.
- The lateness of growth in tourism and entrance into ecotourism, enabling it to benefit by observing and learning to avoid the mistakes made by others.
- High educational level of the population and complete access to schools and the media.
- Forty-year tradition of popular participation in decision making and carrying out objectives.

In the sections that follow in this chapter, we lay out some definitions of sustainable tourism and ecotourism, and then describe how these concepts have been implemented in the National System of Protected Areas in Cuba, often with the direct support of government policies.

Definitions and Concepts

Sustainable tourism refers to the type of tourism that is based on either natural or man-made resources and contributes to sustainable development. It is a form of tourism that needs to be managed in such a way that all activity focused on a patrimonial resource (natural or cultural) may continue indefinitely. The definition recognizes the necessity of an integrated development approach addressing the relationships between natural and cultural resources, the tourist sector and other activities, as well as processes and value systems where tourism takes place.

Ecotourism is nature-based tourism that attempts to promote conservation. Lindberg and McKercher (1997) argue that, from the mid 1990s, ecotourism has entered a period of maturity (Eagles, 1992; Weiler and Richins, 1995). Many of the first definitions of ecotourism tended to be descriptive. They helped foster a proliferation of tours centred on ecology, but without a solid ecological base (Wight, 1994). More recently, prescriptive definitions of ecotourism have been developed. These now include a greater range of benefits, such as preservation for destinations, educational programmes, minimal impact from visitors, and socio-economic benefits associated with small-scale facilities established by the local populations. Any rational tourist plan contains the preservation of the environment as a fundamental component (Inskeep, 1991). The translation of theory into practice has not been simple, and in the majority of cases ecotourism has not lived up to the expectations.

To define ecotourism in practice has been problematic (Brandon, 1996). There are at least 35 related terms (Mowforth, 1992). Among the most well-known are: nature tourism, wilderness tourism, adventure tourism, green tourism, alternative tourism, sustainable tourism, respectful tourism, holidays in nature, study tourism, scientific tourism, cultural tourism, low-impact tourism, rural tourism and soft tourism (Backman *et al.*, 1994; Wall, 1994). All of these terms share the fact that they are an alternative to mass-consumption tourism, but they are not synonyms of ecotourism. Ecotourism joins tourism and nature (Farrell and Runyan, 1991), but it must also demonstrate clear ecological and sociocultural objectives (Inskeep, 1987).

Protected Areas in Cuba

Healthy ecosystems are a prerequisite for high-quality ecotourism products. Parks and protected areas are particularly appealing to ecotourists. Cuba has 35 legally recognized protected areas, including areas of national and local significance. A group of 32 additional areas are currently seeking approval. The representativeness of the National System of Protected Areas of Cuba is good because the system includes a high percentage of endemic and threatened species of plants; endemic, native and migratory bird species; many endemic, threatened and rare vertebrates; and places with the highest abundance of Cuban land vertebrates.

Law 81 of the Environment of Cuba, enacted on 11 July 1997, laid the groundwork that guides Cuba's environmental policy. The passage of this law filled an important legislative gap because it set out the objectives and basic principles that govern the functioning of the country's National System of Protected Areas. Article 8 of this law defines protected areas within the national territory, and mandates the protection of biological diversity and of the natural historical and cultural resources associated with it.

Among the various objectives of the National System of Protected Areas Plan of 2002, Clause No. 1 is noteworthy because of its close and direct relation with tourism: 'To make recreation and the development of tourism possible in a way that is compatible with the management category of the area'. Also notable is Decree Law 201 on Protected Areas National System (enacted on 22 December 1999), which established the legal regimen for the National System of Protected Areas. It addresses: management categories and plans; proposal and declaration of protected areas and buffer zones; protection regimens, granting of authorizations for activities in protected areas and their buffer zones; regulations for control and administration, as well as public use.

In this Decree Law regulations for public use of protected areas, as well as other uses related to tourism, are as follows:

1. Construction projects within the protected areas will be carried out in accordance with sustainability criteria, in a way that guarantees the preservation of the area's characteristics and the integrity of its surroundings.
2. There will be ongoing monitoring of environmental impacts in visited areas to update regulations needed for its use and protection.
3. Tracks or trails inside each area will have to be designed on scientific bases, to permit observation without alterations of the natural and historic cultural values.
4. The tourist entities and other institutions must coordinate with each area's administrative authorities regarding the number of visits, visitors, periodicity and activities.
5. Visitors must be accompanied by a guide when they visit sensitive places.
6. Wildlife observation by visitors will be done from trails or special observation posts for this purpose, or in zones designated in the management plan.

Among the management categories that have specific objectives in order to provide opportunities for the development of tourism and recreation are the following:

- *National park*: this area is a combination of terrestrial and marine ecosystems, in wild or semi-wild status, with scarce or absent human populations. It is designated to protect the ecological integrity of one or more ecosystems of international, regional or national relevance, and managed principally with the objective of ecosystem conservation.
- *Ecological reserve*: the reserve is a combination of terrestrial and marine areas, in wild or semi-wild status. It is designated to protect the ecological integrity of parts of or entire ecosystems of international, regional or national relevance, and managed principally with the objective of ecosystem conservation.
- *Natural outstanding element*: this is an area that contains one or more natural characteristics of outstanding or exceptional value because of their implicit rarity and representative or aesthetic qualities, and that can contain historic cultural values. These areas are managed with the aim to preserve the above characteristics and values.

- *Managed floristic reserve*: this natural or semi-natural area needs active management interventions to achieve protection and maintenance of natural complexes or ecosystems, in order to guarantee the existence of specific plant communities or floristic species. The reserve could present imbalances due to harmful processes or particular features that require habitat or species manipulation, with the aim to supply optimal conditions for their restoration or suitable protection, according to specific circumstances.
- *Fauna refuge*: this is a combination of terrestrial and marine areas in which the protection and habitats of the species prove to be essential to sustain migratory wildlife or significant resident populations. It is not required for this refuge to include only natural territories. Human activity linked to resource management is permitted whenever it does not contradict the established regulations of the area's specific objectives.
- *Natural protected landscape*: this is a combination of terrestrial and marine areas of wild or semi-wild status, managed principally with objectives of protection and maintenance of natural conditions, as well as environmental services and sustainable tourism development.
- *Protected area of managed resources*: these terrestrial and marine areas, or combination of both, in wild or semi-wild status, are the object of management activities that guarantee protection and main-tenance of biological diversity and provide, at the same time, a sustainable flow of natural products and services to satisfy local or national needs. In relation to its functioning, it must be contained inside protected areas of a more strict management category.
- *Special region of sustainable development*: this area is also described as a multi-use area, and it constitutes a special protected area type which, due to its extensive characteristics, high grade of human influence, economic potential, important natural values and fragile ecosystems, differs substantially from the rest of the established management categories.

Ecotourism Industry in Cuba

In Cuba, tourism is considered a strategic priority as an instrument for development in specific sections of the country. It is approached as an integral programme in which, directly or indirectly, all sectors of society and economy intervene. For the Ministry of Tourism in Cuba, economic, environmental and sociocultural sustainability are prerequisites for the development of the tourism sector. Tourist numbers and income generated are the traditional arenas from which tourism success can be measured. These traditional measures are bowing to ways of more strategic character, where the rate of sustainability reached by the destinations has a relevant place. The Constitution of the Republic of Cuba establishes that sustainable development constitutes a basic principle of the country's policy.

For Cuban tourism, sustainability is defined as something that contributes to the integral development of the country, raising its contributions to the economy, increasing job opportunities, increasing quality of life for people, and contributing at the same time to the preservation and/or restoration of natural and cultural resources for current and future responsible use. As a member country of The Association of Caribbean States, Cuba is committed to working towards the Sustainable Tourism Zone of the Caribbean. Fulfilling the objective of sustainability, in addition to bringing environmental, cultural and social benefits to the country, constitutes one of the pillars for tourism development.

In 1995, 16 tourist regions were established in Cuba, eight of them designated as 'Regions of Greater Development'. These include: Havana, Varadero, Jardines del Rey, Norte de Camagüey, Norte de Holguín, Santiago de Cuba, Costa Sur and the Canarreos' Archipelago. The remaining eight regions, named 'Developing Regions', are: Guanahacabibes, Viñales-Soroa, Ciénaga de Zapata, Sagua la Grande, Caibarién, Norte de Las Tunas, Baracoa and Sur del Granma. Besides these regions, Cuba has three tourism poles and seven isolated tourist centres.

Following the initial national and territorial evaluation of the development potential for ecotourism, areas were defined that could be integrated in a first implementation stage. The areas identified were: Sierra del Rosario, Ciénaga de Zapata, Valle de Viñales, Centro Histórico de Trinidad y Valle de los Ingenios, Mil Cumbres, La Guabina, Topes de Collantes, Cayo Saetía, Bahía de Naranjos, Pinares de Mayaríl and Sierra Maestra. Also included were 16 hotels and 40 other tourism facilities (Figs 12.1 and 12.2).

However, in terms of their architecture, technological conditions and services offered, most of these were developed more for mass tourism. The services that are offered in these facilities are similar and rudimentary; there is practically no distinction between the areas. Most of them lack necessary features of ecotourism, such as interpretation centres, specialized guides and detailed information in maps and brochures, among others. Nevertheless, there are facilities in which recreational activities are linked with ecotourism, such as the Center for Caiman Reproduction in Zapata Swamp, the Soroa Orchid Garden, some peasant farmsteads, and others.

From the hotels and other facilities, 75 optional tours are advertised, including hikes on interpretative trails, horseback riding, visits to towns and places with historic and cultural attractions, peasant farmsteads, and others related to the native and cultural characteristics of the region. The low numbers of people per tour is acceptable, considering the low levels of average tourist stays.

The marketing of ecotourism in Cuba is still incipient, despite the fact that a lot of information is readily available for a variety of audiences. It is very important to establish coherent criteria for Cuba's promotion as an ecotourism destination. Consequently, the definition of a clear image is

Fig. 12.1. Cable ride in Cuba. (Photo: Karen Lee Wald.)

Fig. 12.2. Room with tree branch at Las Terrazas, Cuba. (Photo: Karen Lee Wald.)

essential, not only in form but in content. The Cuban image as an ecotourism destination is currently being developed and we are just at the appropriate time to correctly project policy to follow in this regard.

Opportunities for the Development of Ecotourism in Cuba

Cuba currently shows the highest tourism growth of the insular Caribbean, and it is relatively well positioned to receive tourists from countries that represent the main markets for ecotourism, i.e. France, Germany, Canada, Italy and Spain. Cuba possesses well-preserved natural and cultural resources of high tourist interest, with great landscape diversity and an attractive combination of beaches and coastal resources with other natural landscapes. In addition, Cuba shows favourable climatic conditions that make ecotourism feasible throughout the year. Also, Cuba is socially stable, safe, has a good health-care system, and has good transport services in the form of highways, ports and airport systems that permit access to natural places, facilities for lodging and tourist services in natural areas. There are also scientific and non-profit organizations focused on environmental research and protection that increase the potential for ecotourism development.

As the demand for ecotourism increases, the products offered must be continuously and substantially modified. To this end, the Ministry of Tourism in Cuba is working to direct its strategies on tourist product diversification, where ecotourism has a priority. In this context, there is a possibility to 'insert' ecotourism products in combined programmes (mixed products) aimed at the conventional tourism market (sun and beach) for which the majority of tourists choose Cuba.

Obstacles to the Development of Ecotourism in Cuba

An analysis of the obstacles to ecotourism products, conducted by Cuban specialists, focused on the Cuban tourist sector and also on international aspects of ecotourism. Neighbouring countries in Central America and the Caribbean already have established an image and products of ecotourism, while Cuba does not have a well-defined image as an ecotourism destination. Other countries have strong marketing campaigns and the tourism competition is high. Practically all of the Caribbean countries are engaging in ample development programmes, including adequate lodging capacities and capabilities. In Cuba, marketing efforts and knowledge are still relatively insufficient.

Nevertheless, Cuba aims to insert itself in this market by highlighting its individuality. Cuba's insularity, beaches, climate, and cultural and natural resources are superlative compared with other Caribbean destinations. Yet, Cuba is not on an equal footing with other Caribbean nations because of the US economic blockage, which precludes financing and the transfer of knowledge in many different aspects. Because of this geopolitical reality over the past several decades, almost all hotels and tourist facilities were built mainly for conventional tourism, which means they lack the facilities and specialized services needed for ecotourism. In particular, they do not have ecologically friendly technologies for the construction and operation of hotels, including liquid and solid waste treatment and renewable energy. Collaboration and coordination between the different entities that develop tourism in Cuba, linked with research and environmental non-profit organizations, is not enough to meet the need. At the same time, codes of conduct for tourists, or other incentives, do not yet exist. A system of questionnaires for tourists needs to be developed in order to get reliable statistics on tourist arrivals, countries of origin, degree of satisfaction, etc.

Government Recognition of Sustainability

Tourism is an industry that has the potential to provide a strong and stable economy for the country (Gunn, 1994). Indeed, for many countries tourism is an important component of a national strategy for economic development. The goal in Cuba is to achieve profit in this service industry while also contributing to the country's sustainable development.

Local communities receive economic benefits in the form of earnings and jobs; often these profits come from the sale of handicrafts, providing guide services and the issuance of licenses and lodges. In Cuba, residents in local communities are favoured and given priority for jobs in the tourist facilities. Local products, services, and both traditional and contemporary cultural activities, are offered. With the exception of a small handful of advisors and collaborators, all those who work in tourism are Cubans, and more than 90% of the labour force is comprised of residents in the locality and municipality of the tourist enterprise.

To this end, the Cuban Ministry of Science, Technology and Environment created a nationwide system to grant official environmental recognition, to distinguish entities that provide sustainable solutions for tourism activities, products or services that might otherwise have negative impacts. To gain this recognition, these tourism programmes must also have accepted the standards established for the protection of workers, nearby communities and the local environment.

Tourism has been one of the principal economic sectors interested in gaining this environmental recognition from government, partly because doing so makes the opening of new markets easier. This is especially true as some tourists prefer environmentally certified facilities. The recognition also has the potential to stimulate innovation, raise the value of tourist facilities, increase the confidence of investors and stakeholders, improve relations with local communities, and create a platform from which to meet other environmental standards, such as those regarding waste water and emissions. The Melía Varadero Hotel was the first to obtain this official recognition in Cuba.

Beyond its potential as a driver for economic development, many people are convinced that ecotourism is a sound strategy for conserving natural resources. Others question its true conservation value. Ehrenfield (1992) noted that market-based approaches to conservation, like ecotourism, are problematic due to biological and economic complexity. In addition, it is evident that although ecotourism may provide economic incentives for conservation, it can also destroy the resources on which it depends (Berle, 1990). The principal environmental impacts of tourism are pollution, especially from inadequate solid and liquid waste management, and biodiversity loss due to habitat destruction, among others. Besides these direct environmental impacts, social and cultural effects of tourism can indirectly lead to degradation. The Cuban environmental policy, which is based on principles and sustained by specialized legislation, identifies actions for preventing and controlling these impacts.

Included is an emphasis on sustainable technologies, such as green construction materials, the use of alternative energy sources, and systems of low consumption for treatment and recycling of liquid and solid waste. Tourism is permanently integrated into efforts the country undertakes in order to face climate change and natural disasters. This is achieved by developing quick information systems and applying the required measures to mitigate and to minimize possible damages that could be produced.

Joint Resolution for Tourism

In summary, the Cuban policy regarding touristic uses of natural, rural and culturally valuable locations and areas is based on the concept of sustainable tourism. The accelerated growth of tourism has, in many cases, exceeded the scarce regulations that for years ruled tourist activity in Cuba, making them notoriously obsolete. For this, and many other reasons, the need for a coherent and new legal framework became evident. To this end, the Ministry of Science, Technology and Environment, through the National Environmental Strategy, dictated guidelines for the creation of a specific environmental regulatory body for the tourist sector – the Ministry of Tourism. In May 1999, the Ministry of Tourism, the Ministry of Science, Technology and Environment and the Ministry of Agriculture signed a joint Resolution for the development and regulation of tourism in the country. The Resolution is currently being assessed after its initial years in action.

In various ways Cuba has contributed to the reaffirmation of Caribbean identity and the protection of cultural values of the countries of the region, aiming to create a common but diverse image. Promotion and collaboration for the development of events and sociocultural activities is permanently ongoing, making the link between culture and tourism stronger. Important work is being done for the rescue and responsible use of places with historical value, based on the declaration of relevant natural and historic places as World Heritage Sites. Institutions, groups and communities that work for the preservation of genuine cultural expressions are stimulated and supported.

Cuba's experience with land-use planning in general, and tourism development in particular, has proved a good procedure to promote the conscious participation of the population in the decision-making process. Cuba actively participated with members of The Association of Caribbean States in the wording of strategies, actions, declarations and protocols and the conceptualization of indicators that will serve to assess the degree of sustainability. In addition, Cuba aided the creation of instruments and legally binding procedures for the Caribbean Zone of Sustainable Tourism.

The Cuban Ministry of Tourism works to develop and implement models for conservation and sustainable use of the environment in the tourist-use spaces. They emphasize strict compliance with the environmental legislation, quality control, sustainability certification, use of adequate technologies, and the fulfilment of the environmental impact assessment process.

Environmental impact assessment is primarily concerned with protection of the environment, and for this purpose it must evaluate and provide information to decision makers on the probable environmental effects. This assessment will then permit, approve with conditionality or deny the execution of a project or activity, and establish adequate procedures. New tourist facilities, in particular those that could affect coastal ecosystems, are required to apply for approval from the Ministry of Science, Technology and Environment. They must then carry out the corresponding Environmental Impact Assessment Process.

High diversity or fragile ecosystems with tourist use are protected through regulations that include tourist behaviour. In specially protected areas, for example coastal ecosystems, the protection of beaches, coral reefs and mangroves is legally supported by Decree Law 212 of 2000 on Management of the Coastal Zone. Several projects for the rehabilitation of high-quality beaches in the tourist poles, affected by erosive processes and bad construction procedures in the past, are being executed with the financial support of the tourist sector.

Through the Tourism Education System, environmental education has been guaranteed for all executives and employees, including such topics as capacity building, training and re-qualification. The personnel of tourism facilities take part in actions that contribute to the awareness of the local population on environmental issues.

With the aim of contributing to the increase of the tourist flow to the region, the Cuban tourist sector establishes that sustainability principles in the economic, sociocultural and environmental fields are an indispensable condition to fulfil. Additionally, as a way to increase the value of our products, the destinations are highlighting their own identities at the national and regional levels. The creation of multiple-destination products is enhanced, having the differentiation between them as a basis.

Conclusions

Ecosystems are dynamic, and they change over the course of time. Human beings, however, are the principal agents for change in nature. Human activity, as a whole, must become sustainable, and tourism is not an exception. Sustainable tourism in natural areas can be converted into a vital tool to preserve the natural and cultural heritage, as well as for the improvement of quality of life, principally for communities in less developed rural zones.

Sustainable tourism in natural areas is an overarching concept that fuses the ideas of sustainable development with the tourism industry. It is an attempt to balance a variety of economic, sociocultural and ecological concerns at the international, national and local levels. The uncontrolled development of tourism in natural areas and destinations with human settlements has proved to be unsustainable. The degradation of the areas and the loss of biological and cultural diversity will destroy the natural and cultural attractions on which this industry relies. A focus on sustainability in tourism can help prevent this from occurring, but only if it constitutes a real incentive to protect natural areas and local cultures.

In our country, many conditions are different now from those of prior years. The understanding of the economic role of tourism has increased. Cuban society has created 'antibodies' against demoralizing tendencies. The constructive capabilities of the sector have been gaining efficiency. Domestic products participate in a substantial way in satisfying increasing amounts of tourist demand. Artistic expression, and culture in general, have become the essential tourist product, and, internationally, Cuban destinations have acquired a more consistent and recognized position. The national agencies and the grassroots entities demonstrate more and more of Cuba's potential in the creation of products of great attraction for tourists.

References

Backman, K.E., Wright, B.A. and Backman, S.J. (1994) Ecotourism: a short descriptive explanation. *Trends* 31(2), 23–27.

Berle, P. (1990) Two faces of ecotourism. *Audubon* 92, 6.

Brandon, K. (1996) *Ecotourism and Conservation: A Review of Key Issues.* ESD Paper No. 033. World Bank, Washington, DC.

Eagles, P.F.J. (1992) The travel motivations of Canadian ecotourists. *Journal of Travel Research* 21, 3–7.

Ehrenfield, D. (1992) The business of conservation. *Conservation Biology* 6, 1–3.

Farrell, B.H. and Runyan, D. (1991) Ecology and tourism. *Annals of Tourism Research* 18, 26–40.

Gunn, C.A. (1994) *Tourism Planning*, 3rd edn. Taylor and Francis, Washington, DC.

Inskeep, E. (1987) Environmental planning for tourism. *Annals of Tourism Research* 14, 118–135.

Inskeep, E. (1991) *Tourism Planning: An Integrated and Sustainable Approach.* Van Nostrand Reinhold, New York.

Lindberg, K. and McKercher, B. (1997) Ecotourism: a critical overview. *Pacific Tourism Review* 1, 65–79.

Mowforth, M. (1992) *Ecotourism: Terminology and Definitions*. Research Report. University of Plymouth, Plymouth, UK.

Wall, G. (1994) Ecotourism: old wine in new bottles? *Trends* 31(2): 4–9.

Weiler, B. and Richins, H. (1995) Extreme, extravagant and elite: a profile of ecotourists on Earthwatch expeditions. *Tourism, Recreation Research* 20, 29–36.

Wight, P.A. (1994) Environmentally responsible marketing of tourism. In: Cater, E. and Lowman, G. (eds) *Ecotourism: A Sustainable Option?* John Wiley and Sons, Toronto, Canada, pp. 39–56.

13 Ecotourism and Ecolodge Development in the 21st Century

H. CEBALLOS-LASCURAIN

*Program of International Consultancy on Ecotourism (PICE),
Mexico DF, Mexico*

Introduction

In the first decade of the new millennium, ecotourism is already a global phenomenon that is starting to provide tangible benefits for many developed and developing countries. It has become one of the fastest-growing segments of tourism activities around the world.

Tourism more generally is the world's most important civil industry, valued at roughly US$3.5 trillion annually and employing 127 million workers (one in 15 workers worldwide). The segment of tourism undergoing the fastest growth is nature-based tourism, which includes ecotourism. Nature-based tourism has been estimated to account for between 10% and 20% of all international travel expenditures, according to the World Tourism and Travel Council (WTTC), and that figure seems to be increasing rapidly (WTTC, 2000). Unless this growth receives careful and professional guidance by tourism experts and authorities, serious negative consequences – some of which may have terminal effects – are a real possibility.

Ecotourism, as defined by The World Conservation Union, is:

> environmentally responsible travel and visitation to relatively undisturbed natural areas, in order to enjoy, study and appreciate nature (and any accompanying cultural features – both past and present), that promotes conservation, has low negative visitor impact, and provides for beneficially active socio-economic involvement of local populations. (Ceballos-Lascurain, 1996).

In other words, ecotourism denotes nature tourism with a normative element. It has only recently emerged as a feasible option for both conserving the natural and cultural heritage of nations and regions and contributing to sustainable development. Natural areas, and especially legally protected areas, their landscape, wildlife and flora – together with any existing cultural features – constitute major attractions for the peoples of the countries in which they are found and for tourists around the world.

Since the late 1980s ecotourism activities have increased remarkably. Governments of the most varied countries are showing heretofore-unknown interest in ecotourism, recognizing its enormous capabilities for conserving the natural and cultural heritage of their nations and also its rich potential for ensuring sustainable development. Conservation non-governmental organizations (NGOs) around the planet are also embarking upon ecotourism projects, recognizing in them an important ally. Ecotourism operators and professional membership organizations are sprouting everywhere. Local communities in remote localities, which until very recently had very little contact with 'modern' civilization, are now attracting ecotourists to their settlements in the jungle, the desert or the island (Ceballos-Lascurain, 2001; Rodríguez, Chapter 10, this volume).

Unfortunately, accurate statistics on ecotourism are still lacking. Institutions such as the World Tourism Organization and the WTTC are urging both governments and private firms to generate trustworthy data in order to evaluate the true magnitude of ecotourism around the world. Some preliminary studies indicate that perhaps 15% of international tourism is ecotourism-oriented and that the annual rate of growth of this type of tourism is also around 15%, compared with a growth rate of 4% for overall tourism in the 1990s (Honey, 1999).

International agencies such as the World Bank, the United Nations Development Programme, the United Nations Environment Programme, the European Union, the World Wildlife Fund, The World Conservation Union, The Nature Conservancy and Conservation International are all involved in promoting and developing studies and specific projects in different fields of ecotourism around the world.

Countries with Success in Ecotourism

Countries that are generating success stories in the realm of ecotourism, such Kenya, Costa Rica, South Africa, Australia, New Zealand, Ecuador and Belize, are doing so in part because they are managing to attain a degree of more or less appropriate coordination among the different stakeholders involved: government, the tourism industry, NGOs, local communities and universities, among others. All of these countries have extraordinary natural assets (landscape, fauna and flora), in some cases complemented by a rich cultural heritage, effective protected area net-works, and a vocal and pro-active ecotourism industry sector, interested in achieving conservation and sustainable development goals, as well as good business.

These countries are also very competitive in the ecotourism industry because, apart from their singular assets, there has generally been a joint interest on behalf of both government and private industry to develop ecotourism, as both sectors recognize important benefits to reap from ecotourism. The example in this volume from Cuba by Borges Hernándes and colleagues illustrates this kind of government involvement.

Following is a brief description of recent ecotourism development in Costa Rica and Belize. These two countries have achieved a relatively good coordination between governments and the private sector.

Costa Rica

The Costa Rican government has long considered tourism as critical for generating employment and other economic benefits, promoting foreign investment, and supporting development that is compatible with environment conservation and the maintenance of rural heritage. The government has faced the challenge of integrating ecotourism into a diverse mosaic of tourist activities and attractions, with the aim of offering a single extensive tourist product, or what Zamora and Obando (2001) call 'a peaceful, green, and clean country'. This is not an easy task, as there seems to be a dual policy of heavily marketing Costa Rica's natural areas and ecotourism attractions while at the same time trying to augment visitor numbers by means of mass beach resorts and urban hotels owned by transnational chains, cruise ships and prepaid air charter tours (Honey, 1999).

Since 1994, tourism and ecotourism have been Costa Rica's top earners. In 2000, the country hosted 1,088,000 international and domestic tourists, 800,000 of whom visited protected areas, generating about US$2.5 million in admission fees and payment of services (Zamora and Obando, 2001). The number of domestic visitors now exceeds the number of international tourists visiting protected areas in Costa Rica. Apart from the government-managed protected areas, Costa Rica has an important and very successful network of private reserves, established as non-profit entities. Most of these reserves are involved in some form of ecotourism.

In spite of the many bright points of ecotourism development in Costa Rica, there are still a number of shortcomings in the harmonious interaction between tourism and conservation, which can be summarized in three closely interrelated issues: (i) lack of effective coordination between some of the responsible parties; (ii) serious negative environmental impact of non-planned tourism; and (iii) a generalized lack of environmental awareness in society. Currently, the big challenge for Costa Rica is maintaining a high quality level for its ecotourism industry while at the same time finding ways to provide more tangible benefits for the national park system and biodiversity conservation programmes.

Belize

Tourism is a major source of revenue for the Belizean economy. In 2000, tourism contributed 25% of total foreign exchange earnings. With its combination of rainforest ecosystems, Maya archaeological sites, living

Maya culture and the second longest barrier reef in the world, this small country has an enviable ecotourism resource base to present to the world.

Visitation to six key national parks and reserves and to the Maya archaeological sites amounted to more than 150,000 visitors in 2000. In 1991 the then Ministry of Tourism and the Environment produced an Integrated Tourism Policy and Strategy Statement, which re-valued many important assets, widely recognizing that tourism in Belize is directly tied to the diversity of natural and cultural resources, and that protection of these resources is crucial to the industry's future. National tourism marketing and development efforts in Belize focus primarily on ecotourism (Wiezsman, 2001).

However, as in Costa Rica, the potential for ecotourism in Belize faces a number of challenges. One is the fact that enforcement of environmental laws and regulations is weak due to a lack of financial resources. Second, institutional capacity tends to be insufficient to carry out necessary land-use planning, park management activities, environmental inventories and impact assessments. Third, parks receive little government funding and instead most are supported by international NGOs. Finally, there is a perceived lack of political commitment to engage fully in implementing conservation programmes and developing a sound ecotourism strategy.

Throughout most of the world, the rise of ecotourism has coincided with the promotion of free markets and economic globalization, with the private sector hailed as the main engine for development. In many countries, state-run enterprises, including those in the tourism industry, are being sold off or shut down. This push towards privatization has been propelled by the international lending and aid agencies and major corporate players, who try to avoid excessive bureaucracy and inefficiency. In most successful ecotourism destination countries, however, even if there is a drive towards privatization, the governments (through their Ministry of Tourism or Tourism Board) are actively promoting the ecotourism attractions of their countries in a very energetic way in international forums and through the media. Evidently, it pays off more to promote partnerships than to enforce strict regulations.

And, of course, the ecotourists themselves are pushing the market around the world. Over 30 million Americans, for example, belong to environmental organizations or profess an interest in environmental protection. A National Survey on Recreation and the Environment indicates that in the USA there are about 69 million birdwatchers, of whom about 25 million travel away from their homes every year to go and watch birds (NSRE, 2000). In the UK, recent estimates indicate that there are over one million 'serious' birdwatchers or birders. Children ardently watching television documentaries on nature and distant 'exotic' lands will want to visit these wonders themselves and many will perhaps become ecotourists when they grow older.

But not everything about ecotourism has a bright side. There are also serious problems. As the term 'ecotourism' has currently become very popular and is overused and misused in numerous instances, many pseudo-ecotour outfits are being set up, masquerading as 'green operations' when in reality they are seeking only a fast profit and engaging in no real conservation efforts. In other cases, projects with the intention of being 'ecotouristic' have failed because the training aspects were neglected, or the active involvement of the local communities was not achieved, or for a number of other reasons. Also, tourist 'mega-projects' continue to be rampant in many countries, especially in beach environments, with their well-known ravaging effects on the natural and cultural environment.

But genuine, well-planned ecotourism projects are definitely becoming more numerous and popular. With luck, they will establish a trend for the 21st century and make tourism generally more sustainable everywhere. The question is no longer if tourism may perform a role in the conservation of the natural and cultural heritage of our planet, but rather what are the specific steps that need to be taken in different countries to carry out activities that will ensure a true symbiosis between tourism, conservation and sustainable development.

The Ecolodge Concept

One product of the ecotourism industry is packaged lodge accommodations in remote, natural areas. According to The International Ecotourism Society, the term 'ecolodge' is an 'industry label used to identify a nature-dependent tourist lodge that meets the philosophy of ecotourism' (Hawkins *et al.*, 1995). At a purist level, an ecolodge will offer a tourist an educational and participatory experience, be developed and managed in an environmentally sensitive manner, and protect its operating environment. An ecolodge is different from mainstream lodges, like fishing and ski lodges and luxury retreats. It is the philosophy of ecological sensitivity that must underlie, and ultimately define, each operation.

It must be stressed that the most important thing about an ecolodge is that the ecolodge is not the most important thing (Ceballos-Lascurain, 1997). That is, it is the quality of the surrounding environment that counts most – the nearby natural and cultural attractions – and the way ecotourism circuits and itineraries are set up, operated and marketed. It is also the manner and extent to which local populations are actively involved in the process (see Durham, Chapter 5, this volume; de Vasconcellos Pêgas and Stronza, Chapter 11, this volume).

A primary draw of any ecolodge is its capacity to provide tourists with opportunities to be in close contact with nature. A major distinction between an ecolodge and a traditional lodge is that in the latter the main attractions are of an artificial character, as well as the facilities and activities that take place there (golf, tennis, gymnasiums, water-jetting and water-skiing, windsurfing, swimming pools, etc.). By contrast, the main attractions of an ecolodge are its natural setting and nature-based activities, which allow for a better appreciation and enjoyment of wildlife and wild habitats. In the conventional resort-type lodge, much of the site is typically reconfigured (patios, terraces, lawns, garden compositions, sporting fields, water basins, swimming pools, etc.) and the tourists' experiences are heavily controlled and programmed, reflecting in general an anthropocentric view of the earth's natural resources (i.e. they are there for our use).

In any ecolodge project, there is a need to apply a new approach to architecture, now widely termed as ecological design or 'ecodesign'. Ecodesign may be defined as any form of design that is integrated with surrounding ecosystems and helps minimize negative environmental impacts (Ceballos-Lascurain, 1997). Ecodesign is an integrative and ecologically responsible design discipline. It consists of joining isolated efforts in what has been loosely termed as 'green architecture'.

Ecolodges should be designed in an environmentally friendly way, as they are frequently located in areas of great scenic beauty and ecological significance. Application of appropriate waste treatment methods and the use of alternative energy sources (especially in remote locations) are especially important items to be considered. Physical facilities should be technologically viable and adequate, and also socially acceptable and economically feasible. Joint ventures between communities and the private and non-profit sectors can help meet the expense of such technologies. Physical planning and building (planning for expansion) should always be long-term endeavours. It is important to remember that economic benefits to all parties involved in the ecotourism process come from environmentally friendly facilities and technologies.

Ecolodges are often located in parks or other remote and wild areas, and therefore very few typical infrastructural elements and services found in more traditional settings are available, such as access by paved highway, public transportation services, electric and telephone lines, piped potable water, public drainage and sewage, refuse collection and disposal, nearby school and medical services, shopping areas, etc. For this reason, a totally new and different approach to physical planning is required, one based on a high level of functional, energy and food self-sufficiency. Before designing and building an ecolodge, it is critical to identify clearly and realistically the characteristics of access to infrastructure and public services, and define beforehand the level of self-sufficiency wished to be attained (Mehta and Ceballos-Lascurain, 2002).

Many nature tourists do not expect, in a poor rural area, the facilities found in rich cities and beach resorts. Some enjoy roughing it for a while, and are even prepared to pay more for the privilege. Certain standards will always remain non-negotiable though – especially security and basic hygiene.

It is always important to connect tourism facilities as much as possible with the surrounding environment (both natural and cultural), using architectural forms in harmony with the natural landscape (vegetation and land forms), and designing with long-term environmental criteria in mind. A tourism facility should always possess a sense of place.

The design of an ecolodge must be inspired and inspiring. The subject and application of ecodesign are still incipient in many parts of the world, and it is hoped that clear and appropriate guidelines will soon be applied more widely (Ceballos-Lascurain and Mehta, 2002).

Five main principles of ecodesign are the following:

- *Solutions grow from place*: design should always grow out of specific site conditions and limitations, as well as values of the designers and users. Some of the most beautiful and appropriate examples of architecture around the world have been built by non-architects who expanded their houses and other buildings over time as they learned about the peculiarities of their site, developing precise knowledge of place and making original and unique design responses (Rudofsky, 1964; Van der Ryn and Cowan, 1996).

- *Ecological accounting informs design*: no conventional design is carried out without a careful accounting of all economic costs. Likewise, no conventional design is executed with a careful accounting of all *ecological* costs, from resource depletion to pollution and habitat destruction. Tracing the full set of ecological impacts of a design is obviously a prerequisite for ameliorating those impacts.

- *Design with nature*: by working with the patterns and processes favoured by the living world, we can dramatically reduce the ecological impacts of our designs. We also respect the needs of all species while meeting our own. For example, in nature, materials are continuously broken into their basic components and rebuilt into new living forms. When garbage becomes compost for human use, an essential structure within nature is revealed.

- *Everyone is a designer*: good ecodesign evolves from listening to people with a problem. A design evolves and is adopted because it fits the needs of a particular community of people with shared values and circumstances. The best design experiences occur when no one can claim credit for the solution – when the solution grows and evolves organically out of a particular situation, process and pattern of com-munication. Listen to every voice in the design process. No one is participant only or designer only: everyone should be a participant-designer.

- *Make nature visible*: every user (and builder) of a good ecodesign should learn from using (and building) a specific technology based on ecological principles. Don't hide solutions; rather, let people see how the different parts of buildings work. In the case of sanitary facilities, 'flush and forget' technology does not encourage mindfulness or a sense of responsibility. The design and construction of a composting toilet, for example, usually requires people's involvement, and that involvement necessarily connects them with their own biological processes. De-natured environments ignore our need and our potential for learning. Making natural cycles and processes visible brings the designed environment back to life (Van der Ryn and Cowan, 1996).

Ecolodge Development in the Americas

Ecolodge development is a new phenomenon, and lessons are being learned every day around the world in this fascinating and fast-growing field. There are several areas where ecolodge development is being successfully implemented. Some key areas of ecolodge development around the world include Costa Rica, Belize, Ecuador, Peru, Brazil (mainly the Amazonian area), Venezuela, Australia, New Zealand, Malaysia, Kenya, Tanzania, South Africa, Malawi and Botswana.

There are many recent good examples of ecodesign of tourism facilities around the world. In the Americas the following three examples are noteworthy.

Kapawi Ecolodge

Kapawi is an ecotourism/ecolodge project in a rainforest locality of the Amazonian region of Ecuador. Kapawi is operated by a Quito-based nature tour operator, CANODROS S.A., with community-based participation (members of the Achuar nation), providing a model of environmentally friendly design and also a model of how private capital investments can be integrated with local community goals, with minimum cultural and environmental impacts (Rodríguez, Chapter 10, this volume).

Living in the remotest area of south-eastern Ecuador, the Achuar had little contact with Westerners before the arrival of missionaries in the late 1960s. Even today Western influence is minimal and the Achuar remain nearly self-sufficient in their territory, still able to obtain most of what they need from the forest. The traditional Achuar architecture represents a traditional knowledge of technologies and concepts that have evolved in order to fulfil the conditions imposed by the tropical rainforest. The structure is simple and harmonious with the environment.

The techniques used for the building of the Kapawi Ecolodge followed this traditional concept of architecture and were performed only by members of the Achuar community. Within this framework, a few foreign elements were added to the original Achuar design, such as individual rooms within each house, installing electrical systems powered by solar energy, and bathrooms with sanitary installations that required non-traditional materials such as wires, cement, metallic mosquito netting, furniture, modern waste management, organic black water treatment, etc., yet without invalidating the traditional concept. The Kapawi Ecolodge was built on the edge of a lagoon, accommodating a maximum of 70 people, including guests and staff, this being not larger than a medium-size Achuar village. The Kapawi Ecolodge consists of 21 huts (double rooms), each room with a private bathroom and a terrace facing the lagoon. By building the huts on stilts, less impact was caused to the surrounding vegetation. The complex includes a kitchen, dining room, bar, reading room and boutique, various houses to accommodate staff, storage rooms for food, camping equipment and fuel, a workshop, two docks (one at the nearby river, another at the lake) and a shelter for backup generators (Rodríguez, 1999).

A well provides sediment-free water to the Kapawi Ecolodge. The water is pumped into five plastic reservoirs of 2000 l capacity each, fed by the pump at a rate of 15 l per minute. Submersible solar-powered pumps pressurize the system and distribute the water to the different parts of the ecolodge. The water is filtered in a carbon filter where a silver-nitrate element kills microorganisms. Sun showers provide 10 l of warm water per passenger at the end of the day. Throughout the day there is unlimited cold water.

Canguçu Ecological Center

Located between Araguaia National Park and Cantão State Park in the State of Tocantins, southern Brazil, Canguçu Ecological Center was created by a Brazilian NGO, Instituto Ecológica, originally for developing ecological research (especially in the field of carbon sequestration in the region of Bananal Island). Soon it was decided that, alongside the scientific projects undertaken there, it was important to develop ecotourism as a form of self-sustainability and to provide additional income to the Instituto. An ecolodge was designed and built in Canguçu by the architect, Luis Hildebrando Ferreira Paz.

The ecolodge is built as a wooden structure on stilts, with thatched roof made of piaçaba palm, and is well integrated with the rainforest surroundings. It has a 20 m high observation tower from where tourists can get an expansive view of the Javea River and look for birds in the forest canopy. To operate the ecolodge and promote ecotourism to Canguçu, a tour operator company called Bananal Ecotour was created, working in parallel with the Instituto Ecológica. The goal is to provide a self-financing mechanism for research carried out in the area.

Manu Lodge

Manu Lodge, located in the Amazonian rainforest, is a rustic facility established in 1987 by Manu Nature Tours, using local building materials (wood, palm leaves, bamboo), designed in such a way that it is practically hidden in the forest – its building height is well below the treeline. Situated in Manu Biosphere Reserve, one of the areas of major biodiversity in the world (1100 species of birds), the lodge attracts ecotourists from around the world, especially US birdwatchers, who are willing to pay US$200 per night without having such conventional amenities as electric light (kerosene lamps are used instead) or air conditioning.

A number of activities are organized for visiting ecotourists, including birdwatching, canoe rides to observe giant otters and ethnobotanical walks. There are expert naturalist guides who provide excellent interpretation services to visitors. Two observation towers are provided for watching birds in the canopy. During the low season, Peruvians (including students with high grades) are offered special low-price packages to stay at Manu Lodge.

Conclusion

It is hoped that, in the not too distant future, all ecotourism activities and facilities will be designed with the utmost concern for ecological sustainability. One goal of this endeavour is to make the interest and investments in ecotourism contribute meaningfully to conservation of the planet's natural and cultural heritage. Ultimately, the paradigms and models of ecotourism and ecolodge development may positively influence the ways in which all other types of tourism are carried out. All tourism, including mass tourism, will surely benefit from a trend towards sustainability.

References

Ceballos-Lascurain, H. (1996) *Tourism, Ecotourism and Protected Areas*. International Union for the Conservation of Nature and Natural Resources, Gland, Switzerland.

Ceballos-Lascurain, H. (1997) *Ecolodge Guidelines for the Red Sea Coast of Egypt*. Winrock Organization, Washington, DC.

Ceballos-Lascurain, H. (2001) Integrating Biodiversity into the Tourism Sector: Best Practice and Country Case Studies. Prepared for UNDP/UNEP/GEF Biodiversity Planning Support Programme. United Nations Environment Programme, Nairobi; available at http://www.unep.org/bpsp/Tourism/Tourism%20Synthesis%20Report.pdf (accessed February 2008).

Ceballos-Lascurain, H. and Mehta, H. (2002) Architectural design. In: Mehta, H., Baez, A.L. and O'Loughlin, P. (eds) *International Ecolodge Guidelines*. The International Ecotourism Society, Burlington, Vermont, pp. 55–92.

Hawkins, D.E., Epler Wood, M. and Bittman, S. (1995) *The Ecolodge Sourcebook*. The International Ecotourism Society, Burlington, Vermont.

Honey, M. (1999) *Ecotourism and Sustainable Development*. Island Press, Washington, DC.

Mehta, H. and Ceballos-Lascurain, H. (2002) Site selection, planning and design. In: Mehta, H., Baez, A.L. and O'Loughlin, P. (eds) *International Ecolodge Guidelines*. The International Ecotourism Society, Burlington, Vermont, pp. 7–34.

NSRE (2000) *National Survey of Fishing, Hunting, and Wildlife-associated Recreation*. US Fish & Wildlife Service, Washington, DC.

Rodríguez, A. (1999) *Kapawi, A Model of Sustainable Development in Ecuadorian Amazonia with Community-based Participation and Private Investment*. CANODROS S.A., Quito.

Rudofsky, B. (1964) *Architecture without Architects*. The Museum of Modern Art, New York.

Spenceley, A. (2001) South Africa Case Study. Prepared for UNDP/UNEP/GEF Biodiversity Planning Support Programme. United Nations Environment Programme, Nairobi; available at http://www.unep.org/bpsp/Tourism/Case%20Studies%20(pdf)/SOUTH %20AFRICA%20(Tourism).pdf (accessed February 2008).

Van der Ryn, S. and Cowan, S. (1996) *Ecological Design*. Island Press, Washington, DC.

Wiezsman, P. (2001) Case Study: Tourism and Biodiversity (Ecotourism – A Sustainable Development Tool, A Case for Belize). Prepared for UNDP/UNEP/GEF Biodiversity Planning Support Programme. United Nations Environment Programme, Nairobi; available at http://www.unep.org/bpsp/Tourism/Case%20Studies%20(pdf)/Belize (Tourism).pdf (accessed February 2008).

WTTC (2000) *Update on World Tourism*. World Travel and Tourism Council, Brussels.

Zamora, N. and Obando, V. (2001) Biodiversity and Tourism in Costa Rica. Prepared for UNDP/UNEP/GEF Biodiversity Planning Support Programme. United Nations Environment Programme, Nairobi; available at http://www.unep.org/bpsp/Tourism/ Case%20Studies%20(pdf)/COSTA%20RICA%20(Tourism).pdf (accessed February 2008).

Part VIII

Guidelines and Standards

_____

14 An Ecotourism Project Analysis and Evaluation Framework for International Development Donors

M. EPLER WOOD

EplerWood International, Burlington, Vermont, USA

Introduction

The effort to set sustainability standards for ecotourism has focused primarily on the private sector since the late 1980s. The process of introducing standards for ecotourism development was steady in the 1990s with guidelines developed for nature tour operators (TIES, 1993), ecolodges (Mehta *et al.*, 2002) and marine ecotourism (Halpenny, 2002; see also Stonich, Chapter 4, this volume). Certification standards for ecotourism businesses or the more inclusive field of sustainable tourism have been established in Australia, Costa Rica, Kenya and Jamaica, among other countries, and an active effort to coordinate these activities and create a global certification system has been promoted extensively by non-governmental organizations (NGOs) (Rainforest Alliance, 2003). While private sector guidelines and certification were the focus of much NGO activity since 2000, few initiatives have focused on the accurate monitoring and evaluation of donor-funded ecotourism projects. Investment in donor-funded sustainable tourism projects, many of which are managed by NGOs, reached over US$7 billion between 1998 and 2002, making donors the largest investors in sustainable tourism and ecotourism development worldwide (Christ *et al.*, 2003).

This chapter documents that one of the most influential sectors in the ecotourism development process – donors (defined as private foundations, and bilateral and multilateral agencies) – have not yet developed clear and transparent monitoring and evaluation indicators for ecotourism projects, to ensure that the ecotourism projects they fund worldwide meet triple bottom-line standards. The chapter responds to this important gap by exploring the literature regarding standards for ecotourism development projects, and discusses how such standards could be developed in the future, in terms of data analysis needs, multiple-stakeholder input and a review of existing recommendations from previous forums worldwide.

The *World Ecotourism Summit Final and Preparatory Meeting Reports* (WTO, 2002a) provided important guidance on the progress of governments, NGOs, communities and the private sector in establishing a framework for sustainability. The World Tourism Organization (WTO) also has published an important text entitled *Indicators of Sustainable Development for Tourism Destinations: A Guidebook*, which provides key guidance to local and municipal governments on how to monitor the development of their destinations (WTO, 2004a). Hawkins and Lamoureux (2006) published a paper on indicators and performance monitoring systems that can guide a destination's stakeholders in decision making and that can benefit the local tourism industry and community, as well as visitors who have chosen their tourism destination. They conclude that while there are some successes in the area of monitoring, far greater attention needs to be placed on recognizing the need for comprehensive monitoring systems with indicators.

I propose the development of a project monitoring and evaluation framework that defines indicators for conservation, community development and business competitiveness that can be accessed online intersectorally and reviewed by university researchers, donor evaluators, NGOs, communities and the private sector. Proposals for improving the sustainable nature of this sector are being updated at all times, and the process of developing useable guidelines for donor projects will take time and the participation of stakeholders around the world, especially those who have participated in donor-funded projects. In this chapter I offer a proposal for a framework to begin the process of input and review. It is not intended to be a final product. None the less, I suggest that a consistent project-monitoring and -evaluation framework for donors funding ecotourism is urgently needed and is crucial to the success of donor support for this new and innovative field.

Donor Support History

A study by researchers from The George Washington University (GWU), Conservation International (CI) and the United Nations Environment Programme (UNEP) resulted in a database with details of over 320 tourism-related projects. The aim was to determine the amount of donor funds channelled into tourism development and the types of projects funded in 2002. The investment totalled US$7 billion over 5 years. Only 17% of the projects included 'tourism' in the title, while most referenced environmental protection. The authors concluded that this lack of definition of tourism as a sectoral area of support has made it extremely difficult for donors to evaluate the outcomes of tourism-related projects (Christ *et al.*, 2003).

European researchers found that most European development agencies link biodiversity conservation with poverty reduction within local communities, local cultural preservation, sensitive promotion to visitors and biodiversity improvements (SECA, 2000). However, there were few strict criteria and evaluation procedures. Only informal approaches for funding have been identified. This indicates the need for an immediate effort to establish a consistent monitoring and evaluation framework that can be adapted for use by donor organizations around the world.

In 1998, I undertook an analysis of European and US donor-supported projects in Ecuador for The Nature Conservancy, where a confluence of donor-supported ecotourism and biodiversity projects was well under way (Epler Wood, 1998). Some 33 community-based ecotourism projects were documented in Ecuador at that time, most of which had received donor support (Wesche and Drumm, 1999). I concluded that new funding guidelines were urgently needed to prevent project failures. This publication was distributed widely by The International Ecotourism Society and The Nature Conservancy in Spanish and English, and incorporated into the recommendations of other publications on the development of community-based ecotourism projects (Denman, 2001; Hausler and Strasdas, 2002).

The GWU/CI/UNEP publication *Tourism and Biodiversity: Mapping Tourism's Global Footprint* notes that development agencies do not view themselves as important in setting the stage for sustainable tourism development (Christ *et al.*, 2003). However, their research with 35 ecotourism experts showed that while development agencies may be unaware of their role in influencing actors on the ground during critical phases of siting, land-use planning, design and choice of technologies and materials, experts found development agencies to be influential in their decision-making processes.

The consistent lack of recognition of the donor role in ecotourism and sustainable tourism development, and the lack of definition of tourism as a specific area for donor support, has led to many problems. These were confirmed in 1999 when donor representatives from the Inter-American Development Bank, the World Bank and German, French and Norwegian bilateral aid representatives met to discuss with ecotourism leaders how to set standards for ecotourism projects. The results of this Ecotourism Development Policy Forum were summarized with the following points: (i) there are critical gaps in existing knowledge and information regarding ecotourism; (ii) ecotourism projects in the donor community lack coordination and have high overlap; and (iii) donor packages intended to conserve biological diversity have often failed to properly account for tourism market realities (Epler Wood, 2002).

In response to these gaps in donor advance analysis, excellent procedures for technical assistance were formulated by the German bilateral support agency GTZ, which looked at the first stage of ecotourism technical assistance (Steck *et al.*, 1999). These guidelines stress the importance of analysis of existing laws and regulations in force, the collection of statistical data to gauge the development of ecotourism, the consolidation of legal frameworks and financial adjustment mechanisms to avoid or reduce disparities brought about by tourism development.

More recently, a document was produced for the US Agency for International Development (USAID) which reviewed how sustainable and ecotourism projects were implemented by USAID worldwide between 1995 and 2005. This study found that sustainable tourism was primarily used as a tool to meet objectives like biodiversity conservation, gender equality or poverty alleviation. The study recommended good monitoring and evaluation not only during the project but also after it ended. It pointed out that all too often anecdotal evidence has been used as a measure of success. Finally, it recommended clarifying the goals and objectives of sustainable tourism and making certain that they can be measured from the outset of every project (NRIC, 2005).

The USAID document also recommended learning from the mistakes of others (NRIC, 2005). An effort to coordinate knowledge and advance cooperation between donors took place in 2004. The WTO Sustainable Tourism Policy Forum gathered leaders from donor organizations around the world and produced a Washington Declaration on Tourism as a Sustainable Development Strategy (WTO, 2004b), which called for more collaboration between international donors, researchers, policy makers and educators in the field of sustainable tourism. But the mechanism for implementing such cooperation was not made clear.

I suggest that donors need to endorse a triple bottom-line monitoring and evaluation framework for ecotourism and sustainable tourism, which includes conservation, community and business competitiveness development indicators that can be reviewed and accessed by researchers and consultants, and updated via research meetings every 3 to 5 years. While good efforts have now taken place to review lessons learned and coordination among donors is increasing, a more standardized monitoring and evaluation structure for donor projects is still lacking and remains as a high priority in this field.

Evaluation Framework for Ecotourism as a Conservation Strategy

As stated above, ecotourism principles, standards and guidelines have evolved for private business, but evaluation standards are only now being discussed for organizations carrying out ecotourism projects as a strategy for conservation. An informal inquiry sent to The Nature Conservancy, CI and RARE in 2002 resulted in the finding that the development of evaluation and monitoring systems is still in the early stages. An historical analysis of The Nature Conservancy's 5-year ecotourism programme for USAID-funded Parks in Peril 2000 found no standardized, measurable monitoring and evaluation criteria for projects (Jones, 2007). The Biodiversity Support Network's final publication included ecotourism projects in a general framework of evaluation, but used indirect measures of conservation achievement (Margoulis *et al.*, 2000). A 'threat reduction assessment' approach was used to represent the conservation impact at each site. This technique examines the ability of the project to achieve biodiversity conservation by evaluating the area, intensity and urgency of each threat, as well as the degree to which all threats have been addressed by project activities.

A review of recent papers that include field examples helped to formulate an initial list of questions for ecotourism evaluation that would help donors and NGOs evaluate ecotourism as a conservation tool.

1. How does ecotourism contribute to costs of managing protected areas?

There is no international database regarding the use of visitor fees to parks, but anecdotal evidence indicates they have been introduced and/or increased at many developed and developing country natural areas in the 1990s (Lindberg, 2001). Giongo *et al.* (1993) surveyed 319 protected areas in the world and found that over 50% of revenues for protected areas in developing countries were from visitor entrance fees. However, to study real conservation impact it must also be noted exactly what portion of the fees are used directly in the protected area. Giongo *et al.*'s study showed that 32% of these fees were returned to the protected areas.

Recent developments around the world indicate that more tourism funds are being earmarked for conservation. The US Fee Demonstration Project provides 80% of the new fees worth a total of $176 million in 2000/1 to the park or forest that collects it (Lindberg, 2001). In Belize, the Protected Area Conservation Trust (PACT) collects departure taxes for a fund used to finance natural area conservation. The proposed fee for PACT was reduced from US$10 to US$3.75 because of opposition to fees from the tourism industry (Spergel, 1996). None the less, according to PACT's *2000 Annual Report* (PACT, 2001), US$500,000 in conservation fees were being collected per annum, and between April 2000 and March 2001, US$275,000 in grants were awarded in amounts between US$10,000 and US$35,000 to both terrestrial and marine reserves.

It is well documented that funding of protected areas is not adequate around the world. The World Conservation Union (IUCN) estimates that 80% of protected areas' budgets are not being covered by any source, and that an estimated 'US$20–30 billion annually over the next 30 years [is] required to establish and maintain a comprehensive protected area system including terrestrial, wetland, and marine ecosystems' (IUCN, 2003).

One of the problems identified in the 'Financial Security for Protected Areas' recommendations of the 2003 World Parks and Protected Area Congress was that 'revenues from tourist income… [are] not being earmarked for protected area management' (IUCN, 2003). Advance project analysis and evaluation questions should therefore include a focus on how much total revenue ecotourism is providing to protected areas, what percentage is being earmarked for conservation in specific protected areas, and what proportion of total protected area budgets is being covered by ecotourism.

2. What are the biophysical impacts of tourism in natural areas?

The significance of biophysical visitor impacts on natural areas worldwide has never been quantified biologically. Tracking impacts is dependent on having or obtaining baseline data, but it is frequently unavailable. Giongo *et al.* (1993) found that monitoring of impacts was taking place in just over 50% of parks in developed countries and in less than 35% in developing countries. The 'Tourism as a Vehicle for Conservation and Support of Protected Areas' recommendations of the 2003 World Parks and Protected Area Congress touch only lightly on this issue, stating that optimum types and levels of protected area visitation should be determined. The mandate should be stronger, given the critical nature of monitoring as a primary tool to prevent tourism impacts on natural ecosystems. The publication *Sustainable Tourism in Protected Areas: Guidelines for Planning and Management*, published jointly by UNEP, IUCN and WTO, makes the case more strongly: 'Monitoring is an essential component of any planning or management process, for without monitoring managers know nothing about progress towards the objectives that have been set' for visitor management (Eagles *et al.*, 2002).

If biophysical monitoring is not taking place, an evaluation framework can categorize the biophysical categories of impact and the percentage area being affected. A study based on interviews with US park superintendents in 51 parks found 30% of the parks had significant impacts on vegetation, 37% on wildlife, 22% on water quality and 15% on air quality (Wang and Miko, 1997). This study did not inquire what percentage areas of the parks referenced were having these difficulties, a sorely needed piece of information. Giongo *et al.* (1993) showed that managers had concerns about erosion, site spreading, trail depth, water quality and vegetation impacts. These problems were cited as being an issue in fewer than 20% of the parks in developed countries and in fewer than 5% in developing countries, again without information on the percentage area being affected. Developed world parks had particular concerns about trail depth, site spreading and erosion, which were found to have exceeded acceptable levels in twice as many parks in developed countries than in developing ones.

Another evaluation focal point for the impacts of tourism in natural areas is the existence of direct management strategies, including zoning, required guides, citations and fines, campsite designation, limitation of visit duration, reservation systems and visitor number limits. Ten years ago these strategies were used by less than 50% of developed world parks and less than 40% of most developing world parks (Giongo *et al.*, 1993). The existence of regulations to manage visitation in parks and protected areas around the world may be an important indicator of progress in the future to understand if ecotourism is having an impact on conservation of natural areas. However, Giongo *et al.* (1993) note that protected areas tend to avoid direct regulation of visitors as much as possible, preferring indirect management techniques.

Direct impact management indicators on the biophysical environment near trails and campsites must be accounted for as well as indicators of impacts on wildlife, water and air quality. Indirect management techniques include signs, patrols, tour operators, introductory talks, written material, displays, etc. These management approaches can also be tracked as part of an evaluation framework, to understand how well natural areas are using information to educate visitors.

3. How are ecotourism impacts managed in buffer zones of protected areas?

While some attention is generally paid to visitor impacts on areas within the borders of protected areas, startlingly little attention has been paid to the management of visitor impacts outside the borders of protected areas. The lack of controls on the use of land by both private landowners and commercial developers outside protected areas can have a devastating effect, and this must be tracked in order to understand the impacts of ecotourism on natural areas. Very little data on this topic exist. The Nature Conservancy guidelines for visitor monitoring (Rome, 1999) recommended monitoring outside protected areas because of the impacts of tourism on local communities.

Different approaches to managing tourism growth have been documented (e.g. Bosselman *et al.*, 1999) and these growth management strategies should be reviewed as part of a framework of evaluation when looking at regions affected by ecotourism development. Zoning and controlling visitor quantity using a variety of zones designated according to type of use constitute the most common approach to controlling visitor impacts, and can be considered a fundamental tool to protect areas from visitor impacts. Tourism plans are another strategy that can help the affected communities to understand what their goals are for protection, and allow community members to begin the process of establishing either zoning or limitation strategies. Design planning can help areas establish the types of exterior elements desired, such as architecture, vegetation buffers and density of each building site. This type of planning helps the community to control its own sense of 'self' and maintain control of outside development influences.

Regulatory mechanisms must also be tracked, such as the municipality's ability to control density of land use and the types of environmental impact analyses required to gain building permits. In many areas, municipalities still have no ability to limit commercial buildings that do not have sewage treatment or other basic health and safety requirements. The *World Ecotourism Summit Final and Preparatory Meeting Reports* offer volumes of data on the lack of adequate government tourism policies to protect the environment and health standards (WTO, 2002a). I performed a regional and international ecotourism policy gap analysis for the World Bank/International Finance Corporation (IFC)/Global Environment Facility (GEF) using these data and found there was no monitoring of tourism impacts and no land-use planning in most parts of the developing world (EplerWood International, 2003). Furthermore, inspections and monitoring for health standards were considerably weak worldwide (see Table 14.1).

It is difficult to imagine progress towards sustainable tourism unless important regulatory and policy gaps are addressed. In just one case study in Belize, the authors of the report *Rural Ecotourism Assessment Program (REAP)* found that while significant donor funds are flowing towards NGO projects focused on biodiversity conservation off the coast of Belize within marine protected areas, local communities living below the poverty line in buffer zones directly adjacent to marine protected areas have no sewage treatment system and no source of financial support from their government or donors to develop such a system (Lash and Austin, 2003).

Indicators to review for managing buffer zone impacts therefore include the existence of zoning, community tourism and design plans and regulatory mechanisms, which include financial commitment for enforcement and legislative requirements for proper sewage treatment and other fundamentals of environmental health and safety in all tourism development zones.

4. What impact is ecotourism having on biological diversity?

While tourism's impacts on wildlife and vegetation have been tracked by protected area managers in the past decades to a limited degree (see question 1), efforts to track tourism's impacts on biological diversity are just beginning. Excellent progress was made with the publication of the GWU/CI/UNEP report *Tourism and Biodiversity*, which maps tourism's global footprint (Christ *et al.*, 2003).

Technically, tracking biodiversity impacts in hotspot regions, in terms of collecting data on populations of indicator species, may be a greater challenge. Baseline data will be hard to obtain in most biologically rich areas. The analysis of biodiversity impacts of tourism and the monitoring of such impacts will be a cost-intensive process dependent on the participation of institutions that are willing to work in cooperation with donor projects. It is likely that monitoring costs are often viewed by donors as prohibitive and therefore biodiversity monitoring of tourism impacts is often not pursued in terms of technically tracking indicator species.

A great deal of valuable data can be obtained by creating a supportive environment for researchers. Some basic methods of establishing research cooperation are recommended here based on my experience with donor projects and a review of ideas included in the UNEP/IUCN/WTO guidelines for research cooperation in protected areas (Eagles *et al.*, 2002). These are: (i) sharing employment costs for research between university and donor projects; (ii) creating research cooperation agreements for donor projects; (iii) developing an accessible library of studies with databases for the use of all researchers during the life of a donor project; and (iv) providing transport and encouraging researchers to work on-site

Table 14.1. International ecotourism policy analysis. (From *World Ecotourism Summit Final Report, Theme A* (WTO 2002a).)

Policy-making body/policy type	Policy tool	Policy action
Legislative body and executive branch		
Legal frameworks	Legal review of tourism policies	Integrate needs of ecotourism businesses in legal policies for tourism
Legislative frameworks	Review of relevant legislations	Integrate needs of ecotourism businesses in municipal and local legislation
Fiscal commitment	Budget review	Incorporate ecotourism legislative, legal and policy frameworks into budget for economic development
Tourism board		
National marketing	Internet and trade fairs	Incorporate ecotourism information in national travel market campaigns
Market intelligence	Market research	Quality research of ecotourism market sector for nation
Regional marketing	Regional ecotourism networks	Financial and logistical support for marketing networks
Inter-ministerial cooperation		
Transboundary initiatives	Transnational policies	Meetings between countries to establish cooperation
Inter-ministerial planning	Integrated planning	Inter-ministerial working groups
Tourism ministry		
Policy frameworks	National ecotourism plans and policies	Integrate policy with other national development and conservation goals
Health standards	Inspections and monitoring	Ensure facilities meeting health standards
Environment and natural resources		
Development planning	Zoning, land-use planning	Limit scale of tourism development
Monitoring	Enforcement	Funds to enforce development regulations
Protected areas	Visitor management	Funds for baseline data, manage impacts
Provincial or municipal government		
Participative planning	Participative policy planning	Incorporate community and indigenous populations in planning for ecotourism development
Land tenure	Reform of land titling	Review of land titling issues in ecotourism development zones
Land use	Zoning, land-use planning	Develop Ecotourism Development Zones
Infrastructural support	Signage, roads, communication, electricity, water, solid waste, sewage treatment	Review needs in ecotourism zones, target development as appropriate
Economic development		
Public–private cooperation	Private sector advisory board	Develop Advisory Board
Sustainable growth	National tourism accounting system reform	Develop economic indicators for tourism development in different zones. Review incentives for development in poor and rural areas, triple bottom-line results

during project development as part of a monitoring team that both gathers scientific data and monitors specific agreed-upon data points, obtained via participatory processes, during the life of the project.

There are many benefits to creating research agreements to monitor biodiversity (and other) impacts with local research institutions. Research cooperation can result in educating students attending biology programmes in developing countries, who can learn a great deal from participating in monitoring programmes. Donor support for such cooperation can help support local university programmes and help advance the state of knowledge of tourism impacts. Databases for biodiversity monitoring of tourism projects is distinct from scientific biodiversity monitoring, and indicators must be established via participatory processes with local communities in accordance with standard visitor management practices (Eagles *et al.*, 2002). Such monitoring indicators should be established and maintained by local institutions that have a research agenda, in order for them to become a valuable part of the intellectual capital for the region. Such databases provide vital information for future tourism impact/ biodiversity monitoring projects. Once established with local universities they can become valuable assets for future use, in cooperation with government entities, such as natural resource and protected area agencies, that are traditionally extremely short on funds to undertake monitoring in parks and protected areas.

5. What impact is ecotourism having on new government policies?

At the World Ecotourism Summit (WES) in May 2002 in Quebec, Canada, there was an effort to collate and synthesize all preparatory meetings and presentations made during the event. Table 14.1 provides a breakdown of the recommendations made at WES according to the policy type needed, policy tools recommended and policy actions required.

At the international level, it is clear from the results at WES that legislative and legal frameworks for ecotourism are still lacking. There will need to be a long-term effort to integrate the needs of donor projects into legal policies for tourism at the national, provincial and local level. There is also a pressing need to require the incorporation of tourism legal and regulatory frameworks into the budget at all levels of government. Until fiscal commitment is achieved, planning will not result in action.

Evaluation of government policies should be a part of any donor evaluation framework. A possible framework for the evaluation of government policies is presented in Box 14.1.

6. Is ecotourism building environmental and social awareness of destinations?

The role of ecotourism in educating visitors and the community has been stressed throughout the world, but in particular in Australia. Interpretation is an integral component of ecotourism, as it can help visitors gain a better awareness, appreciation and understanding of the natural areas they visit

---

Box 14.1. Starting points for government ecotourism programmes. (From Epler Wood, 2002.)

1. Establish an Inter-ministerial Working Group that combines expertise of the Ministries of Tourism, Environment and the agency or agencies charged with rural development.
2. Empower and fund a secretariat of experts that work in the fields of natural resource management, community development and tourism.
3. Develop a participatory planning programme that involves stakeholders from throughout the country or region, including rural and indigenous communities.
4. Establish objectives for a programme based on stakeholder input, such as increased rural economic development, increased budgets for management of protected areas and better management of visitors in fragile areas.
5. Develop training programmes for tourism ministry and other relevant government personnel.
6. Review transportation corridors, trail systems, small-scale non-commercial river transportation systems, small aircraft access and other infrastructure necessary to develop ecotourism. Develop a transportation plan that facilitates good ecotourism itineraries; stresses low environmental impact, low energy use, visitor safety and scenic qualities; and provides quality visitor information.
7. Develop both policies to meet objectives and budgetary mechanisms to fund them. Seek legislative approvals where necessary.
8. Develop a visitor information programme and niche market plan.
9. Develop a long-term community training programme to develop community participation in ecotourism development.
10. Establish biological and social carrying capacity benchmarks through research that establishes long-term monitoring of tourism impacts.
11. Develop finance mechanisms for the development of small ecolodges that provide incentives to conserve land and train local people.
12. Develop an information base and best practice information through university research programmes for biological monitoring of ecotourism impacts.
13. Develop land-use planning capacity in local municipalities through exposure to the benefits of zoning and regulatory techniques. Limit dense development in buffer zones of protected lands and other important ecotourism attractions.

(Charters and Law, 2000; see also Kohl, Chapter 8, this volume). Understanding how ecotourism delivers information about the environment and local cultures is fundamental to evaluating it. Interpretive programmes should be evaluated by the quality of their design and by other components summarized below:

- It is critical that the interpretive activity is based on sound information that is presented in a balanced manner so that visitors are able to form their own opinions.
- There should be a clear distinction between facts and opinions.
- There should be cooperation between the agency and the ecotourism operator to ensure the integrity of the content of interpretation.
- There should be an interpretive strategy that focuses on messages to be delivered and appropriate techniques to deliver the message.
- There should be training of interpretive staff.

The six questions identified above are fundamental to the understanding of how well ecotourism interpretation programmes are designed, which makes the assessment process less complex and vulnerable to assumptions of the researcher or the project designer. They are summarized below in Box 14.2.

Ecotourism as a Community Development Strategy

The discussion of how well ecotourism contributes to sustainability relies not just on a conservation bottom line, which has been argued by certain experts (Brandon and Margoluis, 1996). Sustainable development literature has shown that the triple bottom line of conservation, economic and cultural/social benefits needs to be considered equally (SustainAbility, 1996).

How ecotourism contributes to the social bottom line, or local 'well-being', is the most complex analysis with the fewest parameters agreed upon in the literature or with donors.

Ecotourism strives to be not only a conservation mechanism and an economic development tool, but also a development process that seeks to remain harmonious with local cultural and social needs. Assessing these factors has been difficult, although studies by the Organization of Labour in Bolivia, Peru and Ecuador (Maldonado, 2001, 2002) and the Pro-Poor Tourism Programme (Ashley *et al.*, 2001) have led the way with good evaluative frameworks. The authors of these studies agree that: (i) tourism must deliver net benefits to the poor as a goal in itself (Ashley *et al.*, 2001); and (ii) economic development cannot be justified for its own sake, but rather there must be a validation of social capital and a contribution to the preservation of cultural identity to genuinely contribute to the community (Maldonado, 2002). These two guiding principles will be interwoven into all aspects of the proposed framework as follows.

Box 14.2. Interpretation Benchmarks.

Design	Methodology	Information Quality
An interpretation strategy must guide all materials and presentations	Cooperation between tourism operators or other private sector entities and protected area agencies must guide the process of programme development	Text and presentations must be based on referenced information
Materials must include useful visualizations of key points and clear text	Training for all guides and interpretive staff must be ongoing	Content must be balanced with a clear distinction between facts and opinion

7. Has ecotourism contributed to the expansion of local business opportunities?

Tourism is a labour-intensive sector and has the potential of reducing poverty through employment. The Pro-Poor Tourism Programme case studies evaluate complementary tourism enterprises as being equally important to the actual supply of the tourism products themselves, such as craft initiatives. Lessons learned from the Pro-Poor tourism study show that credit and training are fundamental to the success of tourism as a tool to expand local business opportunities for the poor.

Maldonado (2001, 2002) finds that while business opportunities may expand, the pay for service can be extremely low and communities manage poorly the concepts of cost of goods, depreciation, amortization and the use of profits to build a business. Lessons learned from this study suggest that the training of community members in the management of funds could produce significant benefits and avoid possible conflicts among community members.

An evaluation framework could therefore include questions about credit availability for micro businesses and training for the management of small business finances. The value of labour could also be assessed in the area and compared with what local community members are earning in the ecotourism project.

8. Are economic opportunities from ecotourism reaching new segments of the population?

Maldonado (2001, 2002) looks at the question of how much economic opportunity has resulted from ecotourism in each country he studied – Bolivia, Peru and Ecuador. What he finds is that Bolivia offers very few legitimate examples of economic opportunity for local and indigenous communities in ecotourism, while Ecuador and Peru show increasing evidence of growth. He points out that the characteristics of products from these rural segments of society are often limited and quite dependent on outside forces, largely due to the centralization of the economies of the countries he studied. He explains that nearly all capital is held largely in the cities with the economic elite. The marginalization and lack of attention to rural areas by state institutions in all three countries are a significant problem. As a result, the private sector is less likely to invest in rural areas because the potential for yields are reduced by the lack of infrastructure. None the less, he points out that the Government of Ecuador has had a positive impact by investing in the legalization of community business and assisting with community ecotourism develop-ment. He also notes the Government of Peru has assisted with community-based product development. He discusses NGO investment as well, but points out that much of this investment has been lost due to a lack of understanding of business development. What is helpful and enlightening

about Maldonado's study is that it seeks to lay out the existing social/
political economic framework of the rural poor first before analysing what
ecotourism can contribute to the development process.

All of the Pro-Poor case studies were among poor, marginalized
peoples around the world of a variety of ethnic and indigenous origins
(Ashley *et al.*, 2001). The authors found that individuals in case study
projects would not otherwise have been employed because there were few
other viable economic activities in the areas studied. The core groups
working earned enough to bring them above the poverty line. In three case
studies a high percentage of the earners were women.

In formulating an evaluation framework, it appears that both macro and
micro conditions need to be considered. The pre-existing development
scenario must be clearly outlined by a research process that seeks to identify
the impacts of just one development tool such as ecotourism. In terms of
inputs to this pre-existing situation, the involvement of government in
developing business opportunities for marginalized populations is one
significant evaluation factor. Other micro factors to consider would include
the earnings of individuals who were previously below the poverty line or
may not have worked before due to a lack of other economic activities in the
area. Finally, how many women gain opportunity through ecotourism and
related businesses could be evaluated.

9. Have collective benefits to the communities been enhanced?

The collective benefits to be considered are numerous, and they go well
beyond income and employment generated. Understanding collective
benefits will help the evaluator to understand whether ecotourism is
contributing to the well-being of local people.

The Pro-Poor study of Ashley *et al.* (2001) included the following
categories to consider for collective benefits:

- Human capital: skills, education and health.
- Physical capital: roads, water, other infrastructure and tools.
- Financial capital: credit and collective income.
- Social capital and community organizations.
- Access to information.
- Policy context.
- Market opportunities, livelihood options.
- Cultural values.
- Optimism, pride and participation.
- Exposure to risk and exploitation.

As Maldonado (2001) points out, the communities he studied confront
many restrictions due to the structure of society, the market and the State,
where they continue to be excluded and discriminated against in terms of
their access to resources, public services, development opportunity,
education, professional training and health. All of this results in their

lessened ability to genuinely take part in ecotourism or any development opportunity. In studying specific communities in the Andean region, he found that they seek better access to public services, health, education and welfare. This study therefore confirms that in order to evaluate ecotourism as a sustainable development tool, its ability to contribute to community collective benefits is a fundamental point.

In addition to the points above, Maldonado also adds that communities must have their legal and land rights guaranteed. While ecotourism should not be evaluated according to its ability to deliver legal rights, legal land rights must be viewed as a basic minimum standard in order for ecotourism development to properly proceed.

10. What are the social and cultural impacts of ecotourism?

This evaluation point is difficult indeed, and deserves still more background research at the field level. The International Year of Ecotourism Preparatory Meeting results on monitoring social and cultural impacts for Mesoamerica offered wisdom based on the cumulative experience of participants from communities and community projects in Central America.

One thing they agreed is that sensible, rapid and inexpensive evaluation and monitoring tools are needed to evaluate the economic, social and environmental impacts of ecotourism. At present few donors provide assistance or mechanisms for monitoring, and the open marketplace does not require the use of social or environmental impact monitoring tools. There is little technical clarity on how to measure social impacts (WTO, 2002b).

There are few consistent guidelines on this topic. But to review some recent recommendations (Maldonado, 2001), there could be the following points for evaluation:

- Provision of education and training for the delivery of tourism products that is equitable.
- Full respect and protection of the values, symbols and cultural expressions of the community's identity, language, customs and traditions.
- Strengthening of the organizational abilities of the community for representation at a regional and national level.
- Development of a process of exchange between communities to enable them to develop a strong sense of solidarity with other communities and cultures around the world.

The potential well-known negative social and cultural impacts of tourism (Epler Wood, 2002) must also be evaluated with feedback mechanisms for project redesign, such as:

- Loss of local traditions.
- Commercialization of local products.
- Erosion of self-worth.

- Undermining of family structure.
- Loss of interest in land stewardship.
- Fighting among those who benefit and those who do not.
- Crime and adoption of illegal underground economies.

Most ecotourism researchers and practitioners agree all ecotourism should have the following preconditions:

- Prior informed consent from the community.
- Participatory community pre-assessment when requested with experienced third-party professionals and community discussion of results.
- Participation of a representative group of community members including ethnic minorities and women in all phases of the tourism development process must be funded within the project design.
- Training for all community members interested to understand the basis of tourism development with follow-up for those who will be active in the development process.

Finally, a Declaration of Otavalo, written on behalf of communities that met to discuss sustainable, competitive tourism within the communities, suggests that there must be federal, state and municipal policies that respect rights and seek to redress the historical reality of marginalized groups that have not had adequate representation in the past (Otavalo, 2001).

11. Has ecotourism improved access to information and allowed for more participation within society?

While the rights of communities to reject development is paramount, a great many communities seek access to information and have a desire to be less marginalized via participatory community, municipal and civil society processes that include them. Ecotourism could be evaluated according to the kinds of 'strategic alliances' that the community has gained as a result of its involvement in tourism, with the private sector, NGOs, other communities or civil society associations.

Ecotourism could also be evaluated according to the communications mechanisms brought to the community, such as short-wave radios, computers and Internet, or other tools that give the community access to technical (not entertainment) information desired or needed for development.

There might be a review of how many community members actually take part in community-, municipal- and state-level meetings in order to determine if ecotourism has enhanced or decreased the participatory nature of the local culture and society. The ability for women or marginalized ethnic groups to participate should be analysed not only at the state level but also at the community level. The 'Community Benefit Questions' are summarized in Box 14.3.

Box 14.3. Community Development Benchmarks.

Economic Opportunity	Collective Benefits	Social and Cultural Benefits	Quality of Participatory Process
Expansion of local business opportunity	Enhancement of human, physical, financial, and social capital	Educational opportunities improved	Prior informed consent before programme is initiated
Income generation that reaches new segments of society	Policy background and context provided	Cultural values protected	Participaotry pre-assessment process facilitated by neutral outside experts
New market opportunities	Improved access to information via communication technologies	Organizational abilities strengthened	Participation of representative groups including ethnic minorities and women
Diversified market opportunities		Improved options for exchange and solidarity	Training

Ecotourism as a Competitive Business Strategy

Studies of the business of ecolodges and ecotourism have been few and far between. The ground-breaking study by Sanders and Halpenny (2000) represented a first step in creating a more systematic set of data on the economics and financing of ecolodges. Genuine ecolodges have been in operation for less than 10 years, and many have been profitable for only several years. Until 2003, studies on ecolodges had been unable to look at business models or success parameters, because many lodges were too informal to provide sufficient business background or had not been in business long enough to become profitable. In addition, there was insufficient understanding of ecolodge standards to evaluate how well ecolodges were meeting triple bottom-line standards.

Recent research for the World Bank/IFC/GEF presents excellent evidence that the private sector can be a very successful purveyor of triple bottom-line benefits for developing countries (EplerWood International, 2003). The authors of the report concluded that fostering profitable businesses in partnership with local communities should be the primary goal, because these businesses are the most likely to deliver conservation results and social benefits. The 15 private businesses studied fostered 73 smaller partner businesses – all with triple bottom-line success including highly innovative forms of long-term community equity in project outcomes.

More recently the World Economic Forum has published the first *Travel and Tourism Competitiveness Index* (Blanke and Chiesa, 2007). This index is organized into 13 categories within three broad categories: (i) regulatory framework; (ii) business environment and infrastructure; and (iii) human, cultural and natural resources. The business category captures such indicators as air transport infrastructure, tourism infrastructure, ground transport infrastructure, and price competitiveness. The top ten countries are all developed with the number one country being Switzerland. While this new Index provides an important and sophisticated monitoring system for countries, it is not designed for donors working in developing countries and it is not a system designed for sustainable tourism or ecotourism.

This study looks at market and business indicators of importance for donors seeking to evaluate the potential viability of ecotourism business models in developing countries. Some of the key findings from the World Bank/IFC/GEF study indicate that there are some very clear factors that give ecotourism enterprises a market edge (EplerWood International, 2003).

- *Destination*: the destination where the business is located must be perceived by the market as attractive in terms of providing the desired experience within a safe context. What makes a destination attractive often relates to the charisma of the natural or wildlife attraction, good government policies that foster local businesses, promote ecotourism and cover some of the costs for preserving the environment and providing local infrastructure, and the international media's interest in the area as expressed through magazine, television and newspaper coverage.
- *Value*: successful ecotourism businesses are those capable of distinguishing themselves from the competition in ways that make their product more attractive in a manner where clients perceive they are receiving more value for their ecotourism dollar.
- *Interpretation and other activities*: attractions such as unique species, congregations of mega fauna and unique cultural experiences are all important elements in making the destination attractive, but it is the interesting activities, high-quality interpretation and other perceived benefits which define success.
- *Accessibility*: accessibility generally impacts the cost of the product and determines the size of the client market. Operators that are on daily commercial flight schedules with easy connections to international flights have a clear advantage over others that have less reliable air service.
- *Management*: good management is a very broad category and encompasses areas such as marketing, financial management, logistics, human resource management and systems implementations. Successful businesses appear to have a healthy balance of passion for the business combined with the right mix of technical skills and vision.
- *Marketing*: the ability to market the product and diversify the client base stands out as one of the core competencies required for success. A large marketing budget is not necessarily a requirement for success, although larger budgets could improve sales results and sustainability. Marketing success requires a clear vision of how to position oneself in the market with pricing, services and strategic marketing. This is

complemented by a strategy on how to access the market through contacts, strategic alliances, word of mouth, articles, research projects, awards in ecotourism, etc. Diversification of the client base also reduces the reliance on one business source and limits the business exposure to a decline in demand in one market segment.

- *Access to capital*: multiple sources of capital and the creative combination of these resources enable businesses to finance their start-ups. Financing structures that allow for longer-term return on investment perspectives and have a low amount of leverage (debt) appear to be a common characteristic. Patient investor capital with realistic expectations for their return horizon and relatively small debt service payments to total cash flow both contribute to a more sustainable financial structure when equity or debt financing is involved.

Applying such business model criteria to donor projects that seek to enhance both conservation and local benefits in the future might greatly increase the sustainability of projects. Box 14.4 summarizes the framework for business competitiveness.

The Future of International Donor Support for Ecotourism

Experts in the field of sustainable tourism development and ecotourism think that bilateral and multilateral aid agencies will be the leading source of funds for ecotourism development projects in the future (Hawkins *et al.*, 2002). But these agencies lack expertise. Of the 29 donor agency respondents for the study of Hawkins *et al.* (2002), 20 indicated that their organization would benefit from an education programme focused on sustainable tourism with specific focus areas on project design, linking sustainable tourism to resource management, financial aspects of sustainable tourism, economic rationale, strategic approaches and maximization of community involvement, among others.

The stakes are high for successful new interventions in sustainable tourism and ecotourism. A study by the Worldwatch Institute in Washington, DC found that 'tourism is the only economic sector where developing countries consistently run a trade surplus' (Mastny, 2001, p. 6). It is especially significant in poorer countries that have few other options: 'for the world's 49 so-called least developed countries…tourism is now the second largest source of foreign exchange after oil' (Mastny, 2001, p. 19).

Tourism's contribution to the gross domestic products of developing countries has been climbing dramatically in the past decade. It is the only service industry where there is a growing positive balance of trade flowing from the developed countries to the poorest nations, with 41 of the 50 poorest countries now earning over 10% of their exports from tourism. It is a principal export of 31 of the 49 least-developed countries and number one for seven; and it is in the top five exports for more than 80% of developing countries (Roe *et al.*, 2004). The WTO's research indicates that

Box 14.4. Competitive Ecotourism Business Benchmarks.

Destination Quality	Value for Price	Interpretation Quality	Accessibility	Management	Marketing	Access to Capital
Safety – low external threats	Cost based on competition in equivalent destinations	Quality of guided programmes in terms of service and structuring of groups while safely viewing attractions	Reliable access to an international airport within one day by land or air	Capacity to manage finances and generate accounting reports	Ability to achieve strategic positioning in the marketplace	Ability to combine multiple sources of capital
Good charisma of wildlife or natural attraction	Cost based on service quality	Uniqueness of informational content provided		Ability to deliver smooth logistical arrangements	Strong partnerships and strategic alliances	Access to patient capital
Policies that foster local business	Cost based on uniqueness of experience	Capacity to deliver information in a way that captivates and provides context		Good human resource management	Good ability to work with the media or be positioned with the media	Ability to leverage equity with low debt service costs
Reasonable or good local infrastructure	Cost based on quality of interpretative services					
Media interest						

tourism's role in developing economies will continue to accelerate, becoming increasingly important in South America, Southern Africa, South-east Asia and Oceania (WTO, 2006).

The investment of US$7 billion in donor projects related to sustainable tourism and ecotourism, with over 178 projects active in 2002, represents significant capital investment. None the less, evidence is mounting that many donor-funded NGO ecotourism projects disappear after the donor funding cycle is over. Maldonado (2002), a strong advocate for ecotourism as a tool for community development, notes that much donor investment has been lost due to NGOs' lack of business acumen. Hawkins *et al.* (2002) note that:

> many NGOs and donor agencies have attempted to work with communities, identify their needs and provide communities with what they want (tented camps, craft villages). Often these initiatives have been supply-based, have not involved the private sector, and their sustainability is questionable.

Future donor development projects would benefit greatly from a macro strategy of donor investment opportunities based on the potential for financially sustainable long-term results in developing countries. Such decisions cannot be based on biodiversity criteria alone or on pro-poor criteria either. Triple bottom-line approaches should appear in the monitoring and evaluation systems of all NGOs and donors. Donor assistance for ecotourism development in the future will have to be progressive, market-savvy and highly proactive in order to generate more profitable businesses, while at the same time applying strict project development and monitoring criteria for community benefits/pro-poor results and environmental conservation objectives.

Conclusion

Ecotourism needs to be monitored and evaluated according to the triple bottom-line of conservation, community development/pro-poor benefits and business competitiveness. While coming to global agreement on the criteria for monitoring and evaluation of donor projects is challenging, there is an urgent need for such an agreement. All of the major donors funding ecotourism should require triple bottom-line monitoring and evaluation. Rather than having each project develop its own indicators, a centralized system that is donor-approved should be available online. Such a system would save millions of dollars in labour and effort.

NGOs receiving donor funding should immediately use a greater portion of their programmatic resources to monitor and evaluate their projects, moving beyond lessons learned and anecdotal evaluations of project success. A significant effort will be required to train NGO project managers around the world to implement monitoring and evaluation systems. This will require that all the major NGOs implementing ecotourism with donor funds establish measurable indicators at the beginning of projects and keep consistent records based on indicators during the lives of their projects. The private sector should also apply strict criteria for the use of donor funds and have monitoring systems in place.

This chapter has sought to use recent literature, participatory stakeholder meeting results and other evaluation frameworks for sustainable development to determine if a set of basic questions for ecotourism development evaluation could be derived. It appears that in fact this would be possible. A final draft framework of questions is provided as Table 14.2. Without such a framework in the future, ecotourism will lack proper oversight and put donor investments at risk. A final framework that has the benefit of multiple-stakeholder review will be a valuable contribution of great importance to NGOs, communities, the private sector and donors worldwide.

Table 14.2. Draft evaluation framework questions for ecotourism.

Conservation indicators

1. How does ecotourism contribute to costs of managing protected areas?

   Total revenue provided to protected or natural area system?
   Percentage earmarked for conservation in specific protected or natural areas?
   Percentage of budget provided by ecotourism to total protected or natural area system?
   Percentage provided to individual park or natural area budget?

2. What are the biophysical impacts of tourism in natural areas?

   Is monitoring of impacts taking place?
   Is baseline data being collected?
   What categories of biophysical impacts are there?

   a. wildlife
   b. vegetation
   c. water quality
   d. air quality
   e. erosion

   What percentage of the natural area is being affected?
   What direct management techniques are being used?

   a. zoning
   b. required guides
   c. citations and fines
   d. campsite designation
   e. limitation of duration of visit
   f. reservation systems
   g. visitor number limits

   What indirect management techniques are being used?
   a. signs
   b. patrols
   c. tour operator concessions
   d. introductory talks
   e. written guidelines
   f. displays

   Is a management response system in place?

Table 14.2. – *Continued.*

3. How are ecotourism impacts managed in buffer zones of protected areas?

Are growth management strategies being used?

a. zoning
b. carrying capacity limits
c. tourism plans
d. design plans

Are regulatory mechanisms being used?

a. building permit with environmental standards
b. environmental impact statements
c. standards for sewage treatment
d. watershed protection

What capabilities do local authorities have to implement these mechanisms?

4. What impact is ecotourism having on biological diversity?

What is the management structure of the project?

a. community-based
b non-governmental organization
c. private sector
d. joint venture

What is the degree of threat to the biodiversity of the area?
Which project design addresses threats to the area most effectively?

5. What impact is ecotourism having on new government policies?

What legal frameworks exist to provide incentives for sustainable tourism development?
Are there participatory planning programmes that include rural and indigenous communities?
Is there an ecotourism plan?
What budgetary mechanisms are in place to support ecotourism plans?
What training programmes are in place to support community participation?
What finance mechanisms are in place for small businesses?

6. Is ecotourism building environmental and social awareness of destinations?

Are interpretive activities based on sound information and presented in a balanced manner?
Is there cooperation between natural areas and private sector to develop interpretive programmes?
Is there an interpretive plan or strategy for natural areas?
Is there training for interpretive staff?

Community development indicators

7. Has ecotourism contributed to the expansion of local business opportunities?

What form of credit is available for micro businesses and small business at the community level?
What training is available for small business at the community level?
How do community enterprise benefits and wages compare with other businesses in area?
What are the earnings of the local population presently and how has ecotourism impacted this?

Continued

Table 14.2. – *Continued.*

8. Are economic opportunities from ecotourism reaching new segments of the population?

   What are pre-existing opportunities for marginalized/rural people in terms of business and employment?

   Are indigenous/rural poor/women seeing more business or earning opportunity?

9. Have collective benefits to local communities been enhanced?

   Skills, education and health?

   Roads, water and other infrastructure that is sustainable?

   Credit and collective income?

   Social capital and community organizational strength?

   Information on local, regional and national policies available?

   Information on livelihood options?

   Exposure to risk and exploitation?

10. What are the social and cultural impacts of ecotourism?

    Respect for values, symbols and cultural expressions?

    Preservation of language, customs and traditions?

    Organizational abilities in community?

    Representation at regional and national levels?

    Use of traditional skills?

    Interest in land stewardship?

    In-fighting?

    Crime and adoption of illegal underground commerce?

11. Has ecotourism improved access to information and allowed for more participation within society?

    Number of strategic alliances with private sector, non-governmental organizations or other communities?

    Communications mechanisms obtained for technical information?

    Participation level in community municipal- and state-level meetings?

Business competitiveness indicators

12. Have ecotourism enterprise development models been carefully reviewed to ensure there are good prospects for business viability?

    Is the destination perceived by the market as attractive and safe?

    Are there charismatic wildlife-viewing opportunities?

    Can the ecotourism project distinguish itself in the marketplace and compete in terms of value?

    Are there excellent guides and opportunities to learn in an interactive/active outdoor context that will exceed or fulfil demanding client expectations?

    Will the accommodation be comfortable, while remaining rustic?

    Will the destination be reasonably accessible with daily flight schedules with reasonable connections from an international gateway?

    Does the destination have other interesting attractions within reasonable distance?

    Does management have the capability of targeting a niche market and carrying out cost-effective, efficient marketing programmes that appeal to the targeted client base? Is the targeted client base sufficiently diverse?

    Does management have the capability of handling financial and operating systems for a business?

    Is there patient capital available for the long-term with realistic expectations on return?

    Will debt service remain relatively small in relationship to total cash flow?

References

Ashley, C., Roe, D. and Goodwin, H. (2001) *Pro-Poor Tourism Strategies: Making Tourism Work for the Poor*. Pro-Poor Tourism Report No. 1. Overseas Development Institute, Nottingham, UK.

Blangy, S. and Epler Wood, M. (1993) *Developing and Implementing Ecotourism Guidelines for Wildlands and Neighboring Communities in Ecotourism: A Guide for Planners & Managers*, Vol. I. The International Ecotourism Society, Burlington, Vermont.

Blanke, J. and Chiesa, T. (eds) (2007) *Travel and Tourism Competitiveness Index Report 2007: Furthering the Process of Economic Development*. World Economic Forum, Geneva, Switzerland.

Bosselman, F.P., Petersen, C.A. and McCarthy, C. (eds) (1999) *Managing Growth Strategies*. Island Press, Washington, DC.

Brandon, K. and Margoluis, R. (1996) *The Bottom Line: Getting Biodiversity Conservation Back into Ecotourism in The Ecotourism Equation*. Bulletin No. 99. Yale University, New Haven, Connecticut.

Charters, T. and Law, K. (eds) (2000) *Best Practice Ecotourism in Queensland*. Tourism Queensland, Queensland, Australia.

Christ, C., Hillel, O., Matus, S. and Sweeting, J. (2003) *Tourism and Biodiversity: Mapping Tourism's Global Footprint*. Conservation International, Washington, DC.

Denman, R. (2001) *Guidelines for Community-based Ecotourism Development*, World Wide Fund for Nature, Gland, Switzerland.

Eagles, P., McCool, S.F. and Haynes, C.D. (2002) *Sustainable Tourism in Protected Areas: Guidelines for Planning and Management*. International Union for the Conservation of Nature and Natural Resources, Gland, Switzerland.

Epler Wood, M. (1998) *Meeting the Global Challenge of Community Participation in Ecotourism*. Working Paper No. 2, *America Verde*. The Nature Conservancy, Arlington, Virginia.

Epler Wood, M. (2002) *Ecotourism: Principles, Practices & Policies for Sustainability*. United Nations Environment Programme, Paris and The International Ecotourism Society, Burlington, Vermont.

EplerWood International (2003) *A Review of International Markets, Business, Finance & Technical Assistance Models for Ecolodges in Developing Countries*. World Bank/International Finance Corporation/Global Environment Facility, Washington, DC.

Giongo F., Bosco-Nizeye, J. and Wallace, G. (1993) *A Study of Visitor Management in the World's National Parks and Protected Areas*. Professional Paper. Colorado State University, Fort Collins, Colorado.

Halpenny, E. (2002) *Marine Ecotourism Guidelines*. The International Ecotourism Society, Burlington, Vermont.

Hausler, N. and Strasdas, W. (2002) *Training Manual for Community-based Tourism*. InWEnt – Capacity Building International, Zschortau, Germany.

Hawkins, D., Lamoureux, K. and Poon, A. (2002) *The Relationship of Tourism Development to Biodiversity Conservation and the Sustainable Use of Energy and Water Resources*. Report to the United Nations Environment Programme. UNEP, Paris.

Hawkins, D.E. and Lamoureux, K. (2006) *Performance Monitoring Programs and Performance Indicators for Sustainable Tourism*. Industry and Environment Programme, Paris.

IUCN (2003) *Financial Security for Protected Areas. WPC Recommendation 07, Vth World Parks Congress*. International Union for the Conservation of Nature and Natural Resources, Gland, Switzerland.

Jones, H. (2007) *Historical Analysis of Parks in Peril 2000*. The Nature Conservancy, Arlington, Virginia.

Lash, G. and Austin, A. (2003) *Rural Ecotourism Assessment Program (REAP)*. EplerWood International, Burlington, Vermont.

Lindberg, K. (2001) *Protected Area Visitor Fees: Overview*. The International Ecotourism Society, Burlington, Vermont.

Maldonado, C. (2001) *Turismo: Mercado y Sostenibilidad, Equipo Tecnico Multidisciplinario Para Los Paises Andinos*. Oficina Internacional Del Trabajo, Geneva, Switzerland.

Maldonado, C. (2002) *Servicios Empresariales Para el Desarrollo del Etnoturismo Comunitario en Bolivia, Ecuador, y Peru, Equipo Tecnico Multidisciplinario Para Los Paises Andinos*. Oficina Internacional Del Trabajo, Geneva, Switzerland.

Margoulis, R., Margoulis, C., Brandon, K. and Salafsky, N. (2000) *In Good Company*. Biodiversity Support Program, Washington, DC.

Mastny, L. (2001) *Traveling Light: New Paths for International Tourism*. Worldwatch Paper No. 159. Worldwatch Institute, Washington, DC.

Mehta, H., Baez, A. and O'Laughlin, P. (2002) International Ecolodge Guidelines. The International Ecotourism Society, Burlington, Vermont.

NRIC (2005) *USAID and Sustainable Tourism: Meeting Development Objectives*. Report prepared by The Natural Resources Information Clearinghouse. US Agency for International Development, Washington, DC.

Otavalo (2001) *Declaracion de Otavalo sobre Turismo Sostenible, Competitivo, Comunitario y con Identidad*. Otavalo, Imbabura, Ecuador.

PACT (2001) *2000 Annual Report*. Protected Areas Conservation Trust, Belmopan, Belize.

Rainforest Alliance (2003) Sustainable Tourism Stewardship Council Final Report. Rainforest Alliance, New York; available at http://www.rainforest-alliance.org/tourism.cfm?id=council (accessed February 2008).

Roe, D., Ashley, C., Page, S. & Meyer, D. (2004) *Tourism and the Poor: Analysing and Interpreting Tourism Statistics from a Poverty Perspective*. Pro-Poor Tourism Working Paper No. 16. Overseas Development Institute, Nottingham, UK.

Rome, A. (1999) *Ecotourism Impact Monitoring: A Review of Methodologies and Recommendations for Developing Monitoring Programs in Latin America*. The Nature Conservancy, Arlington, Virginia.

Sanders, E.G. and Halpenny, E. (2000) *The Business of Ecolodges*. The International Ecotourism Society, Burlington, Vermont.

SECA (2000) *European Donor Funding of Ecotourism within Environmental Programmes*. SECA, Montpellier, France.

Spergel, B. (1996) *Belize's Protected Area Conservation Trust: A Case Study*. World Wildlife Fund–US, Washington, DC.

Steck, B., Strasdas, W., and Gustedt, E. (1999) *Tourism in Technical Cooperation: A Guide to the Conception, Planning, and Implementation of Project Accompanying Measures in Regional Rural Development and Nature Conservation*. GTZ, Eschborn, Germany.

SustainAbility (1996) *Engaging Stakeholders*. Vol. 1. *The Benchmark Survey*. SustainAbility Ltd, London.

TIES (1993) *Ecotourism Guidelines for Nature Tour Operators*. The International Ecotourism Society, Burlington, Vermont.

Wang, C. and Miko, P.S. (1997) Environmental impacts of tourism on US national parks. *Journal of Travel Research* 35(4), 31–36.

Wesche, R. and Drumm, A. (1999) *Defending our Rainforest: A Guide to Community Based Ecotourism in the Ecuadorian Amazon*. Accion Amazonica, Quito, Ecuador.

WTO (2002a) *World Ecotourism Summit Final and Preparatory Meeting Reports*. World Tourism Organization, Madrid.

WTO (2002b) Meeting Conclusions, Mesoamerica Regional Meeting, Belize City, Belize, 26–28 November 2001. World Tourism Organization, Madrid; available at http://www.world-tourism.org/sustainable/IYE/quebec/cd/regional/pdfs/rmesoaen.pdf (accessed February 2008).

WTO (2004a) *Indicators of Sustainable Development for Tourism Destinations: A Guidebook.* World Tourism Organization, Madrid.

WTO (2004b) *Washington Declaration on Tourism as a Sustainable Development Strategy.* World Tourism Organization, Madrid.

WTO (2006) *Sustainable Tourism – Eliminating Poverty.* World Tourism Organization, Madrid.

15 Setting Standards: Certification Programmes for Ecotourism and Sustainable Tourism

M. HONEY

Center on Ecotourism and Sustainable Development (CESD), Washington, DC, USA

Introduction

In September 2007, tourism experts from several United Nations (UN) agencies and major environmental organizations met at the Washington, DC offices of the UN Foundation to discuss a collective effort to create, for the first time, a globally agreed upon set of sustainable tourism *certification* criteria. They examined a hefty document that compared some 30 certification and ecolabelling programmes, codes of conduct and international guidelines, and proposed a finite set of 'baseline' social, environmental and economic criteria to measure the impacts of tourism businesses (Solimar International *et al.*, 2007). This was the latest step on the long road towards creating a global *accreditation* body, known as the Sustainable Tourism Stewardship Council (STSC). This initiative within tourism parallels similar efforts in a number of other industries that have resulted, for instance, in an accreditation body to monitor sustainability in wood products (Forest Stewardship Council) and in fisheries (Marine Stewardship Council). Since the late 1990s, the route towards creating an STSC had had many twists and turns and there had been road blocks and near derailments. But now, it seemed, the certification train was emerging from the tunnel, and the end – the STSC signpost – appeared to be on the near horizon.

Certification is widely viewed as a vital tool for helping to control tourism, often ranked as the world's largest industry, and put teeth into *ecotourism*, in order to 'separate the wheat from the chaff' (see Box 15.1). If ecotourism is going to move from a good concept to good practices, it must be measured against clear standards. In addition, over the last decade or more, there have been a range of initiatives aimed at 'greening' mainstream tourism: taking the principles of ecotourism and applying them to larger businesses (including chains, resorts and urban hotels, as well as ski lifts,

---

Box 15.1. Definitions.

- *Certification*: a voluntary procedure that assesses, monitors and gives written assurance that a business, product, process, service or management system conforms to specific requirements. It awards a marketable logo or seal to those that meet or exceed baseline standards, i.e. those that at a minimum comply with national and regional regulations, and, typically, fulfil other declared or negotiated standards prescribed by the programme.
- *Accreditation*: a procedure by which an authoritative body formally recognizes that a certifier is competent to carry out specific tasks. In other words, an accreditation programme certifies the certifier.

Note: these definitions are not universally accepted. In a number of countries, including Australia and New Zealand, 'accreditation' is used for what is defined in the USA, Europe, Latin America and elsewhere as 'certification'.

---

golf courses and marinas) throughout the more conventional tourism industry. This is known as *sustainable tourism*. Both ecotourism and sustainable tourism are grounded in the concept of *sustainable development*, as most famously articulated in the Brundtland Report, *Our Common Future* (see Box 15.2). And both ecotourism and sustainable tourism need to be ground-tested against concrete criteria in order to prevent *greenwashing*. Voluntary certification programmes offer a tool for curbing greenwashing and recognizing socially and environmentally responsible companies. As Michael Conroy writes in *Branded: How the 'Certification Revolution' is Transforming Global Corporations*, in which he traces the history of certification initiatives in a range of industries: 'the certification revolution has shown remarkable success in creating the conditions that help transform corporate practices towards greater social and environmental accountability' (Conroy, 2007).

Today the topic of setting standards and measuring impacts is one of the most fertile within responsible tourism circles. This new impetus for certification is coming strongly from several directions, driven in part by the 'green' values and disposable income of baby boomers and in part by growing end-of-the-world-as-we-know-it fears of global warming. Tourism is increasingly viewed as both a contributor to (particularly air transport) and a victim of (rising seas, melting ice caps, weather swings) greenhouse

---

Box 15.2. Definitions.

- *Ecotourism*: 'responsible travel to natural areas, which conserves the environment and improves the welfare of local people' (TIES, 1990).
- *Sustainable tourism*: 'tourism that is economically viable, but does not destroy the resources on which the future of tourism will depend, notably the physical environment, and the social fabric of the host community' (Swarbrooke, 1999).
- *Greenwashing*: the practice of falsely claiming to be sustainable; false advertising.
- *Sustainable development*: 'meets the needs of the present without compromising the ability of future generations to meet their own needs' (Brundtland, 1987).

gas emissions and climate change. One response has been a dramatic upswing in voluntary carbon offset programmes for airline travel, designed to mitigate carbon emissions by contributing to alternative energy projects or old growth forests.

More broadly, we appear to be on the cusp of a new 'green' popular movement. The first global environmental movement that emerged during the 1970s and gave birth to Greenpeace and scores of other non-governmental organizations (NGOs) was mostly focused on influencing government policies. The 'green' movement mushrooming in this new millennium is driven once again by NGOs, but now is focused most squarely on corporations, with demands of corporate social responsibility (CSR), including certification. The link between baby boomers and this new 'green' consumer movement, which includes ecotourism, was noted, for instance, in a US State Department report as early as 2002. It states:

> Trends in the US ecotourism industry indicate growing numbers of educated ecotourists with average or above average annual family incomes, increases in the number of nature education and conservation programs, and increasing concern among the population about the degradation of resources due to poor management or overuse of ecotourism destinations (US State Department, 2002).

By 2007, ecotourism had become chic in the press and with the public. Take, for instance, the *Knoxville News Sentinel*'s feature run on 31 December 2006. It begins: 'ecotourism – once a tiny niche in the travel industry – has grown into a worldwide multi-million dollar business'. After ticking off a list of benefits that come from tourism done right, the writer proposes:

> With 2007 approaching in a few hours, perhaps it's wise to make a New Year's resolution to uphold guidelines for responsible travel. Whether a destination is in the USA or abroad, the environment and cultural heritage need protection from harmful outside elements (Lange, 2006).

The growth of 'green' certification programmes is just one of the signs of the rise and mainstreaming of a new environmentalism in the USA. In 2008, for instance, the American Hotel & Lodging Association (AH&LA), the hotel industry's leading trade organization, announced plans to focus its annual conference on 'educating the industry's leaders on best practices and the importance of environmentally-friendly "green hotels"'. As the conference chair, Jim Burba, put it, 'while a small number of people in the hotel industry have been promoting the logic and merits of "green"/sustainable development and operations for decades, the interest in the past few years has shot up like a rocket'. He added, 'green is now being embraced by developers and owners and is being discussed in the boardrooms of the largest companies in the travel industry' (AH&LA, 2007). Similar trends were reported by *USA Weekend Magazine*, which wrote, 'travellers in most US cities now can choose to stay in "green" hotels whose Earth-friendly practices minimize their environmental impact' (Lisagor, 2005). And an article in *SmartMoney* was even more emphatic: 'the eco-revolution has officially hit the hotel industry, with everyone from staid business chains to hipper-than-thou boutiques now billing themselves as green' (Bellstrom, 2007).

This all seems a far cry from where we were just 8 years ago. In 2000, a colleague and I organized the first international conference on 'green' tourism certification. We brought together some 80 people who had created and were running tourism certification programmes around the world. People came from tourism certification programmes in Australia, Germany, Ecuador, Brazil, Costa Rica, New Zealand, South Africa, Kenya and Canada. No one came representing a 'green' tourism certification programme in the USA. Even worse, we had a terrible time finding a suitable venue for this conference. Since those invited were, in essence, the world's leading experts in 'green' tourism certification programmes, it was clear that we needed to hold the conference in a sustainable hotel – one that had more than the option of not changing sheets and towels every day. After coming up dry in the greater Washington area, we cast our net further afield. We finally found the Mohonk Mountain House, a magnificent 265-room, Victorian castle and one of the country's oldest family-owned resorts, located in heart of New York's Hudson Valley. When ecotourism expert Amos Bien arrived from Costa Rica, he was thrilled; he said that, being originally from New York, he had long heard of Mohonk, which he called 'the US's first and oldest ecolodge'. Since Amos' own ecolodge, Rara Avis, holds a similar distinction in Costa Rica, I took this as gospel, breathed a sigh of relief, and we all settled into this grand old, respectably 'green' resort for what turned out to be a historic conference within the esoteric annals of ecotourism and sustainable tourism certification.

Several important decisions were taken at Mohonk. One was that the delegates wrote and passed the 'Mohonk Agreement', a four-page document outlining the most important social, environmental and economic criteria that need to be part of any legitimate certification programme (Mohonk Agreement, 2000). The Agreement also proposed that there be two levels of certification, one for sustainable tourism and another, with additional criteria to fit the needs of ecotourism businesses and destinations. In addition, the conference delegates decided that the Rainforest Alliance should take the lead in conducting global negotiations around first a feasibility study and then implementation of a new accreditation body, the STSC. With funding from the Ford Foundation and later the Inter-American Development Bank (IDB), the Rainforest Alliance's Sustainable Tourism programme, competently directed by Ronald Sanabria, undertook both global consultations around conceptualizing and creating an STSC and on-the-ground initiatives in the Americas to help create new certification programmes, strengthen existing ones and link them together through the Sustainable Tourism Network of the Americas, a regional association of all those involved in 'green' tourism certification (Conroy, 2007; Rainforest Alliance, 2007; Solimar International *et al.*, 2007).

Since Mohonk, tourism certification has grown. Today, there are several national certification programmes in the USA and more than a dozen state-based ecolabelling programmes (including in Florida, Pennsylvania, Maine and Wisconsin) measuring and awarding ecolabels to hotels that meet environmental – though usually not social – performance criteria. Worldwide, there are close to 100 certification programmes in the field of ecotourism and sustainable tourism, either up and running or in development. The Americas has become the fastest-growing region in the world with, in addition to the US programmes, several programmes in Canada and the Caribbean and at least a dozen running or close to launch in Latin America. In order to understand more fully how we got to this promising point, it is useful to take a closer look at the roots of ecotourism and the origins and growth of certification as a tool for sustainable development.

Historical Roots of 'Green' Certification for the Tourism Industry

The term 'ecotourism' first appeared in the 1970s, a decade that saw the rise of a global environmental movement and a convergence of demand for sustainable and socially responsible forms of tourism. It grew, initially in scattered experiments and without a name, in response to deepening concerns about the negative effects of conventional tourism (Budowski, 1976). Countries in Latin America, Africa and Asia, which viewed tourism as a development tool and foreign exchange earner, were becoming increasingly disillusioned with the economic leakage of tourist dollars and the negative social and environmental impacts of mass tourism. Citizen movements, spearheaded by church groups in Thailand, mounted a campaign for 'responsible tourism' that sought to counter child prostitution and other social ills connected with mass tourism. Simultaneously, scientists, parks officials and environmental organizations in various parts of the world were becoming increasingly alarmed by the loss of rainforest and other habitat and of rhino, elephant, tiger and other endangered wildlife. They began to argue that protected areas would only survive if the people in and around these fragile ecosystems saw some tangible benefits from tourism.

Mounting criticism of the collateral damage caused by tourism – leakage of profits and social and environmental ills – led the World Bank and the IDB, which had invested heavily in large tourism projects, to conclude that tourism was not a sound development strategy. In the late 1970s, both institutions closed down their tourism departments and ceased lending for tourism. (They moved back into providing loans for tourism projects only in the 1990s, this time under the rubric of ecotourism.) In parallel with these trends, a portion of the travelling public was becoming increasingly turned off by packaged cruises, overcrowded campsites and high-rise beach hotels, and began seeking less crowded and more unspoiled natural areas. Spurred by relatively affordable and plentiful airline routes, increasing numbers of nature lovers began seeking serenity and pristine beauty overseas. And, gradually as well, the travel and tourism industry came to view protection of the physical environment – its income base – as important to its own survival and began to see that there was a growing market among the travelling public for 'green' tourism.

Gradually these different interests began to coalesce into a new field that, between the late 1970s and mid-1980s, was labelled 'ecotourism'. This alternative to traditional tourism really gained notice after the publication of the World Conference on Environment and Development document *Our Common Future*. Commonly referred to as the Brundtland Report, this publication is responsible for the current conceptualization of sustainability as having three equally important dimensions: economic, environmental and social (Brundtland, 1987). Ecotourism, properly understood, holds that each of these three facets must be implemented.

Ecotourism is often described as a specialized or 'niche' market within the travel industry, similar to other subsets such as 'nature' and 'adventure' tourism (Goodwin, 1996). But what is clear from comparing the definitions in Box 15.3 is that tourism, nature tourism and adventure tourism focus on *what* the tourist or travel is seeking or doing, while ecotourism focuses on the *impact* of this travel on the traveller, the environment and the people in the host country (Fennell, 2001), and posits that this impact must be *positive*. As such, ecotourism is closely linked to the concept of sustainable development (Honey, 1999). Rather than being simply a niche market within tourism or a subset of nature tourism, properly understood, ecotourism is a set of principles and practices for how the public should travel and for how the travel industry should operate (Wood, 2002).

Back in 1991, when David Western, Costas Christ, Megan Epler Wood and other tourism and conservation experts came together to found The International Ecotourism Society (TIES), they spent much of one night hammering out the succinct, 16-word description that remains today the most popular and commonly cited definition. 'Afterwards', recalls Costas Christ, Chair of the World Travel and Tourism Council's Tourism for Tomorrow Awards, 'we looked around at each other and said, "okay, who among us is really doing what we have just defined?" No one spoke up'. Christ says, 'we were all achieving various aspects of the definition, but none among us (and we were the committed of the committed!) was hitting in our practices all that ecotourism means' (C. Christ, Washington, DC, personal communication, 1998).

Box 15.3. Different types of tourism.

- *Tourism*: travel undertaken for pleasure.
- *Nature tourism*: travel to unspoiled places to experience and enjoy nature.
- *Adventure tourism*: nature tourism that involves physical endurance and risk taking.
- *Ecotourism*: 'responsible travel to natural areas, which conserves the environment and improves the welfare of local people' (TIES, 1990).

During the 1990s, propelled in part by both the UN's 1992 Earth Summit and a rapidly growing tourism industry, ecotourism literally exploded. By the mid-1990s, ecotourism (together with nature tourism) was being hailed as the fastest-growing sector of the travel and tourism industry. According to the World Resources Institute, at the beginning of the 1990s, tourism overall was growing at a rate of 4% a year, while nature travel was increasing at 10% to 30% annually. According to the UN World Tourism Organization (UNWTO), global spending on ecotourism is currently increasing by 20% per year, or about five times faster than the tourism industry as a whole (TIES, 2005). In 1999, Hector Ceballos-Lascurain, the well-known Mexican architect and conservationist, declared:

> Ecotourism is no longer a mere concept or subject of wishful thinking. On the contrary, ecotourism has become a global reality... There seem to be very few countries in the world in which some type of ecotourism development or discussion is not presently taking place (Ceballos-Lascurain, 1999).

Indeed, a review of surveys and polls in the USA and Europe taken since 2001 found the demand for responsible tourism to be strong and growing, as evidenced by the following: (i) a majority of tourists are interested in the social, cultural and environmental issues relevant to the destinations they visit. They want to learn about the issues both before they travel and while they are at their destination; (ii) many travellers seek out pristine environments to visit, and it is important to the vast majority of them that their trip does not damage local ecosystems. They are interested in patronizing hotels that are committed to protecting the local environment, and increasingly view local environmental and social stewardship as a responsibility of the businesses they support; and (iii) only a small percentage of tourists, however, actually ask about hotel environmental policies; even fewer report changing their plans due to responsible tourism issues (Chafe, 2005). What this indicates is that there is broad consumer desire for responsible travel – a survey released in 2007 put US consumer spending for ecotourism at US$24.2 billion – but that these consumers don't tend to be activists. They will do the right thing if it is made easy (Chafe, 2005; GreenMoney Journal, 2007). For this reason as well, 'green' certification programmes and ecolabels are important.

Parallel to ecotourism's global reach and recognition have also come concerns, most articulately and persistently voiced by those in the global South, that the radical tenets of ecotourism would not continue to take root and grow in the new century. Despite success stories (e.g. Gordillo Jordan *et al.*, Chapter 3, this volume), there is ample evidence that, in many places, ecotourism's principles and core practices are being corrupted and watered down, hijacked and perverted, or have failed altogether (West and Carrier, 2004). Indeed, what is currently being served up as ecotourism includes a mixed grill with three rather distinct varieties: (i) ecotourism 'lite' businesses which adopt a few environmental practices (such as not washing sheets and towels each day or using energy-saving shower heads); (ii) 'greenwashing' scams and shams which use 'green' rhetoric in their marketing but follow none of the principles and practices; and (iii) genuine ecotourism, or those businesses that are genuinely striving to implement environmentally and socially responsible practices (Honey, 1999).

Since the late 1990s it has become increasingly clear that if ecotourism is to fulfil its transformative potential, it must move from imprecision to a set of clear tools, standards and criteria (Sanabria, 1999; Sasidharan *et al.*, 2000; Wood, 2002; Yunis, 2002a,b; Madinah, 2005). Ecotourism needs to be not just conceptualized, but also codified. It is here that 'green' certification programmes have a central role to play. While ecotourism seeks to provide tangible benefits for both conservation and local communities, certification that includes socio-economic and environmental criteria seeks to set standards and measure what are the benefits to host countries, local communities and the environment (Jamal *et al.*, 2006).

Background to Certification

The 1992 UN Conference on Environment and Development, known as the 'Earth Summit', held in Rio de Janeiro, provided impetus for a variety of efforts to set environmental standards through voluntary compliance, governmental regulation and international agreements and treaties. In this mix of reforms and regulations, certification is increasingly viewed as an important tool for enduring sustainability. The Earth Summit made scant reference to tourism, the world's largest industry (Mastny, 2002). However, during the 1990s, ecotourism mushroomed, becoming, by many accounts, the fastest-growing sector of the tourism industry. Since the Earth Summit, certification initiatives have grown within tourism and many other major industries (including coffee, wood, fisheries, organic foods, cut flowers, aquarium fish, and appliances for the home, school and office) as a way to promote sustainable development (Lucier and Shepard, 1997; Vlosky *et al.*, 1999; Gobbi, 2000).

In 2002, the UN declared the International Year of Ecotourism (IYE), signifying that ecotourism had taken on global importance. Over the course of a year, regional forums were held around the world, with certification being one of the topics for discussion and consultation (Vlosky *et al.*, 1999; Mastny, 2001; Hoad, 2002). In 2001, a study commissioned by the UNWTO identified 59 ecolabels that were 'very comprehensive, state of the art' certification programmes (UNWTO, 2002). During the year, two certification programmes were created by national ecotourism organizations: the Swedish Ecotourism Association launched Nature's Best and the Ecotourism Society of Kenya (ESOK, later renamed Ecotourism Kenya) rolled out its Eco-Rating System, the first in Africa. In May 2002, the UN's IYE process culminated as more than one thousand delegates from 132 countries took part in the World Ecotourism Summit in Quebec City, Canada. The nine-page 'Quebec Declaration on Ecotourism' issued at the conclusion of the Summit called on governments, at the local, regional and national levels, to 'use internationally approved and reviewed guidelines to develop certification schemes, ecolabels and other voluntary initiatives geared towards sustainability in ecotourism' (UNEP, 2002). At Quebec, delegates announced plans to develop at least nine more new certification programmes, including ones in Fiji, Ecuador and Japan, although not all of these were subsequently launched.

With the IYE and the global summit, tourism, via the concept of ecotourism, was now viewed, perhaps more than any other global industry, as a tool for both conservation and local community development. '[E]cotourism embraces the principles of sustainable tourism, concerning the economic, social and environmental impacts of tourism', states the Quebec Declaration. It goes on to affirm that:

> Different forms of tourism, especially ecotourism, if managed in a
> sustainable manner can represent a valuable economic opportunity for local
> and indigenous populations and their cultures and for the conservation and
> sustainable use of nature for future generations, and can be a leading source
> of revenues for protected areas (UNEP, 2002).

The very concept of ecotourism questions the impacts of tourism – who benefits and who pays – and it argues that, done properly, these impacts should benefit both conservation and communities.

The Quebec Declaration was forwarded to the World Summit on Sustainable Development (WSSD), held several months later in Johannesburg, South Africa to mark the tenth anniversary of the Rio Earth Summit. The Quebec Declaration clearly stated that, unlike at the Earth Summit, the tourism industry could no longer be overlooked and that its 'green' variant, ecotourism, was now closely linked to sustainable development. '[T]he sustainability of tourism', stated the Quebec Declaration, 'should be a priority at WSSD due to its potential contribution to poverty alleviation and environmental protection in endangered ecosystems' (UNEP, 2002).

Since 2002, there has been a steady stream of regional and global conferences on ecotourism or on other topics at which ecotourism and certification were prominently discussed. The World Conservation Union's (IUCN) Vth World Parks Congress, held in September 2003 in Durban, South Africa, became another important venue for promoting 'green' certification programmes. The IUCN's South Africa office used the occasion to unveil its new hotel certification programme, Fair Trade in Tourism South Africa (FTTSA), which emphasizes social criteria such as fair wages and good working conditions that are in line with South Africa's commitment to using tourism as a tool for poverty alleviation. In addition, the United Nations Environment Programme (UNEP), in partnership with four other organizations – Rainforest Alliance, TIES, the Center on Ecotourism and Sustainable Development and the UNWTO – presented a half-day workshop on certification, specifically geared to protected area managers. It also marked the official findings of the feasibility study and the announcement of an international initiative to create, within the next few years, the STSC as a global accreditation body for sustainable tourism and ecotourism certification programmes (Font *et al.*, 2003; Rainforest Alliance, 2008).

Over the following years, other important conferences that included certification workshops were held in Bar Harbor, Maine; Rio de Janeiro, Brazil; Oslo, Norway; and elsewhere. A number of new certification programmes were launched, often with the help of the Rainforest Alliance. One of the most important of these was in Brazil, where the Sustainable Tourism Certification Program (PCTS) had important institutional and financial support from the government, NGOs, industry and the IDB (Rainforest Alliance 2007; Solimar International *et al.*, 2007). By 2007, the Rainforest Alliance had put together a business and organization plan, and was moving to the next step: looking for political and financial support from leading global organizations as well as key national governments.

'Green' Certification: a Tool for Our Times

Despite the proliferation of 'green' certification programmes, the rigour and quality of many of these programmes are uneven. Indeed, one expert's characterization back in 1990 is equally fitting today:

> Certification programs are similar to dandelions. First, there is one certification program. Overnight, a whole field of certification programs seems to spring up! Once dandelions get a hold in your yard, it is difficult if not impossible to eliminate them – the same is true of certification programs. The answer to the question 'are dandelions weeds or flowers?' is determined by the beholder as is the value of certification (Torigny, 1990).

Whether viewed as a weed or a flower, 'green' certification is a voluntary, market-based tool that seeks to reward sound environmental and social practices. As such, it is uniquely suited to our times. The prevailing notion for much of the 20th century was that social, economic and environmental problems should and could be solved by government intervention. However, over the last several decades, the role of the state has been rolled back, as corporations have moved outside national boundaries, developing new institutions of global corporate governance (World Trade Organization, North American Free Trade Alliance, Asia Pacific Economic Cooperation, etc.) and pushing a new ideology, dubbed the 'Washington Consensus', which trumpets free trade, privatization, deregulation and economic globalization.

In response to the widening gap between rich and poor within and across countries, a dynamic global justice movement took to the streets in Seattle, Washington, DC, Prague, Davos, Quebec City, Genoa, Porto Alegre, Barcelona, and elsewhere. Youth, labour, environmentalists, human rights, social justice and peace activists and other constituencies have joined forces to protest against the World Trade Organization, World Bank, World

Economic Forum and other institutions dominated by the wealthiest countries and corporations. Parallel with these protests, a variety of efforts, many spearheaded by NGOs, have sought to engage with industry and find tools for setting socially and environmentally responsible standards. According to an analysis by Duke University researchers, 'while certification will never replace the state, it is quickly becoming a powerful tool for promoting worker [host country, and local community] rights and protecting the environment in an era of free trade' (Gereffi *et al.* 2001). Certification programmes are all based on the assumption that there is a market – a public demand – for environmentally and socially responsible products. They assume that an informed public will both reward socially and environmentally responsible businesses by purchasing its goods and services and punish (through boycotts, court cases, stockholder battles and other methods) those that are not. Gereffi *et al.* (2001) conclude that certification programmes, as a 'voluntary governance mechanism', are 'transforming traditional power relationships in the global arena'.

Complexities of the Tourism Industry

Tourism, as the world's largest industry, is found in virtually every country. It employs directly and indirectly an estimated 234.3 million people (about one in ten people) and accounts for 10.3% of the world gross domestic product (WTTC, 2007). Unlike other 'green' and socially responsible certification programmes for a single product – wood, bananas, coffee, aquarium fish – where the chain of custody can be fairly easily established from the point of origin to wholesalers, retailers and the consumer, tourism is both multifaceted and nonlinear, and involves a wide variety of both services and products. According to the UNEP, tourism-related businesses include travel agents, tour operators, guides, transport companies (airlines, car rental companies, buses, railways, taxis, boats, etc.), accommodations (hotels, resorts, lodges, guesthouses, hostels, camping sites), cafés and restaurants, shops (clothing, souvenir, handicraft, art), entertainment centres (theatres, museums, theme parks, cinemas), and sport and recreation facilities (stadiums, athletic centres, diving and fishing clubs, golf courses, ski resorts, marinas, chartered transport, safaris and other guided visits) (UNEP, 2001). In addition, there is the physical environment on which tourism depends, including parks and protected areas (private and government), rural areas, beaches, marine protected areas, mountains, towns and cities, and cultural and heritage sites.

In addition, some early certification programmes in the USA, Europe and Canada sought to certify tourism professionals. Of these, the oldest US programme, the Certified Travel Counselor (CTC), was introduced in 1965 by the Institute of Certified Travel Agents as a voluntary programme to rate and recognize the competence of individual travel agents. Other programmes certified a range of professionals within the tourism and travel industry, including hotel administrators, meeting professionals and exhibit managers. By the early 1990s, there were some dozen programmes in the USA to certify tourism professionals. This type of certification programme was designed to demonstrate professional competence and performance and to promote self-assessment and improvement (Morrison *et al.*, 1992). While the programmes helped to attest to the integrity of individuals, they were not linked to setting or measuring environmentally and socially responsible criteria for the industry.

Even older were the certification programmes that measure quality, price and service of tourism businesses and were linked to the growth of the automobile for family vacations. Beginning in 1900, Michelin, the French tyre company, published its first guidebook measuring and rating hotels and restaurants. Shortly afterwards, the American Automobile Association or AAA, made up of US automobile clubs, also began producing motorist handbooks that used a series of stars to rate the quality and cost of accommodations and restaurants located along highways. Gradually the 5-star quality and safety rating system for accommodations has spread around the world, although the criteria vary from country to country. Today, in Europe, Costa Rica, Australia and elsewhere, these 5-star certification programmes often exist side by side with newer 'green' certification programmes. In New Zealand, efforts have been under way for several years to integrate environmental and cultural criteria into their traditional 5-star quality programme, known as Qualmark® (www.qualmark.co.nz), which is a joint venture between the automobile association and the government's national tourism organization (Honey and Rome, 2001).

Nearly all of the 'green' certification programmes within the tourism industry began in the 1990s. The majority have focused on accommodations, but there are a growing number of certification programmes covering other sectors of the tourism industry, including golf courses, protected areas, beaches, tour boats, cruise ships, naturalist guides and tour operators. They certify tourism professionals (guides and tour operators), businesses, products, attractions, destinations or services (Fig. 15.1).

Most certification programmes are either national or regional programmes, with the heaviest concentration in Europe; North and South America has the next largest number, and seven are worldwide programmes. The UNWTO study found that, in 2002, neither Africa nor the USA had any certification programmes for ecotourism or sustainable tourism (UNWTO, 2002). Robert Toth, an engineer who has worked on many certification initiatives, describes tourism certification programmes as a three-legged stool (Toth, 2002). One leg measures and rates quality, service and price; a second measures health, hygiene and safety; and a third measures sustainability (Fig. 15.2).

Toth explains that government generally regulates health and safety standards and most tourists take them for granted. The price and quality standards, which have typically been most important to travellers, have often been set and measured by industry associations, such as AAA or Michelin. While the focus of the mass or conventional tourism industry has historically been on visitor satisfaction as defined by rating these first

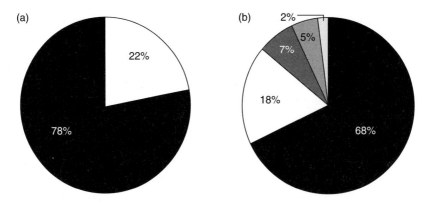

Fig. 15.1. Sustainable and ecotourism certification programmes: (a) geographic distribution (■, Europe; □, outside Europe); (b) tourist industry sectors (■, accommodations; □, destinations; ■, tour operators; ■, sports/leisure facilities; , transportation). (From UNWTO, 2002.)

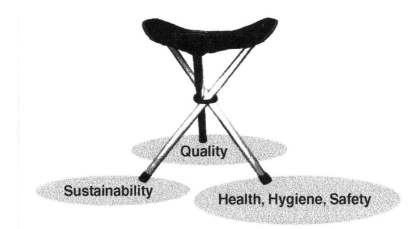

Fig. 15.2. Three legs of certification programmes. (From Toth, 2002.)

two legs – health and safety and cost and quality – the newer 'green' certification programmes hold that tourism businesses also measure environmental and socio-economic impacts and consider the satisfaction of the host community as well as that of the traveller. The origins of this third leg of certification – sustainability – can be traced directly to the rise of the ecotourism movement.

Common Components of Certification Programmes

In analysing the current array of 'green' certification programmes within the tourism industry, it can be seen that they are all united by some common components. However, these programmes are divided as well by their methodology – process versus performance – and by the sector of the industry they cover – conventional tourism, sustainable tourism and ecotourism. Examining both the common components and broad distinctions helps to illuminate the strengths and weaknesses of these programmes and to lay out the basic framework and principles that need to be part of any environmentally and socially responsible programme. While certification programmes within the travel and tourism industry vary widely, they do all have several common features. These include:

- *Voluntary enrolment*: at present, all certification programmes in the travel and tourism industry are voluntary, i.e. businesses can decide whether to apply for certification. Most do so because they believe that certification can provide technical assistance and help them adopt cost-saving measures and/or because certification will bring them market distinction and increased business. Businesses often view voluntary certification as a way to ward off government regulation and consumer boycott.
- *Logo*: all programmes award a selective logo, seal or brand designed to be recognizable to consumers. Most permit the logo to be used only after certification is achieved and for a specified period of time before another audit is required. Many certification programmes give logos for different levels of achievement: one to five suns, stars or leaves, for instance. This allows businesses to display a combination of logos as they progress through different levels. While this encourages continual improvement by the business, it may prove confusing to consumers (C. Balfe, Divisional President, HVS International, personal communication, December 2001).
- *Standards and criteria*: the *standard* is a document approved by a recognized body that provides for common and repeated use of a prescribed set of rules, conditions or requirements (Toth, 2002). The *criteria* (and indicators) are the specific measurements against which a business is being judged. All certification programmes require that businesses be assessed by measuring their level of compliance with prescribed criteria that either comply with or go beyond government regulations. As described above, the criteria can be viewed as a three-legged stool of safety, quality and service, and sustainability. In addition, certification standards can be achieved by using either process-based or performance-based methodologies. Process-based certification programmes involve setting up an environmental management system tailored to the particular business, while performance-based programmes contain a uniform set of environmental and, usually, socio-economic benchmarks. As discussed below, understanding the process–performance distinction is crucial in evaluating the effectiveness of socially and environmentally responsible programmes within the tourism industry.
- *Assessment and auditing*: all certification programmes award logos based on some kind of assessment or audit. This can be first-party, by the

company itself, typically by completing a written questionnaire; second-party, i.e. by an industry association; or third-party, by an independent organization, usually multiple-stakeholder, that is not connected with either the company seeking certification or the body that grants certification and issues the logo. Auditing can be done by a review of the written materials submitted by the business or on-site. Third-party assessment and on-site auditing is considered the most rigorous and credible because it avoids any conflict of interest (Conroy, 2007).

- *Membership and fees*: while many 'green' certification programmes are initially financed with start-up funds from governments, NGOs, international financial institutions or foundations, the long-run aim is to make them self-supporting. This can come, at least in part, through charging an enrolment fee to those businesses seeking certification. However, this is likely to be insufficient beyond the start-up phase, and therefore ongoing sources of additional funding are necessary to enable certification programmes to be effective. As a study of financing certification programmes states, 'long-term revenue streams must be created through a mix of fees, products and services provided by certification programs; government tax and credit mechanisms; and industry, media, NGO, and financial institution support' (Rome, 2007). One potential source of funds is for governments to provide a portion of the tax revenue from airport departure, hotel, restaurant or other tourism taxes to support certification programmes. As Conroy writes, 'government funding may be more available for tourism certification than for other forms of private voluntary certification. The tourism sector is such an important source of investment and, under the right circumstances, export earnings that governments have an interest in ensuring that each country's tourism sector is competitive in the current market' (Conroy, 2007).

    This money is used by the certification programme for administration and to support advertising and promotion of the logo and of the companies that are certified. If sufficient numbers of companies have been certified, the promotion can also be used to market the country as a sustainable tourism or ecotourism destination. The independent auditing body, which should be separate from the certification programme (to avoid any conflict of interest), also usually charges fees for the on-site assessment. Some programmes such as the CST (Certification for Sustainable Tourism) in Costa Rica and the FTTSA in South Africa have received government support so that they can offer, at least initially and particularly for smaller businesses, free on-site audits. Usually there is a sliding scale with larger and more profitable businesses paying more. These fees vary widely and, as discussed below, tend to be highest for certification based on environmental management systems.

While certification programmes share these common components, they are distinguished by both methodology and the sector of the tourism industry they cover.

Methodologies: Process versus Performance

Broadly stated, 'green' certification programmes within the travel and tourism industry can be divided into two methodologies: (i) *process-based* using an internally created environment management system (EMS) tailored to a particular business; and (ii) *performance-based* using externally set environmental and often sociocultural and economic criteria or benchmarks against which a business is judged. While it is argued that performance standards are vital to measure sustainability and rate businesses against one another, increasingly certification programmes include a mix of both process and performance standards. Understanding the process versus performance distinction is vital to any analysis of the integrity of a certification programme.

Process-based certification programmes

Today, the best-known process-based certification programme is ISO 14001 (or one of its variants), the standard in the ISO 14000 family that contains the specification and framework for creating an EMS for any business, regardless of its size, product, service or sector. (ISO stands for the International Organization for Standardization, a world federation of standards bodies that develops voluntary standards designed to facilitate international manufacturing, trade and communications. Another ISO standard, also widely used by the tourism industry, especially hotels, is the ISO 9000 family that sets up management systems for quality and service. Still another cluster – ISO 28, 65, 66 and 67 – contain guidance for establishing and managing certification systems, while ISO 61 contains the requirements for assessment and accreditation of certification bodies. These are important for creating uniformity in how certification programmes function and are accredited.) ISO 14001 can be applied corporate-wide, at an individual site, or to one particular part of a firm's operations. The exact scope of ISO 14001 is up to the discretion of the company (Honey and Rome, 2001; Toth, 2002).

Certification to ISO 14001 means that a business's EMS conforms to the specifications of the standard, as verified by an audit process. ISO does not do auditing; it simply facilitates the development of EMS standards to monitor certain criteria. Businesses often elect to use an outside commercial firm because they believe that an EMS audit by a qualified, neutral, third party will be more credible. Certification to ISO standards is based on having an acceptable process for developing and revising the EMS; it is not based on implementation of the EMS. For instance, when in 2001, an ISO-certified company in Bangkok was exposed in the Thai press as continuing to pollute, the ISO certifier defended the company, saying, 'ISO doesn't mean that you don't pollute. It means that you have mechanisms in place to clean up' (Krut and Gleckman, 1998; Synergy, 2000; Honey, 2002).

ISO 14001 and other types of EMS are being used by several certification programmes in Europe (Green Tourism Business Schemes for accommodations, visitor attractions and holiday parks in Scotland; Green Flag for green hotels; ECOTUR in Spain; The Nordic Swan and Green Key in Denmark), a few hotel chains (such as the Spanish chain Sol Melia Hotel), and a scattering of individual hotels in Germany, Portugal, Sweden, Jamaica, Hong Kong and elsewhere (ISO, 2001). One is the Costao do Santinho Resort & Spa, located on Santa Catarina Island in southern Brazil, which in November 2000 became that country's first beach resort to receive certification based on ISO 14001.

Costao do Santinho, an enormous beach complex located on the north-west tip of the island, has a staff of 600 and includes hotel rooms and timeshare apartments for 1400 guests, as well as conference facilities, indoor and outdoor pools, spas, sports facilities and a commercial centre. A management team, working with outside consultants, identified several areas they wanted to set up systems to improve. These included building a modern waste treatment plant to protect the beach water and accommodate the resort's expansion; establishing a private nature and archaeological reserve on the property with native species, hiking trails, and signs identifying plants and artefacts; setting up systems for recycling trash and organic composting; and environmental education pamphlets and programmes for guests and area school children. The entire process of creating an EMS to ISO 14001 specifications took a year and the resort spent US$240,000 on staff, outside consultants, auditors and environmental improvements. Josane Rocha Lima, the resort's Coordinator of Quality Control, described the certification initiative as 'a work in progress': by early 2002, the waste treatment plant, for instance, had yet to start using the recycled water to irrigate the lawns. In addition, the hotel management had already removed recycling bins and folders about their environmental initiatives from the rooms because, Rocha says, they decided not to 'push these on the guests', most of whom come for up-scale luxury, surfing and sunbathing on the resort's broad, white sand beach. Yet the resort was certified based on its creation of an EMS, not based on its achievements or performance (J.R. Lima and others, Costao do Santinho, Brazil, personal communications, February 2002).

As Costao do Santinho illustrates, ISO and other forms of process-based certification fit well with how large hotels and chains are organized. The advantages of ISO 14001 are that it is internationally recognized, can operate globally and across tourism sectors, and has standards tailored to the needs of the individual business. The drawbacks are, however, considerable: it is costly (setting up an EMS usually requires hiring commercial consultants and can cost US$20,000 to US$40,000 for a medium-sized company, large hotels can cost as much as US$400,000); it is complicated and heavily engineering-oriented; it focuses on internal environmental operating systems, not a company's social and economic impact on the surrounding area or on how a business compares with others in the field; and it is concerned only with *how* a company operates, not *what* it does. The ISO certification does not guarantee certain standards have been met and does not allow comparisons among resorts. Therefore ISO and other types of process-based management systems are insufficient, by themselves, to generate sustainable tourism practices (Honey and Rome, 2001; Honey, 2002). Process-based certification programmes have two fatal flaws: (i) they do not allow tourists and others to readily compare one certified business with another; and (ii) they do not, ultimately, guarantee sustainability. There is a growing awareness about the shortcomings of this methodology and growing agreement that, to be credible, certification programmes must include performance-based standards.

Performance-based certification programmes

Today, an increasing number of certification programmes are performance-based, and therefore focus on what a business does in a variety of environmental, sociocultural and economic areas. While process-based programmes set up a system for monitoring and improving performance, performance-based methodology states the goals or targets that must be achieved to receive certification and use of a logo. These same performance criteria are then used to measure all companies or products seeking certification under that particular programme. Performance-based programmes tend to be less costly and permit comparisons among businesses since all are audited based on the same criteria. Costa Rica's CST, for instance, has a list of 153 yes/no questions for accommodations, while the Blue Flag programme, which began in Europe and is now global, has two sets of criteria for certifying beaches and marinas. One of the Blue Flag sets contains the 'essential' criteria for certification, and the other contains 'guideline' or desirable criteria. Blue Flag requires, for instance, that any beach meets or surpasses official plans and legislation, has no discharge affecting the beach, and provides microbiological monitoring. Most programmes, including Blue Flag, contract with an independent auditor to do an on-site inspection to determine if the criteria are met (Honey and Rome, 2001; Font and Mihalic, 2002). Following this audit, the applicant is awarded a logo that may have several different levels to indicate current status and to encourage improvement in fulfilling more or higher criteria.

Costa Rica's CST is among those that have several levels and award logos based on the score an applicant obtains (CST, 2008). The questionnaire for hotels, which is usually completed by the manager, is divided into four different areas: (i) physical and biological environment; (ii) infrastructure and services; (iii) external clients; and (iv) socio-economic environment. Each answer, in turn, is weighted in importance from 1 to 3, with 3 the most important. For instance, one question under the socio-economic environment gives 3 points if at least '60% of the hotel's employees are people from the local community'. Another question asks if the hotel 'owns a natural protected area'. If it does, the applicant gets 2 points. The total points received in each category are then calculated, translated into a percentage and then given a rating, based on a scale of 0 to 5. Costa Rican officials say that the different levels in this system help encourage hotels make improvements so that they can receive a higher rating (Bien, 2002).

Performance-based certification programmes are easier to implement because they do not require setting up complex and costly management systems. They are therefore more attractive to small and medium-sized enterprises. In addition, although EMS programmes are typically devised by management and outside consultants, the most effective performance-based programmes are created and implemented by a range of stakeholders (including representatives from industry, government, NGOs, host communities and often academics) and can solicit and integrate opinions from tourists. Blue Flag, for instance, is owned and managed by an NGO, the Foundation for Environmental Education (FEE) in Denmark, has received financial support from the European Commission, and is implemented within each country by a designated NGO that works with the national government and business. CST was created and is run by the Costa Rican government's tourism institute (ICT), and includes the active participation of officials from a local business school connected to Harvard University (INCAE), the tourism industry, consultants, international funding agencies and NGOs.

Performance-based programmes do, however, present some challenges. The yes/no format can be harsh. For instance, under the CST standards, presumably if only 58% (instead of at least 60%) of a hotel's workforce is from the local community, the hotel receives a zero on that particular question. Even more prevalent, many criteria are qualitative, subjective and imprecise, and therefore difficult to measure, and many sustainability targets are undefined. For instance, the CST does not specify the size of a protected area a hotel must have and this permits a hotel that has a small garden to receive the same points as one that has an extensive private reserve. And the next question, 'is the hotel's protected area appropriately managed?', can be open to wide interpretation. Despite these difficulties, certification programmes must strive to cover these and other areas that fall broadly under the sustainability umbrella. As a study done for WWF-UK concludes:

> Only where universal performance levels and targets that tackle sustainability (environmental, social and economic) are specified within and by a standard, and where criteria making their attainment a prerequisite are present, can something akin to sustainability be promised by certification (Synergy, 2000).

Increasingly, many of the newer or revamped programmes, such as Green Globe 21, Eco Certification (formerly NEAP) in Australia, Green Deal in Guatemala and the Nordic Ecolabels for Hotels, represent a hybrid of process-based environmental management systems and performance standards or benchmarks. The WWF-UK study concludes that this combined approach is useful because it:

encourages businesses to establish comprehensive environmental management systems that deliver systematic and continuous improvements, include performance targets and also encourage businesses to invest in technologies that deliver the greatest economic and environmental benefits within a specific region (Synergy 2000).

This type of hybrid is certain to become the norm in the future.

Conventional, Sustainable and Eco-Tourism Certification Programmes

While understanding the distinction between the process and performance methodologies is important, certification programmes can also be categorized using a wider lens than methodology. In terms of developing public policy, model programmes and international standards, it is helpful to distinguish three fundamental types of certification programmes. They are: those covering the conventional (sometimes called mass) tourism, sustainable tourism and ecotourism markets.

Conventional tourism certification programmes

Conventional tourism certification programmes cover companies within the mass or traditional tourism market, i.e. the large sectors of the tourism industry that have been built without following ecotourism principles and practices. They generally include airlines, car rental agencies, hotel chains, cruise ships and other high-volume types of travel and tourism. While historically certification programmes within the conventional tourism sector have focused on quality and cost, the newer 'green' programmes focus on monitoring and improving environmental efficiency within the business by setting up management systems. They emphasize adopting environmentally friendly systems that also save money. For instance, the Hilton Tokyo Bay, which is certified under the ECOTEL programme, saved US$250,000 in 1999 alone by reducing its garbage from 3.5 t daily to 1.7 t (Szuchman, 2000).

These programmes focus on the physical plant or the internal business, not wider conservation and community impacts. For instance, Costao do Santinho, Brazil's first ISO-certified beach resort (discussed above), is harshly criticized by local NGO activists for involvement in unsavoury financial and land deals – areas which are not examined by environmental management systems. Another example is the Committed to Green certification programme developed in 1997 by the European Golf Association Ecology Union. It awards certification to golf courses that set up environmental management systems to reclaim and recycle water, plant native grasses, create buffer zones and use Integrated Pest Management (Reuther, 1999). This golf course certification programme, like most others within the conventional tourism market, focuses internally and does not include criteria to adequately measure the socio-economic impacts on the surrounding environment and community. While these are, in a sense, the narrowest and least effective of the certification models, they are also typically the best-funded, best-known and most-heavily marketed because they have strong industry backing.

In the USA by late 2007, there were at least 13 states with green lodging certification programmes (Florida, Maine, Michigan, Virginia, California, North Carolina, Vermont, Pennsylvania, Maryland, Georgia, New Hampshire, Wisconsin and District of Columbia). These programmes were all developed separately, but all with similar features. They are free or low-cost, voluntary, focused solely on environmental criteria, offer technical advice and assistance in green strategies, provide third-party assessments (and some have on-site audit), and have government support, through either the environmental protection department, waste management or energy offices, or the tourism and visitors bureau. 'The bottom line is that someone in each state needs to champion the idea, gather other interested parties and come up with a plan', writes *Green Lodging News* (Hasek, 2007). It is this state support – with staff, resources, marketing and benefits – that appears crucial to the rapid growth and growing popularity of these programmes. The Florida Green Lodging certification programme, for instance, offers three levels of logo – one, two or three palm trees – and is designed reinforce sustainable practices, promote continual improvements, and 'encourage hotels to understand and improve their environmental performance rather than simply implement a few green practices' (Florida DEP, 2006).

These certification programmes are addressing the heart of the tourism industry where rigorous and responsible standards for environmental and social equity protection are urgently needed. However, most of today's conventional tourism certification programmes fall short in terms of social and economic criteria and in terms of examining impacts to the surrounding area: they are leading to some 'green' innovations, but they are insufficient to generate truly sustainable tourism practices. In essence, the current types of certification for the conventional market usually entail taking useful, but minimal, ecotourism 'lite' measures that fall far short of the sound practices and principles needed to ensure that the business is socially and environmentally sustainable.

Sustainable tourism certification programmes

This type of programme measures a range of environmental and at least some sociocultural and economic equity issues both internally (as pertains to the business, service or product) and externally (on the surrounding community and physical environment). These are primarily or totally performance- or achievement-based programmes, using independent auditors and multi-faceted questionnaires drawn up in consultation with a variety of stakeholders. It may also include creating a management system to help establish more efficient environmental procedures.

Most often sustainable tourism certification involves individual or site-specific businesses or attractions such as hotels. The basic aim or motto of this type of programme can be characterized as 'harm reduction'. A number of the leading programmes today, including CST in Costa Rica, Blue Flag for beaches, Australia's Eco Certification nature tourism level, Brazil's PCTS and a number of the European programmes, cover the sustainable tourism certification category. There is growing consensus that sustainable tourism certification offers the best option in terms of developing global standards and a model programme (Honey and Rome, 2001; Font and Harris, 2004; Solimar International *et al.*, 2007). Its criteria are broad enough to encompass various sizes of businesses and types of tourism, including niche markets such as nature, historic and cultural tourism. At the same time, it can contain specific questions tailored to the conditions of a particular country, state or region and it is administered locally. And, because it focuses on performance both inside and outside the business, it offers a more holistic approach to measuring the effects of a tourism business and allows comparisons among those certified.

Sustainable tourism is, however, a less clear-cut category than either mass tourism or ecotourism and some worry that it can easily be too broadly drawn. Costa Rica's CST programme, while widely praised as an early 'green' tourism certification programme (though it has since been poorly managed and inadequately financed by Costa Rica's tourism institute, ICT), also has its distracters and critics. Some argue that it is not suitable for smaller, low-budget and often locally owned accommodations. In addition, some critics question how, in its first round of audits, the Herradura Hotel, a large urban hotel and convention centre not known for either its community or conservation activities, managed to receive the same high, four-green-leaf rating as four well-respected ecolodges and country inns. CST officials and experts concede privately that this apparent anomaly could reveal glitches in either the criteria questions or auditing procedures. In 2002, CST undertook to modify its criteria slightly and, with a new audit, the Herradura Hotel received only two green leaves. CST also created a separate set of criteria for ecotourism but, as of late 2007, this standard had not been launched (CST officials, hotel owners and consultants, San Jose, personal communications, 2002–2007). CST officials also declined to actively cooperate with Rainforest Alliance's important initiative to build a Sustainable Tourism Certification Network of the Americas to strengthen and harmonize certification programmes throughout North and South America and the Caribbean. Despite its problems, CST continues to have an influence on certification programme development in other countries, although it has refused to be an active participant in the Network of the Americas (Bien, 2003; Rainforest Alliance, 2007).

Ecotourism certification programmes

This third category of certification programmes covers those companies that describe themselves (through brochures, web sites, guidebooks, etc.) as involved in ecotourism. They are invariably located in or near protected areas or other fragile and pristine ecosystems. Given this, ecotourism certification programmes emphasize a business's impact on the local community and the ecosystem in which it operates. While 'green' innovations for mainstream tourism reduce energy consumption and waste, ecotourism standards go beyond questions of eco-efficiency and are more responsive to national and local stakeholder concerns (Crabtree *et al.*, 2002). While sustainable tourism certification strives to reduce negative impacts, ecotourism certification gauges whether companies contribute *positively* to conservation of protected areas and what mechanisms are in place to ensure *benefits* reach local people. Often launched by NGOs and typically covering smaller businesses, ecotourism certification programmes usually lack adequate financing, strong support from industry or adequate marketing capacities. Eco Certification (formerly NEAP) in Australia is the best-known ecotourism certification programme: two of its three levels distinguish and rate enterprises involved in ecotourism; the third category rates nature tourism enterprises, or those more properly defined as involved in sustainable tourism (Honey and Rome, 2001; Chester and Crabtree, 2002). Other examples include the PAN (Protected Areas Network) Parks for protected areas over 25,000 ha and their surrounding communities and businesses in Europe (Honey and Rome 2001; Font and Mihalic, 2002) and Smart Voyager for boats in the Galapagos Islands (Honey and Rome 2001; Sanabria, 2001).

Even though ecotourism constitutes a small sector of the market, measuring and rating these businesses, services and products is clearly vital both because of its effects on local communities and fragile ecosystems and because sound ecotourism can help to ratchet up performance standards for the broader tourism industry. In terms of developing a global certification model, it seems most appropriate that ecotourism certification programmes, which cater to the particular social, cultural and environmental context of each country, be incorporated or 'nested within' sustainable tourism certification programmes with special criteria necessary for ecotourism businesses and destinations. This is what was proposed in the Mohonk Agreement, and it continues to be regarded as important today to link sustainable tourism and ecotourism programmes under one umbrella in order to create the most complete and rigorous standard (Crabtree *et al.*, 2002; Solimar International *et al.*, 2007).

The Road Ahead

Today there are active discussions around the issue of adopting or creating a certification programme for the travel and tourism industry that can serve as a global and/or regional model, and can be used to guide countries or states/provinces that are now developing their own certification programmes. The most successful of the regional initiatives is the Network of the Americas, directed by the Rainforest Alliance. It is argued here that sustainable tourism certification programmes – rather than the weaker and usually process-based conventional tourism certification programmes or the more rigorous but more specialized ecotourism certification programmes – currently offer the best model. Before adoption, any global or regional sustainable certification programme must be thoroughly ground-tested. In addition, it must be accompanied by both an internationally accepted set of guidelines and principles for certification programmes within the tourism industry and an accreditation system.

While a universal certification model seems feasible and desirable, this model should be flexible enough to incorporate local and regional conditions and, in areas with fragile ecotourism and indigenous communities, to include distinct, more rigorous, ecotourism certification criteria. These programmes, while ideally based on an international set of principles and a model programme, must be tailored through broad-based dialogue with local stakeholders to fit the realities of the geographic area it is covering.

Further, it seems most appropriate to implement certification programmes on a country-by-country or in some instances state-by-state basis. It is preferable that auditors and evaluators be locally based to help ensure that they interpret their findings with the utmost sensitivity and knowledge. In addition, the auditors must be independent, third-party experts or consultants – separate from both the businesses and from the certification programme.

Finally, there is a need to adopt a global accreditation programme for the tourism industry that can serve to 'certify the certifiers'. Beginning in 2000, Rainforest Alliance began spearheading a feasibility study to examine the possibilities for creating a global accreditation programme that would assess and certify sustainable tourism and ecotourism certification programmes against a common framework. The first phase of this project, known as the STSC, completed in October 2003, was based on consultations with a wide range of officials from governments, international agencies, environmental and development NGOs, the private sector and existing certification programmes, as well as community activists, academics, consultants and indigenous leaders. The conclusion of that research was a call for the creation of a Sustainable Tourism Stewardship Council that would not replace existing national, regional and international certification systems but rather would identify and accredit those existing systems, and anticipated new systems, that met a stakeholder-based set of minimum global standards. The STSC study concluded that a rigorous and well-functioning accreditation programme of this sort is vital for building public confidence in the credibility of individual certification schemes; and it outlined several options for how, over the next few years, a global accreditation system can be established. Beginning in 2003, with the support of funding from the IDB and other international agencies and foundations, the Rainforest Alliance began both working to create more certification programmes in the Americas and to develop a business plan and organizational model for the STSC (Rainforest Alliance, 2007, 2008). Meanwhile, the UNEP created a Task Force on Sustainable Tourism which proceeded to develop a set of Global Baseline Criteria for Sustainable Tourism, due for completion in late 2008 (UN Foundation *et al.*, 2007). As of early 2008, with further support from the UN Foundation, plans were made for creating a UN Type II Partnership for the launch of the STSC. Participants in this process included the UN Foundation, UNEP, the UNWTO, dozens of tourism business leaders, major environmental NGOs, more than half a dozen national governments and many of the leading tourism certification programmes. Launch of the STSC was set for early 2009.

There are, today, considerable grounds for optimism. One of the remarkable results of an international certification workshop held at Mohonk Mountain House in New York in November 2000 was that the 45 participants representing a dozen existing certification programmes quickly came to see that there already exists a solid body of knowledge and practical experience about how to build credible schemes. Further, it was apparent that there is a great deal of overlap and commonality among existing sustainable tourism and ecotourism certification programmes. Participants reached consensus that new programmes should not have to 'reinvent the wheel'; rather they could be given the basic components or the 'spokes of the wheel' and use these to build a certification programme tailored to their particular needs.

Coming out of the ecotourism movement, 'green' certification programmes are helping to measure the impacts of tourism, to assess who benefits and who pays, and to set concrete standards for environmentally and socially responsible practices for tourism businesses, professionals and travellers. As the UNWTO study concludes, certification programmes and other voluntary initiatives 'are revealing tremendous potential to move the industry towards sustainability, but not without careful nurturing and support from the key industry stakeholders' (UNWTO, 2002). In addition, certification systems should be viewed as only one of a combination of tools, both voluntary and regulatory, that are needed in order to promote both social equity and a sustainable environment. As Michael Conroy, one of certification's leading gurus wisely wrote, 'certification is a type of insurance against social and environmental damage, not totally foolproof, but far better than running unprotected' (Conroy, 2002).

References

AH&LA (2007) ALIS Programming Goes Green. *AH&LA News Release*, 22 August. American Hotel & Lodging Association, Washington, DC.

Bellstrom, K. (2007) Eco-Lodging. *SmartMoney Magazine*, 12 September; available at http://www.smartmoney.com/mag/index.cfm?story=september2007-eco (accessed March 2008).

Bien, A. (2002) Environmental certification for tourism in Central America: CST and other programs. In: Honey, M. (ed.) *Ecotourism and Certification: Setting Standards in Practice*. Island Press, Washington, DC, pp. 133–160.

Bien, A. (2003) *Normalization Proposal for the Brazilian Sustainable Tourism Certification Program*. Instituto de Hospitalidade, Rio de Janeiro, Brazil.

Brundtland, G. (1987) *Our Common Future: The World Commission on Environment and Development*. Oxford University Press, Oxford, UK.

Budowski, G. (1976). Tourism and environmental conservation: conflict, coexistence or symbiosis? *Environmental Conservation* 3, 27–31.

Ceballos-Lascurain, H. (1999) *A National Ecotourism Strategy for Yemen*. World Tourism Organization/United Nations Development Programme/Government of Yemen, Madrid.

Chafe, Z. (2005) *Consumer Demand and Operator Support for Socially and Environmentally Responsible Tourism*. Center for Ecotourism and Sustainable Development/The International Ecotourism Society, Washington, DC; available at http://www.ecotourismcesd.org/webarticles/articlefiles/15-Consumer%20Demand%20April%202005.pdf (accessed February 2008).

Chester, G. and Crabtree, A. (2002) Australia: the nature and ecotourism accreditation program. In: Honey, M. (ed.) *Ecotourism and Certification: Setting Standards in Practice*. Island Press, Washington, DC, pp. 161–185.

Conroy, M. (2002) Certification systems for sustainable tourism and ecotourism: can they transform social and environmental practices? In: Honey, M. (ed.) *Ecotourism and Certification: Setting Standards in Practice*. Island Press, Washington, DC, pp. 103–129.

Conroy, M. (2007) *Branded: How the 'Certification Revolution' is Transforming Global Corporations*. New Society Publishers, Gabriola Island, BC, Canada.

Crabtree, A., O'Reilly, P. and Worboys, G. (2002) Setting a worldwide standard for ecotourism. Sharing expertise in ecotourism certification: developing an international ecotourism standard. Paper prepared for the World Ecotourism Summit, Quebec City, May 2002; available at http://www.ecotourism.org.hk/other%20files/quebeccrause.pdf (accessed February 2008).

CST (2008) All about CST. Certification for Sustainable Tourism homepage, English version; available at http://www.turismo-sostenible.co.cr/EN/home.shtml (accessed March 2008).

Fennell, D. (2001) A content analysis of ecotourism definitions. *Current Issues in Tourism* 4, 403–421.

Florida DEP (2006) Florida Resort Achieves the State's First Two Palm Green Lodging Certification. *News Release*, 9 March. Florida Department of Environmental Protection Press Office, Tallahassee, Florida; available at http://www.dep.state.fl.us/secretary/news/2006/03/0309_02.htm (accessed February 2008).

Font, X. and Harris, C. (2004) Rethinking standards from green to sustainable. *Annals of Tourism Research* 31, 986–1007.

Font, X. and Mihalic, T. (2002) Beyond hotels: nature-based certification in Europe. In: Honey, M. (ed.) *Ecotourism and Certification: Setting Standards in Practice*. Island Press, Washington, DC, pp. 211–263.

Font, X., Sanabria, R. and Skinner, E. (2003) Sustainable tourism and ecotourism certification: raising standards and benefits. *Journal of Ecotourism* 2, 213–218.

Gereffi, G., Garcia-Johnson, R. and Sasser, E. (2001) The NGO–industrial complex. *Foreign Policy*, July–August, 125, 56–65.

Gobbi, J.A. (2000) Is biodiversity-friendly coffee financially viable? An analysis of five different coffee plantation systems in western El Salvador. *Ecological Economics* 33, 267–281.

Goodwin, H. (1996) In pursuit of ecotourism. *Biodiversity and Conservation* 5, 277–291.

GreenMoney Journal (2007) Special 15th Anniversary Issue. *GreenMoney Journal*, Winter 2007/08 issue; available at http://www.greenmoneyjournal.com/ (accessed February 2008).

Hasek, G. (2007) More States Should Develop Green Lodging Certification Programs. *Green Lodging News*, 29 July; available at http://www.greenlodgingnews.com/Content.aspx?=1258 (accessed February 2008).

Hoad, D. (2002) GATS, sustainable tourism and the International Year of Ecotourism (IYE 2002). *Environmental Politics* 11, 159–164.

Honey, M. (1999) *Ecotourism and Sustainable Development: Who Owns Paradise?* Island Press, Washington, DC.

Honey, M. (2002) *Ecotourism and Certification: Setting Standards in Practice.* Island Press, Washington, DC.

Honey, M. and Rome, A. (2001) *Protecting Paradise: Certification Programs for Sustainable Tourism and Ecotourism.* Institute for Policy Studies, Washington, DC.

ISO (2001) *ISO Survey of ISO 9000 and ISO 14000 Certification – Tenth Cycle.* International Organization for Standardization, Geneva, Switzerland.

Jamal, T., Borges, M. and Stronza, A. (2006) The institutionalization of ecotourism: certification, cultural equity, and praxis. *Journal of Ecotourism* 5, 145–175.

Krut, R. and Gleckman, H. (1998) *ISO 14001: A Missed Opportunity for Sustainable Global Industrial Development.* Earthscan, London.

Lange, L. (2006) Growth of ecotourism reflects travellers' desires for responsibility. *Knoxville News Sentinel*, 31 December.

Lisagor, K. (2005) TravelSmart: tap a 'green' hotel. *USA Weekend Magazine*, 24 July.

Lucier, A.A. and Shepard, J.P. (1997) Certification and regulation of forestry practices in the USA: implications for intensively managed plantations. *Biomass and Bioenergy* 13, 193–199.

Madinah, L.K. (2005) Ecotourism and certification: confronting the principle and pragmatics of socially responsible tourism. *Journal of Sustainable Tourism* 13, 281–295.

Mastny, L. (2001) *Traveling Light: New Paths for International Tourism.* Worldwatch Paper No. 159. Worldwatch Institute, Washington, DC.

Mastny, L. (2002) From Rio to Johannesburg: New Paths for International Tourism. *World Summit Policy Briefs* #2, 19 March; available at http://www.worldwatch.org/node/1721 (accessed March 2008).

Mohonk Agreement (2000) Document written and adopted at the Ecotourism and Sustainable Tourism Certification Workshop, Mohonk Mountain House, New York.

Morrison, A., Hsieh, S. and Wang, C.Y. (1992) Certification in the travel and tourism industry: the North American experience. *Journal of Tourism Studies* 3, 32–39.

Rainforest Alliance (2007) Sustainable Tourism Certification Network of the Americas. Rainforest Alliance, New York; available at http://www.rainforest-alliance.org/tourism.cfm?id=network (accessed February 2008).

Rainforest Alliance (2008) Sustainable Tourism. Rainforest Alliance, New York; available at http://www.rainforest-alliance.org/tourism.cfm?id=stsc_study (accessed March 2008).

Reuther, C. (1999) *Towards a Greener Game: A New Environmental Awareness is Slowly Taking Hold in the US Golf Industry.* The Academy of Natural Science, Washington, DC.

Rome, A. (2007) *Financing Tourism Certification Programs.* CESD Certification Handbook #4. Center on Ecotourism and Sustainable Development, Washington, DC and Stanford, California.

Sanabria R. (1999) *Exploring Ecotourism Certification: Creating a Conceptual Framework for the Rainforest Alliance.* Summary, Final Report, JP Morgan Internship. Rainforest Alliance, New York.

Sanabria, R. (2001) Evolving ecotourism alliances conserve biodiversity in the Galapagos Islands. *UNEP Industry and the Environment*, July–December, 33–37.

Sasidharan, V., Sirakaya, E. and Kerstetter, D. (2000) Developing countries and tourism ecolabels. *Tourism Management* 23, 161–174.

Solimar International, Bien, A., Russillo, A., Seek, C. and Luna Kelser, J. (2007) Sustainable Tourism Baseline Criteria Report. Working draft, 17 August. Prepared for the United Nations Foundation and Rainforest Alliance.

Swarbrooke, J. (1999) *Sustainable Tourism Management*. CAB International, Wallingford, UK.

Synergy (2000) *Tourism Certification: An Analysis of Green Globe 21 and Other Tourism Certification Programmes*. Report prepared for WWF-UK. Synergy, London.

Szuchman, P. (2000). Eco-credibility: is your hotel as green as it claims to be? *Conde Nast Traveler*, August, 46.

TIES (1990) Definitions & Principles. The International Ecotourism Society, Washington, DC; available at http://www.ecotourism.org/webmodules/webarticlesnet/templates/eco_template.aspx?articleid=95&zoneid=2 (accessed March 2008).

TIES (2005) *Ecotourism Fact Sheet*. The International Ecotourism Society, Washington, DC.

Torigny, A. (1990). Certification: what, why, and how. In: *Proceedings of the American Society of Association Executives 8th Annual Management Conference*. American Society of Association Executives, Washington, DC, pp. 206–212.

Toth, R. (2002) Exploring the concepts underlying certification. In: Honey, M. (ed.) *Ecotourism and Certification: Setting Standards in Practice*. Island Press, Washington, DC, pp. 73–101.

UNEP (2001) Ecotourism facts and figures. *UNEP Industry and the Environment*, July–December, 5.

UNEP (2002) Quebec Declaration on Ecotourism, 22 May. United Nations Environment Programme; available at http://www.uneptie.org/pc/tourism/documents/ecotourism/WESoutcomes/Quebec-Declar-eng.pdf (accessed February 2008).

UN Foundation *et al.* (2007) Welcome to the Sustainable Tourism Criteria Initiative. United Nations Foundation, United Nations Environment Programme, The World Conservation Union, Rainforest Alliance and Solimar International; available at http://www.sustainabletourismcriteria.org/ (accessed March 2008).

UNWTO (2002) *Voluntary Initiatives for Sustainable Tourism*. World Tourism Organization, Madrid.

US State Department (2002) Overview of Sustainable Ecotourism in the United States of America. Paper submitted to the World Ecotourism Summit, May 2002. US Department of State, Washington, DC; available at http://www.state.gov/g/oes/rls/or/19412.htm (accessed February 2008).

Vlosky, R.P., Ozanne, L.K. and Fontenot, R.J. (1999) A conceptual model of US consumer willingness-to-pay for environmentally certified wood products. *Journal of Consumer Marketing* 16, 122–136.

West, P. and Carrier, J. (2004) Ecotourism and authenticity: getting away from it all? *Current Anthropology*, 45, 483–491.

Wood, M.E. (2002) *Ecotourism: Principles, Practices & Policies for Sustainability*. UNEP Division of Techonology, Industry, and Economics/The International Ecotourism Society, Paris/Burlington, Vermont.

WTTC (2007) *Progress and Priorities 2006/07*. World Travel & Tourism Council, London.

Yunis, E. (2002a) Panel presentation to the International Adventure Travel and Outdoor Show Conference, Chicago, Illinois.

Yunis, E. (2002b) Voluntary initiatives. Paper presented at the International Adventure Travel and Outdoor Show Conference, Chicago, Illinois.

Part IX

Conclusion

_____

16 The Challenge Ahead: Reversing Vicious Cycles through Ecotourism

W.H. DURHAM

Department of Anthropology, Stanford University, Stanford, California, USA

This volume offers a close look at leading experiments under way today in ecotourism in the Americas, a hemisphere where this increasingly important form of tourism flourishes. The chapters explore ecotourism in settings as different as indigenous community lands in the Amazon (Chapters 1, 2 and 10), a luxurious private ecolodge in Montana (Chapter 7), the famous National Park and World Heritage Site of Galapagos (Chapter 5) and in the state-controlled centralized economy of Cuba (Chapter 12). We hope this cross-cutting sample of experiments provides a useful demonstration of the great flexibility and adaptability of the ecotourism concept.

We also hope these and other examples of the volume illustrate the enormous potential of ecotourism to help channel the world's largest legal business towards the solution of environmental and social problems. Particularly noteworthy in this collection are the local benefits of ecotourism operations, especially lodges, in regard to both conservation initiatives and local welfare and employment. Consider conservation first, where there is growing evidence that ecotourism really can make a difference. In these pages we have seen that ecotourism has direct benefits to biodiversity maintenance by creating incentives at the local level for forest reserves, marine and coastal reserves, land concessions and myriad forms of wildlife habitat conservation. Importantly, the evidence here (especially in Chapter 11) suggests that ecotourism also contributes to conservation-enhancing behavioural changes among local inhabitants in cases where people are integrated into decision making about tourism and experience its economic and social benefits.

On top of these direct benefits, the chapters here show that there are also growing indirect contributions from ecotourism in the form of millions of dollars directed to conservation projects from entrance fees, tourist philanthropic donations and ecotourism-operator philanthropy. In just the single case of the Galapagos National Park (Chapter 5), looking only at entrance fees from foreign tourists, an estimated US$4.8 million was generated in one year (2006) for Galapagos conservation organizations and activities. Data like these are convincing that ecotourism can, by direct and indirect means, play a significant positive role in conservation.

By the same token, if ecotourism wishes to claim environmental bragging rights, it will have to do better going forward in regard to carbon usage and climate change. Like most contemporary forms of travel, ecotourism depends heavily on fossil fuel-dependent forms of transportation. This means that 'responsible travel to natural areas' starts out with an environmental debt, so to speak, especially in regard to carbon emissions that must be repaid for there to be a net environmental gain. The time has surely come for ecotourism to incorporate carbon offsets and other creative forms of carbon balancing as part of customary practice, thus reducing its carbon debt from the start. Carbon neutrality will surely be a benchmark of the next phase of maturation in ecotourism.

In terms of benefits to local livelihoods, the chapters of this book offer additional encouraging evidence. Jobs and incomes are growing as a consequence of ecotourism, as are schools, training facilities and handicraft cooperatives. Importantly, these changes are often taking place in rural, high biodiversity areas where alternative livelihoods commonly involve environmentally harmful extractive industries like logging and mining. Under the right conditions, ecotourism makes profitable intact habitat. In one case described here (in Chapter 10), for example, ecotourism operations between 1996 and 2005 at the Kapawi Lodge in Ecuador generated US$1,226,000 in financial contributions to local indigenous communities and the regional indigenous organization. In another of the cases described here (Chapter 3), the Amazon community of Infierno, Peru received more than half a million dollars net income by 2006 for its share of the revenues from the partnership behind the Posada Amazonas Lodge. In addition, Infierno has also received various forms of institutional support, training and capacity building, and a number of 'satellite projects' of social and cultural benefit all stemming from its ecotourism involvement. Parallel benefits were on the rise for the Cofan project as well (described in Chapter 2), until a war between Ecuador and Peru scared off a majority of its visitors. The vulnerability of ecotourism and its local benefits to economic and political vicissitudes is another problem to be addressed in the future development of the industry. Buffering mechanisms are badly needed. But the potential is clearly there for ecotourism to produce many and diverse fruits for local communities.

Finally, ecotourism is also showing itself capable of breaking up the vicious economic cycles that have plagued so many development efforts in the Americas. The operation of such cycles has been particularly well documented in the case of agriculture in Latin America (Painter and Durham, 1995), where repeated efforts to help small-scale producers with new crops and technologies have often generated successes. But ironically, those successes have commonly attracted and abetted the take-over of small producers by large ones, resulting in environmental damage, the displacement of small producers, or both. One might well ask: why is ecotourism different? How can it succeed when so much else has failed to help the rural poor?

Evidence is accumulating through examples like those compiled here that ecotourism is capable of breaking or even reversing the vicious economic cycles of the past. A first key reason is that local knowledge has specific value at the sites where ecotourism is carried out. The environmental experience and wisdom that locals have accumulated by living for generations in these areas can enhance the tourism experience in profound ways. Take the simple example of 'clay-licks' in the Amazon region – almost completely innocuous places known by locals where birds and mammals collect at high density to eat clay and mineral salts. Integrating clay-licks into the tourism experience, especially when augmented with local lore and 'traditional ecological knowledge' (TEK) about the mammals and birds, greatly enhances the probability, quality and appreciation of wildlife sightings and adds to its educational value (on TEK, see Berkes, 1999; Menzies, 2006). Of course, such knowledge can, to an extent, be co-opted by outsiders and integrated into their alternative ecotourism programme. But that is where a second reason comes in.

Where locals have lived in a given environment over generations of time there accrues a special form of 'incumbent advantage' in ecotourism: authenticity. No matter how polished and smooth an outside guide, or well-trained in someone else's TEK, they can never offer the authenticity of a local guide. The same is true for a locally constructed house or lodge, a local garden or agricultural plot, or indeed an entire local village. This advantage is akin to the difference between a painting and a print: people pay premiums and form long lines to see the original. In fact, increasing evidence like that presented here (Chapter 9) points to the cultural experience of ecotourism as being the most meaningful component of all. People embark on ecotourism trips for a variety of reasons – to 'experience nature' in a new setting, to see particular flora and fauna, to advance their own or their children's environmental education, and so on. But what they commonly appreciate most of all, at the end of the trip looking back, are authentic cultural experiences they had along the way. This gives long-term inhabitants unequivocal advantage; it cannot be taken away and sold by outsiders or newcomers. The authenticity advantage, however, can be minimized or voided by exclusionary political actions, the most common of which may be national park formation. In the case of the Galapagos Islands (Chapter 5), for example, the national park has played a crucial conservation role but, inadvertently, it has also given advantage to heavily capitalized outside tour operators who had the best ships for trips to visitor sites at some distance from population centres.

Another reason ecotourism has the potential to succeed for the poor where other forms of development have failed has to do with local and indigenous rights, particularly land rights. Historically, of course, traditional forms of tourism teamed up with state-level conservation efforts to work against local and indigenous communities, frequently resulting in loss of land rights and their displacement from 'protected areas' and national parks (for review see West *et al.*, 2006). Bona fide ecotourism, with its requirement of local benefits, has the capacity to work in precisely the opposite direction, thus to reinforce local and indigenous claims to land. Put simply, ecotourism has an instrumental capacity to support campaigns for territorial rights. On one hand, this capacity stems from the logic that people are more likely to practise sustained conservation in an area when their rights to the area are secure. On the other hand, ecotourism revenues can go a long way towards the realization and defence of land rights, paying for such things as surveying, registration and legal fees. There are now a number of good examples in the Americas – Kapawi Lodge, discussed in Chapter 10, being one of them (Sturdey, 2007) – where ecotourism operations have helped local groups to counter threats from oil exploration and production, mining and mineral extraction, cattle ranches, agribusiness, and the like. The potential is there for ecotourism to work for indigenous and local communities, not against them, in support of their rights to land, education and capacity building, among others.

A final reason ecotourism is resistant to cycles of expansion and concentration has to do with scale. Responsible, low-impact travel to natural areas is generally possible only in small numbers and low densities. The educational goals of ecotourism are also a force for small numbers. Environmentally friendly forms of tourism on a larger scale, without the necessary commitments to conservation and local livelihood, are called instead 'sustainable tourism' (see Chapter 15). They are also more amenable to cyclical consolidation.

Lessons From This Book

In closing, it seems appropriate to return to some of the major lessons learned in these pages about 'ecotourism and conservation in the Americas'. Let me frame them in terms of six questions of more general importance in the study of ecotourism.

1. What is the natural attraction and how strong is its draw for ecotourists? How does one reach the attraction and what are the monetary and carbon costs of getting there?

As this volume has made clear, ecotourism cannot work everywhere. It requires special natural 'draws' that are both uncommon on the planet and available in authentic and aesthetic form only where they naturally occur. The profitability of an ecotourism operation is only as good as its draw, and this caveat must always hold sway. While it is true that ecotourism brings with it a strong and growing market demand, that demand is also one with intrinsic vulnerability to political, social and economic fluctuations. Even with a strong natural attraction, ecotourism can prove fickle. Experience shows (as in Chapters 2 and 10) that ecotourism should thus be but one component among many in a community's or region's greater development strategy. Ease of access, or lower cost of access, can make a site more attractive, other things being equal, and can help reduce the intrinsic carbon debt that comes with fossil fuel-dependent means of transportation. But for ecotourism to remain viable and appealing into the future, unambiguous and untainted means must be found to make ecotourism carbon neutral or better.

2. What do visitors get for their visit? Can the same things be obtained elsewhere?

As argued in these pages (especially Chapters 8 and 9), tourists appreciate many different aspects of ecotourism (aesthetics, entertainment, communion with nature, etc.) but what sustains successful ecotourism is its educational/interpretive value and especially its cultural dimensions. According to research reported here, it is fair to say that people set off to see charismatic species, beautiful landscapes and biodiverse habitats, which they do learn to appreciate and value. But on the return from the trip, what really stand out as most meaningful of all are the cultural experiences and appreciations gained about other cultures and ways of living. Authenticity is also valued in ecotourism, which gives a special intrinsic advantage to operations and facilities run by indigenous peoples and other long-term inhabitants of an area. But just as certification standards are needed to prevent 'greenwashing' in the name of ecotourism (Chapter 15), so too some system of certification may be necessary to protect truly indigenous ecotourism operations.

3. What property relations apply to the site? Who governs access? Who are the stakeholders and what are the social relations among them? What role do locals play?

Property relations and the matter of ownership inevitably have an important influence on ease of access to a valued site, on revenue streams flowing from it and on the motivations for the site's conservation. If an attraction is privately held, employment and philanthropic donations tend to be important pathways for locals to benefit, whereas if an attraction is held as common property by a group of people, net benefits may well be more diverse and greater in magnitude. As we have seen, community involvement in ecotourism is an important predictor of success for both development and conservation. Above and beyond economic benefits, the chapters here (especially Chapter 11) indicate that the more a community is integrated into decision making authority over the business, the more successful the enterprise is likely to be. It is therefore always appropriate to ask, how are locals integrated into decision-making processes of an ecotourism operation, and if they are not so integrated, why not? Again, the decision-making power of local people has a big influence on the eventual success of the venture.

4. What is the institutional setting? What are the physical and social scales of the operation?

This collection of cases and experiments points to two other important variables that influence the success of ecotourism operations: what agencies and organizations, governmental and non-governmental, are involved in a particular area, and what is the resultant scale of the operation? Is the scale appropriate to the physical and social realities of the location? Cases reviewed in this volume show that the involvement of non-governmental organizations (NGOs) and/or private business partners can make ecotourism successful on a scale that would not be appropriate – and sometimes hardly imaginable – without outside assistance. In addition, NGOs and business partners can play an important role in collecting and channelling philanthropic assistance, including private tourist philanthropy, which can play a large role in the overall local benefits of the operation (as through schools, clinics, local infrastructure improvements, and the like).

5. How will the site and project be monitored? What impacts will be measured and by whom?

One of the areas of ecotourism research that surely warrants more attention than it has received to date is monitoring – i.e. the systematic and sustained assessment of conservation and community impacts of ecotourism operations. One reason for this weak spot can be found in ecotourism's business models themselves: only rarely has adequate allowance for long-term monitoring been built into revenue/cost projections. Another reason is the somewhat lethargic response of the social science community to see ecotourism as an appropriate and interesting domain for research, all the more illuminating because of its many experimental forms. We know enough to suggest that ongoing adaptive management, with regular periodic feedback and corrective responses, is crucial to the long-term viability of ecotourism efforts; but we need better measures for monitoring impact, better ways to fund sustained monitoring programmes and better ways to involve locals in the monitoring process.

6. Who wants ecotourism and why? Who benefits and who pays the costs?

Finally, we come to one of the most important questions of all: who wants ecotourism and why? How will its costs and benefits be socially distributed?

The chapters assembled here show overwhelmingly that ecotourism can be empowering for marginalized rural populations, including indigenous peoples and the poor, and it can help in their efforts to gain recognition, rights and resources. But it can do these things only where it is: (i) a successful business that generates profits; and (ii) a socially responsible business that is concerned with doing good and spreading the wealth. Evidence is still fragmentary and incomplete, but there are preliminary signs that sustained success in ecotourism depends on socially distributed decision-making authority. Local and indigenous peoples want more from ecotourism ventures on their lands than shared revenue streams; they also want participation with a measure of decision-making authority. This puts ecotourism in the Americas and elsewhere in a very special position. Unlike so many forms of commercial activity in rural areas whose goal is to pump resources out of a community, ecotourism offers at least the possibility and potential of pumping resources back in. This outcome would be perhaps the most convincing of all signs of 'ecotourism and conservation in the Americas'.

References

Berkes, F. (1999) *Sacred Ecology: Traditional Ecological Knowledge and Resource Management*. Taylor & Francis, Philadelphia, Pennsylvania.

Menzies, C.R. (2006) *Traditional Ecological Knowledge and Resource Management*. University of Nebraska Press, Lincoln, Nebraska.

Painter, M. and Durham, W. (1995) *Social Causes of Environmental Destruction in Latin America*. University of Michigan Press, Ann Arbor, Michigan.

Sturdey, S. (2007) Eco-tourism hope for Ecuador tribes. *BBC News*, 20 February; available at http://news.bbc.co.uk/2/hi/americas/6354887.stm (accessed February 2008).

West, P., Igoe, J. and Brockington, D. (2006) Parks and peoples: the social impacts of protected areas. *Annual Review of Anthropology* 35, 251–277.

Index

Date Due